Presented To:

_____

From:

_____

Date:

_____

Lady
in
Waiting

Lady in Waiting

BECOMING GOD'S BEST WHILE
WAITING FOR MR. RIGHT

JACKIE KENDALL
and
DEBBY JONES

DESTINY IMAGE® PUBLISHERS, INC.

P.O. Box 310, Shippensburg, PA 17257-0310

"Promoting Inspired Lives."

Previously published as Lady in Waiting by Destiny Image
Previous ISBN: 0768423104

Previously published as Say Goodbye to Shame by Treasure House
Previous ISBN: 0768421616

This book and all other Destiny Image, Revival Press, MercyPlace, Fresh Bread, Destiny Image Fiction, and Treasure House books are available at Christian bookstores and distributors worldwide.

For a U.S. bookstore nearest you, call 1-800-722-6774.

For more information on foreign distributors, call 717-532-3040.

Reach us on the Internet: www.destinyimage.com.

ISBN 13 TP: 978-0-7684-4106-2

ISBN 13 Ebook: 978-0-7684-8860-9

For Worldwide Distribution, Printed in the U.S.A.

6 7 8 / 16 15 14 13

DEDICATION

We dedicate this book to all the Ladies in Waiting, especially our daughters Jessica, Christen, and Lauren, who are seeking to become women of God.

CONTENTS

Preface...15

PART I   LADY IN WAITING

Chapter 1   Lady of Reckless Abandonment................................19
Chapter 2   Lady of Diligence..31
Chapter 3   Lady of Faith...45
Chapter 4   Lady of Virtue 57
Chapter 5   Lady of Devotion..69
Chapter 6   Lady of Purity..81
Chapter 7   Lady of Security..97
Chapter 8   Lady of Contentment......................................109
Chapter 9   Lady of Conviction.......................................123
Chapter 10   Lady of Patience...137

PART II   STUDY GUIDE

Chapter 1   Ruth's Reckless Abandonment 153
Chapter 2   Ruth's Diligence...159
Chapter 3   Ruth's Faith...163
Chapter 4   Ruth's Virtue..169
Chapter 5   Ruth's Devotion..175
Chapter 6   Ruth's Purity..181
Chapter 7   Ruth's Security..187
Chapter 8   Ruth's Contentment.......................................193

Chapter 9   Ruth's Convictions 199

Chapter 10   Ruth's Patience. 205

PART III   DEVOTIONAL

          A Word From the Authors. 211

          Helpful Tips for the Lady in Waiting. 213

Day 1   My True Community—*Mother Teresa*. 216

Day 2   A Life Worthy of Eternity—*Susanna Wesley* 218

Day 3   First Love, Divided Love—*Basilea Schlink*. 220

Day 4   Do We Really Love God?—*Hannah More*. 222

Day 5   Waiting for Our Love—*Basilea Schlink*. 224

Day 6   Revelations of Divine Love—*Julian of Norwich*. 226

Day 7   The Effectual Touch in the Will—*Madame Guyon* 228

Day 8   You Must Move In—*Hannah Whitall Smith*. 230

Day 9   A Lesson in the Interior Life—*Hannah Whitall Smith*. 232

Day 10   The Prayer of the Heart—*Madame Guyon*. 233

Day 11   Meditative Reading—*Madame Guyon* 234

Day 12   Distractions in Prayer—*Amy Carmichael* 236

Day 13   Prayer Divinely Explained—*Madame Guyon* 238

Day 14   Loved of God—*Julian of Norwich*. 239

Day 15   The Presence of God—*Jessie Penn-Lewis* 241

Day 16   Religion of the Heart—*Hannah More* 243

Day 17   The Lord Our Dwelling Place—*Hannah Whitall Smith*. . . .245

PART IV   A LUNATIC ON A LIMB WITH JESUS

          Acknowlegements. 249

Story 1   Crime—Keeping Good News to Oneself. 251

Story 2   The Pro and I. 253

Story 3   A Pearl in a Pile of Manure. 255

Story 4   Cautious in Friendship. 257

Story 5   The Spiritually Elite 259

Story 6	A Scholarship on a Silver Tray	261
Story 7	God's New Creature Program	263
Story 8	May I Borrow Your Body?	265
Story 9	The Message at the Red Light	267
Story 10	Overcharged by Worry	269
Story 11	A Human Sparkler	271
Story 12	I Believed a Lie	273
Story 13	Are You Guilty of Achan's Sin?	275
Story 14	Holding Hands After All These Years	277
Story 15	The Ultimate Seduction	279
Story 16	Heavenly Potpourri	281
Story 17	Divine Prayer Encounter	283
Story 18	Motor-Mouth's Heavenly Diary	285
Story 19	The Galatian Disease	287
Story 20	Beloved Doodles and I	289
Story 21	Everyone Needs Friends Like Daniel's	291
Story 22	Bread That Always Rises	293
Story 23	Joy for a Mother's Innermost Being	295
Story 24	God's Love Language	297
Story 25	The Perfect Father's Day Gift	299
Story 26	The Longest Short Trip	301
Story 27	A Heavenly Hug	303
Story 28	How Boldly Can We Pray?	305
Story 29	A No-Excuse Woman	307
Story 30	A Missionary to Beverly Hills	309
Story 31	A Priceless Belt in a Trash Can	311
Story 32	How Do You Say Goodbye to Shame?	313
Story 33	Surrender Your Junior God Badge at the Door, Please	315
Story 34	Liberating the Control Freak	317
Story 35	Fruitful in Suffering	319
Story 36	A Broken Dream in the Making	321

Story 37	Speechless in the Presence of Pain	323
Story 38	Ginger's Song of Victory	325
Story 39	A Miracle Worker	327
Story 40	Gift for the Grieving	329
Story 41	A Man Touched Deeply by My Pain	331
Story 42	Regina's Story	333
Story 43	Blossoms After the Storm	335
Story 44	The Governor on My Gas Pedal	337
Story 45	She Had It All	339
Story 46	A Man's Trip Through the Birth Canal	341
Story 47	From the School Bus Into the Arms of Jesus	343
Story 48	A Snare in My Soul	345
Story 49	He Can Give a Song in Hell	347
Story 50	I Do Not Want to Be Buried With Moses	350
Story 51	Get Behind Me, God	351
Story 52	Everything Said Was Wise and Helpful	353
Story 53	Ailing Heart, Angry Mouth	356
Story 54	If God Is for Me, Who Can Be Against Me?	358
Story 55	Are You Fighting Someone Else's Battle?	360
Story 56	A Worshiper Seduced	362
Story 57	Relying on a Piercing Splinter	364
Story 58	The Abundantly Blessed Wrestler	366
Story 59	No Accelerated Growth Courses	368
Story 60	Sinning in the Face of God's Goodness	370
Story 61	Mining for Concealed Jewels	372
Story 62	"Good" Bad Examples	374
Story 63	The Prosperity of the Wicked—a Mirage	376
Story 64	Security for Our Children	378
Story 65	Toothpicks in Eyeballs	380
Story 66	Get Your Own Marching Orders	382
Story 67	The Best Meal You've Ever Missed	384

Story 68   Outwitted Through Unforgiveness 386

Story 69   The Bride Belongs to the Bridegroom 388

Story 70   Be Careful What You Pray for 390

Story 71   The Secret of the Alabaster Box 392

Story 72   A Busybody and a Murderer.................................394

Story 73   Are You a Pair of Cleats or a Paraclete?...................396

Story 74   One of the Divine Secrets of Yadah Yadah..................398

Story 75   A Holy Wink for Mom......................................401

Story 76   Audacious Prayer Requests................................403

Story 77   God Stoops Down..405

PREFACE

$\mathcal{I}$s this just another book for singles? No! We believe this book is unique because its emphasis is not on a woman's status (single, married, divorced, or widowed), but on the state of her heart. We want to direct a woman's attention toward the One who really understands the longing of her heart. Too many women grow up believing that the inconsolable ache in her heart is for "a man." To love a man, get married, and then have children is thought to be the only script that will satisfy her heart's deepest longing. But no man, woman, or child can appease this longing; it can only be satisfied by the ultimate Bridegroom, Christ Jesus. This book nudges a woman closer to God, while acknowledging any longing she may have to be loved and cherished by a man.

Lady in Waiting is not about finding the right man, but being the right woman. Thus it focuses on ten qualities of a godly woman that are found in the Book of Ruth. These qualities will not only enhance your love relationship with your heavenly Bridegroom, but also guide you as a single woman, guard you while you date, support you in marriage, and comfort you if you are ever widowed or divorced. As you read you will see these characteristics beautifully displayed in the life of Ruth. She recklessly abandons herself to the Lordship of Christ, diligently uses her single days, trusts God with unwavering faith, demonstrates virtue in daily life, loves God with undistracted devotion, stands for physical and emotional purity, lives in security, responds to life with contentment, makes choices based on her convictions, and waits patiently for God to meet her needs.

What are *you* waiting for? Is it for that perfect job, the ideal relationship, a home, a career, a child? What if you get what you are waiting for?

Will it truly bring the fullness of joy you long for? Anything other than a love relationship with the Lord Jesus Christ, regardless of how good that thing may be, will bring you discouragement and disillusionment. So come and explore the life of Ruth and learn what it really means to be a godly woman, "a lady in waiting."

PART I

Lady in Waiting

Chapter 1

LADY OF RECKLESS ABANDONMENT

*T*he big day is over. Your roommate married a wonderful guy, and you were the maid of honor. You shared your roommate's joy, but now you wrestle with envy's painful grip. As the happy couple drives to the perfect honeymoon, you sit alone in an empty apartment, drowning your envy and self-pity with a half-gallon of Heavenly Hash ice cream.

Does this scenario sound familiar?

Have you assumed that your ultimate fulfillment would be found in marriage? Have you privately entertained the notion that the only satisfied women are married women? Have you been expecting your career to satisfy you until you are married? If you have answered "yes" to any of these questions, then you have a prospect of disillusionment looming in the future. On the back cover of the book *Learning to Be a Woman* is a key quotation about fulfillment as a woman:

> A woman is not born a woman. Nor does she become one when she marries a man, bears a child and does their dirty linen, not even when she joins a women's liberation movement. A woman becomes a woman when she becomes what God wants her to be.[1]

This priceless truth can help keep your perspective clear in relation to true fulfillment in life. Too many Christian women think that the inner longings of their heart relate only to love, marriage, and motherhood. Look a little closer and see if that longing isn't ultimately for Jesus. Gary Chapman once remarked in a sermon:

> I feel very strongly that marriage is not a higher calling than the single state. Happy indeed are those people, married or single, who have discovered that happiness is not found in marriage but in a right relationship with God.

Fulfillment for a Christian woman begins with the Lordship of Christ in every area of her life.

A college professor (wife, mother of seven children, singer, and author) told a group of young women that when she was eight years old, her mother told her a secret that has guided her perspective on life. The most important thing her mother would ever tell her was, "No one, not even the man you will marry one day, can make you happy—only Jesus can." What a profound statement for such a little girl. This secret allowed her to grow up following Jesus with reckless abandonment.

Are you still convinced that having Mr. Right will chase away the blues? That's not surprising. On the front of a national magazine, the lead story said, "Hollywood's hottest newcomer is selling more records than Madonna and filling her dance card with movie offers. All that is missing is *Mr. Right!*" Such a mindset bombards singles daily. How can you renew your mind and rise above this stereotype? You can be an exception through understanding "the secret of the alabaster box."

THE SECRET OF THE ALABASTER BOX

In the days Jesus was on earth, when a young woman reached the age of availability for marriage, her family would purchase an alabaster box for her and fill it with precious ointment. The size of the box and the value of the ointment would parallel her family's wealth. This alabaster box would be part of her dowry. When a young man came to ask for her in marriage, she would respond by taking the alabaster box and breaking it at his feet. This gesture of anointing his feet showed him honor.

One day, when Jesus was eating in the house of Simon the leper, a woman came in and broke an alabaster box and poured the valuable ointment on Jesus' head (see Mark 14:3-9). The passage in Luke 7 that refers to this event harshly describes the woman as *"a woman in the city who was a sinner"* (Luke 7:37). This woman found Jesus worthy of such sacrifice and honor. In fact, Jesus memorialized her gesture in Matthew 26:13 (see also Mark 14:9). This gesture had such meaning, for not only did she anoint Jesus for burial, she also gave her all to a heavenly Bridegroom. Yes, she was a sinner (who isn't, according to Romans 3:23?), but this sinner had dreams and wisely broke her alabaster box in the presence of the only One who can make a woman's dreams come true.

What is in your alabaster box? Is your box full of fantasies that began as a little girl while you listened to and watched fairy tales about an enchanting couple living happily ever after? Have you been holding on tightly to your alabaster box of dreams, frantically searching for a man worthy of breaking your box? Take your alabaster box to Jesus and break it in His presence, for He is worthy of such honor. Having responded to your heavenly Bridegroom in such a manner, you can wait with confident assurance that, if it be God's will, He will provide you with an earthly bridegroom.

How do you know if you have broken your alabaster box at the feet of Jesus? Such a decision will be reflected in reckless abandonment to the Lordship of Jesus Christ. When the Lord gives you a difficult assignment, such as another dateless month, you receive His terms without resentment. Your attitude will reflect Mary's response to the angel when she, as a single woman, was given a most difficult assignment. Mary said, *"I belong to the Lord, body and soul...let it happen as you say"* (Luke 1:38 PNT). Take your alabaster box, with your body, soul, and dreams, and entrust them to Jesus. When He is your Lord, you can joyfully walk in the path of life that He has for you.

RUTH'S RECKLESS ABANDONMENT

In the Book of Ruth, a young widow made a critical decision to turn her back on her people, her country, and her gods because her thirsty soul had tasted of the God of Israel. With just a "taste," she recklessly abandoned herself to the only true God. She willingly broke her alabaster box and followed the Lord wherever He would lead her.

> But Ruth said, *"Do not urge me to leave you or turn back from following you; for where you go, I will go, and where you lodge, I will lodge. Your people shall be my people, and your God, my God"* (Ruth 1:16).

As you look at the following three areas of Ruth's life that were affected by her reckless abandonment to God, consider the parallels to your own price tag of commitment to God. Have you broken the valuable alabaster box yet?

NEW FRIENDS

When Ruth told Naomi, "your people shall be my people," she understood that she would not be able to grow closer to the God of Israel if she remained among the Moabites (her own people). Ironically, God called Moab His washbasin (see Ps. 60:8; 108:9). One rinses dirt off in a washbasin. Ruth chose to leave the washbasin and head for Bethlehem, which means the "house of bread."[2]

Even today there exist "Moabites" who will undermine your growth if you spend too much time with them. Sometimes mediocre Christians resist the zeal and commitment of a dedicated single woman. Realizing that one's friends drive you either toward or away from God, you may need to find a "new people" who will encourage your growth and not hinder it. *"He who walks with the wise grows wise, but a companion of fools suffers harm"* (Prov. 13:20 NIV).

Often the choice for deeper commitment produces resentment from people who were once "such good friends." Do not be alarmed; you are in good company. When the woman broke the alabaster box and poured it on Jesus, the disciples did not applaud her act of worship. Instead, with indignation they responded, "Why this waste?" (see Matt. 26:8 NIV). The disciples of Jesus were filled with indignation because the woman obviously wasted the ointment. But from a heavenly perspective, the great cloud of witnesses rejoiced as they beheld the woman giving such honor to Jesus. The broken alabaster box publicly evidenced the woman's reckless abandonment to Jesus. Is there such evidence in your daily life?

This is not to advocate that you distance yourself from all who have not broken their alabaster box at the feet of Jesus. Just consider the ultimate influence your friends have on your commitment to the Lordship of Jesus Christ. Be careful if you spend most of your free time with a girl friend who does not share your commitment to Jesus. It can affect your relationship with the Lord. If a non-Christian or a lukewarm Christian influences you rather than you influencing them, you may be headed for serious trouble. You mirror those who influence you. When a woman stops growing spiritually, the lack of progress can often be traced back to a friendship that undermined her commitment to Jesus.

Take a moment to think about the spiritual depth of the girl friend who influences you the most. Is she daily becoming all that Jesus desires? If so, her growth will challenge you to grow. On the other hand, her apathy may ultimately be contagious. *"Do not be deceived: 'Bad company corrupts good morals'"* (1 Cor. 15:33). Have any of your friendships caused your spiritual life to go into a deep freeze?

Maybe you, like Ruth, need to distance yourself from those who, spiritually speaking, are more like a washbasin than a house of bread. The friends who influence you the most should be women who live by Hebrews 10:24 (NIV): *"And let us consider how we may spur one another on toward love and good deeds."* Your best friends should be cheering you on in your commitment to Jesus.

NEW SURROUNDINGS

Ruth had to relocate in order to be fed spiritually. Likewise, some single women may have to "relocate" because some of their former relationships keep them in a constant state of spiritual "hunger." They have to change jobs or even their church in order to continue to grow. In the same way, be open to a change that may benefit your spiritual growth. Like Ruth, look for something that will stimulate your growth in the Lord.

One young woman had to make a choice between playing on a championship volleyball team or being a part of a discipleship group. She knew that she was free to play volleyball if she wanted. But when she compared volleyball and the discipleship opportunity, the Lord showed her that the good often becomes the enemy of the best in life. Because of her reckless abandonment in following the Lord's leadership, she valued her growing commitment to the Lord more than playing volleyball, and it paid off. The discipleship training prepared her heart to respond to an invitation to serve as a short-term missionary in the Philippines. Another young woman may be called to spend her summer ministering to a volleyball team instead of being in a discipleship group, but the commitment to do as the Lord directs is the key.

Ruth moved from a hedonistic society into a culture that attempted to please the God of the universe rather than the sensuous gods of the flesh. Within our advanced society of the 21st century, we often encounter women engaged in becoming a part of self-serving singles' clubs, singles' dating services, singles' cruises, singles' meet markets… all created to keep singles busy in the waiting time of life. A committed single woman must be sensitive to the inevitable challenges she will meet in her attempt to live unselfishly in such a self-serving society.

One single was persecuted, not by non-Christians but by Christians, because she chose to spend her summer studying at a Bible institute rather than playing in the sunshine with her friends. They actually accused her of thinking she was better than them because she planned to study the Bible intensively for eight weeks. Unfortunately, our self-centered culture in America has penetrated the Church so much that a young woman not only has to choose against the American culture, but sometimes against the more subtle, worldly Christian subculture tainting the Body of Christ.

Part of reckless abandonment is realizing how much our culture has affected our behavior patterns. You want to be Christlike, but your lifestyle is a reflection of *Vogue* magazine or *Cosmopolitan* rather than a new creation in Christ. A.W. Tozer said, "A whole new generation of Christians has come up believing that it is possible to 'accept' Christ without forsaking the world."[3] Ruth had to forsake the familiar and comfortable in order to receive God's best for her life.

NEW FAITH

Ruth moved from a false religion into the only true and eternal relationship. Too many women have been involved in a form of religious worship, but have never had a vital, growing relationship with Jesus. Has your religious experience been like Isaiah 29:13b? *"...Their worship of Me is made up only of rules taught by men"* (NIV). Has your faith been a lifeless ritual rather than a vital love relationship with Jesus? Why not spend some of your free hours as a single woman beginning a journey away from rituals into a deep relationship with Jesus Christ?

One single woman expressed this vital relationship with Jesus in the following way: "I desired that my relationship with the Lord be an adventure. One where I would find out what pleased Him and then do it, devoting as much energy to Jesus as I would in a relationship with a boyfriend. I am falling more in love with Jesus every day." Do you know more about pleasing a boyfriend than you do about pleasing the Lord Jesus?

DIVIDENDS FROM A HIGH PRICE

Ruth's choice was costly, but the return on this high price far outweighed her investment. Matthew 19:29 says, *"And everyone who has left houses or brothers or sisters or father or mother or children or fields for My sake will receive a hundred times as much and will inherit eternal life"* (NIV). Ruth made the choice to turn her back on all that was familiar and begin a whole new life. Her "hundred times as much" was a godly husband, a son who would be the grandfather of King David, and inclusion in the lineage of Jesus Christ. She turned her back on all that was familiar, and God rewarded Ruth's critical choice.

Another costly aspect of Ruth's choice was the time frame in Israel's history. It was the age of the judges, a period of time described as "do your own thing"; *"Everyone did what was right in his own eyes"* (Judg. 21:25b). Ruth chose not only to break her family cycle, but also to challenge the lifestyle that many in Israel embraced. She wanted God's will, not hers; His blueprints, not her elementary scribbling; God's assignment, not her foolish plans.

Whenever a single woman decides to abandon herself completely to Jesus, as Ruth did, she will find herself out of step with society and, sometimes, even with her friends. A single woman today needs the boldness to challenge and break the cycle of the "American way" that exalts a relationship with a man as the answer to life. This "American way" blurs the reality of the ultimate answer to life found in a deep relationship with Jesus Christ. A modern-day Ruth wrote, "My deep satisfaction from my commitment to Jesus is constantly challenged by other believers. They treat me like some kind of Neanderthal, definitely out of step with today's woman."

THE MISSING PUZZLE PIECE

Often a woman will attempt to find delight in a career if Mr. Right has not arrived. In time, even her "great career" will prove to be less than satisfying. A career, a marriage, or even motherhood is not enough to totally satisfy you by itself. God knows that you will never be complete until you really understand that you are complete in Jesus. Colossians 2:9-10 says, *"For in Him all the fullness of Deity dwells in bodily form, and in Him you have been made complete, and He is the head over all rule and authority."* When a single woman enters a career or even marriage without understanding that she is complete in Christ, she will be disillusioned and dissatisfied.

Incompleteness is not the result of being single, but of not being full of Jesus. Only in the process of reckless abandonment to Jesus does any woman ever finally understand that, in Him, she is complete. When two "incomplete" singles get married, their union will not make them complete. Their marriage will be simply two "incomplete" people trying to find completeness in one another. Only when they understand that their fullness is found in a relationship with Jesus will they ever begin to *complement* one another. They can never *complete* one another. You were not created to complete another, but to *complement*. Completion is Jesus' responsibility and complementing is a woman's privilege. A woman not complete in Jesus will be a drain on her husband. Such a woman will expect her husband to fill the gap that only Jesus can fill. Only the single woman who understands this means of being complete in Jesus is mature enough to be a helpmeet (complement). *"For in Christ all the fullness of the Deity lives in bodily form, and you have been given fullness in Christ..."* (Col. 2:9-10 NIV). Are you feeling full yet? Ask the Lord right now to begin this process of revealing to your heart the reality of your fullness in Him. *"But it is good for me to draw near to God..."* (Ps. 73:28a KJV).

In her book, *Loneliness*, Elisabeth Elliot states, "Marriage teaches us that even the most intimate human companionship cannot satisfy the deepest places of the heart. Our hearts are lonely 'til they rest in Him."[4] Elisabeth Elliot has been married three times (twice widowed), and she knows from experience that marriage does not make one complete— only Jesus does.

SATISFIED BY A HEAVENLY FIANCÉ

Does your relationship with Jesus reflect reckless abandonment to Him, or does it reflect only tokenism, a superficial effort toward following Jesus? Are you content to offer to Jesus that which costs you nothing? Are you influencing those around you to consider a life-changing commitment to Jesus Christ? In the Song of Solomon, the Shulammite was so committed to the one she loved that other women wanted to meet him. They were anxious to go with her to seek for him. *"Where has your lover gone, most beautiful of women? Which way did your lover turn, that we may look for him with you?"* (Song of Sol. 6:1 NIV) Who was this one so worthy of such reckless abandonment? Does your commitment to Jesus cause those around you to seriously consider whether Jesus is Lord of their lives? Or does your "token" relationship leave you and others still thirsty?

One of Jackie's single friends stopped by her home one day, glowing and grinning from ear to ear. When questioned about her grin, she replied, "I am on a honeymoon with Jesus." This woman had been through a brutal divorce (including losing custody of her children), and in her hopeless condition she met the One who gives everlasting hope. When she began to recklessly abandon herself to knowing Jesus as Lord, He began to fill the gaps in her heart left by the removal of her husband and children. In Christ she found comfort, healing, direction, and purpose for her life. Do you understand such a relationship with Christ? It doesn't come cheaply, but the high price is worth the results of such a commitment, especially today. The depth of your relationship with God is up to you. God has no favorites; the choice to surrender is yours. A.W. Tozer so brilliantly stated in his book *The Pursuit of God*: "It will require a determined heart and more than a little courage to wrench ourselves loose from the grip of our times and return to Biblical ways."[5]

Ruth had just such a determined heart, and the Lord honored her faith to move away from all that was familiar and take a journey toward the completely unknown. Ruth did not allow her friends, her old surroundings, nor her culture's dead faith to keep her from running hard after God. She did not use the excuse of a dark past to keep her from a bright future that began with her first critical choice: reckless abandonment to Jesus Christ.

Have you made this critical choice or you have settled for a mediocre relationship with Jesus? Amy Carmichael, one of the greatest single woman missionaries who ever lived, once remarked, "The saddest thing one meets is the nominal Christian."[6]

Choose right now to put mediocrity behind you; courageously determine to pursue Jesus with your whole heart, soul, and mind. As a single woman, this is the perfect moment to establish a radical relationship with Jesus and remove any tokenism from your Christian walk.

Becoming a Lady in Waiting begins with reckless abandonment to Jesus. The strength and discipline necessary to be a Lady of Diligence, Faith, Virtue, Devotion, Purity, Security, Contentment, Conviction, and Patience is discovered in this radical way of relating to your heavenly Bridegroom. If you find yourself struggling with any of the qualities discussed in the following chapters, you may want to reexamine your own commitment to Jesus. Is it real and all-encompassing, or merely ornamental? Do you remember a time when you broke your "alabaster box" in the presence of the Lord Jesus? The Lady in Waiting understands the pleasing aroma of the perfume that flows from one's "broken alabaster box." It is the irresistible aroma of reckless abandonment to Jesus Christ.

BECOMING A LADY OF RECKLESS ABANDONMENT

From your perspective, what is the difference between "token commitment" and "reckless abandonment" to Jesus? Is your relationship with Jesus one of sacrifice or convenience? (See Second Samuel 24:24.)

Have you broken your "alabaster box" at the feet of Jesus? (See Mark 14:3-9 and Luke 7:36-39.) Are you afraid to break your box at His feet? Why?

Like Ruth, how has your relationship with Jesus affected your friends, your surroundings, and your faith? (See Matthew 19:29.)

Does your life have public and private evidences of your reckless abandonment to Jesus Christ? Explain.

Read Colossians 2:10. What does being complete in Jesus mean to you? In what ways do you feel incomplete? How can that be changed?

Have you experienced the completeness that comes from the courtship available with your heavenly Fiancé? Consider this dating prerequisite: You must understand you are complete in Jesus before you ever date or marry.

What does the following statement mean to you: "Any woman who does not understand that she is complete in Jesus is susceptible to idolatry"? (This idolatry is dependence on a guy to make her complete—thus putting him in God's place.) Consider this verse: *"How happy are those who know their need for God..."* (Matt. 5:3 PNT).

ENDNOTES

1. Kenneth G. Smith, *Learning to Be a Woman* (Downers Grove, IL: InterVarsity Press, 1970), back cover.

2. *Scofield Bible* (New York, NY: Oxford University Press, 1967), 51, note on Genesis 35:19.

3. A.W. Tozer, The Pursuit of God (Camp Hill, PA: Christian Publications, 1982), 16.

4. Elisabeth Elliot, *Loneliness* (Nashville, TN: Oliver Nelson, 1988), 16.

5. Tozer, *The Pursuit of God*, 29.

6. Quoted in Elisabeth Elliot, *A Chance to Die* (Old Tappan, NJ: Fleming H. Revell Company, 1987), 117.

Chapter 2

LADY OF DILIGENCE

While getting ready for a speaking engagement, she managed to get the kids up, dressed, and fed; fill the lunch boxes; load everyone in the car; and take them to school. Then she hurried home to set her hair and do her makeup. Finally dressed and ready to go speak, she made one last dash for the bathroom. While washing her hands, she noticed that the toilet was overflowing—not a slow drip, but pouring out all over the floor and into her open-toed shoes and nylons. She scrambled for towels and used them to build a dike then rubbed her feet dry and squirted her shoes with perfume. She ran out the door and jumped into the car. Halfway to the church she realized that she had left her Bible and outlines on the kitchen counter.

Such is the drama of Jackie Kendall's daily life. This kind of insanity is not unique to her. Every wife and mother daily deals with the legitimate needs of her husband and children. These needs take precedence over anything she might want to do, regardless of how "noble" her desires are! To be involved in the simplest form of ministry may require the married woman three times as much time to accomplish, in comparison to the single woman. Although a single woman may long for the "chaos" of a family, she must not waste her time wishing for it. She must be diligent to use her single time wisely now. She has more control over her time and choices now than she will probably ever have again. (The single parent is not included in this comparison because her responsibilities are double that of a married woman. She must go "solo" in raising children, increasing the burden of her daily priorities even more.)

The perfect time to make the most of every opportunity is while you are single. Every believer should use time wisely, as Ephesians 5:15-17 (NIV) says,

> *Be very careful, then, how you live—not as unwise but as wise, making the most of every opportunity, because the days are evil. Therefore do not be foolish, but understand what the Lord's will is.*

John Fischer wrote this:

> God has called me to live now. He wants me to realize my full potential as a man right now, to be thankful about where I am, and to enjoy it to the fullest. I have a strange feeling that the single person who is always wishing he were married will probably get married, discover all that is involved, and wish he were single again! He will ask himself, "Why didn't I use that time for the Lord when I didn't have so many other obligations? Why didn't I give myself totally to Him when I was single?"[1]

The single woman can be involved in the Lord's work on a level that a married woman cannot because of the distractions and responsibilities of being a wife and mother. Ironically, some single women can be so distressed by their single state that they become emotionally more distracted than a wife and mother of four children.

Rather than staying home worrying about another "dateless" Saturday night, realize how much valuable time has been entrusted to you at this point in your life. Rather than resent your many single hours, embrace them as a gift from God—a package that contains opportunities to serve Him that are limited only by your own self-pity and lack of obedience.

NO TIME TO WASTE

Understanding God's promised provision for widows, Naomi sent Ruth to gather grain in the field of a kinsman. Ruth was willing to use her life working diligently at whatever her Lord called her to do. She would not be paralyzed by her lack of a husband:

> *And Ruth the Moabitess said to Naomi, "Please let me go to the field and glean among the ears of grain after one in whose*

sight I may find favor." And she said to her, "Go, my daughter" (Ruth 2:2).

She also did not allow the fact that she was a stranger from Moab to cause her to fear while she was gleaning in a strange field. Ruth was the "new girl in town," an obvious newcomer, but she was not afraid to walk into a totally unfamiliar situation. Countless single women stay home rather than travel alone into the unknown. They not only miss out on being encouraged by others, but also are not exposed to new relationships when they remain at home tied up by cords of fear and feeling sorry for themselves.

If a single woman allows the fearful prospect of meeting new people and new challenges to keep her at home, she may find herself bored and lonely while all the time missing many satisfying and fulfilling experiences. Don't stay home as a fearful single woman. Take that step of faith and volunteer. Get involved and see what you have been missing. One single said, "Serving the Lord brings such inexpressible joy." People who are not involved in serving the Lord obviously have never experienced this joy; otherwise, churches wouldn't have to beg them to get involved. If all the singles in the church just realized their "strategic position," churches would not ever need to ask for help with children, youth, or college students. There would probably be so many available single workers that there would be a "surplus of man power"!

FREE TO FOLLOW

Are you busy serving Jesus during your free time, or do you waste hours trying to pursue and snag an available guy? Ruth was a widow, but she did not use her time sponsoring pity parties for all unhappy single women to gather and compare the misery of datelessness. When she and Naomi moved back to Bethlehem, Ruth did not waste a moment feeling sorry for herself. She went right to work. Instead of being drained by her discouraging circumstances, she took advantage of them and diligently embraced each day.

Ruth came to the God of Israel after years of living in darkness, but He gladly received her service even though she was a Moabite foreigner.

She bound herself to the service of the Lord, interweaving her service with Him like the braiding of a heavy rope. Isaiah 56:6-7 (NIV) refers to a foreigner binding himself (or herself) to the Lord and Him willingly receiving their "diligent" service: *"And foreigners who bind themselves to the Lord to serve Him...these I will bring to My holy mountain..."*

Are you tightly bound to the Lord, serving Him diligently, or has your relationship and service been unraveling over the years as you continue to be single and not married? Has resentment and self-pity unraveled what used to be a tightly woven labor for the Lord? You must be sensitive to the things and situations that distract you from redeeming your free time:

> Whatever might blur the vision God had given [Amy Carmichael] of His work, whatever could distract or deceive or tempt others to seek anything but the Lord Jesus Himself she tried to eliminate.[2]

Some singles see the lack of a mate as God denying them something for a more "noble purpose"—*a cross to bear*! Our selfish nature tends to focus on what we do not have rather than on what we do have—free time—that can be used for others and ourselves. Is your life on hold until you have someone to hold?

Sitting in a restaurant across from a beautiful blonde, as the woman's personal story began to unfold, the listener was somewhat overwhelmed. Here was a very attractive woman who had put her life with Jesus on hold after her world fell apart. She had been married for a few years and was trying to conceive a child, when she heard her single best friend was pregnant. What irony: her unmarried friend was with child, and she remained childless. The irony turned into a trauma when this married woman found out that the father was her own husband. Can you imagine the devastation caused in this beautiful young woman's heart? Have you experienced such a crushing emotional blow? The stunned listener began to cry out for wisdom concerning this tragedy. Jesus reminded the listener that God is not intimidated by trauma. In fact, Psalm 34:18 says, *"The Lord is near to the brokenhearted and saves those who are crushed in spirit."* This brokenhearted woman had put her life on hold after her husband divorced her. Such a response is understandable, but that day in the restaurant this now single woman decided to take her broken heart, her empty arms, and her loneliness and give them to Jesus. In exchange, Jesus taught her how to resist feeling sorry for herself and how to stop living in the arena of bitterness. After she made the choice of recklessly abandoning herself to Jesus as Lord, she was free to serve Him. This once brokenhearted single woman has been transformed into a fearless servant of the Lord. In fact, she became a missionary to Quito, Ecuador.

Have you also put your life on hold? Do you have an excuse for not serving Jesus?

A FULL PLACE SETTING

A former college friend remained single longer than any of us ever expected. She had dated incessantly in college, so we assumed if any of the girls would marry, it would be Donna. Ten years after her graduation from college, she was not married. Someone asked what helped her to be so satisfied as a single woman. Her immediate response was, "A full place setting." She had lived for several years eating her meals on paper plates while her good china and flatware were snugly stored in her hope chest. Then the Lord showed her that she did not have to wait for a "mate" to bring beauty to her private world. She unpacked her china and silver and began not only to entertain others in style, but also to daily set out china and crystal for herself. (One Wednesday night at church Donna sat in front of two people who were to become her future in-laws. They did not know each other at the time. On the way home from church, the future father-in-law remarked that he thought Donna would become his daughter-in-law. He was absolutely right. This satisfied single woman has someone sharing her china and crystal today, but her feelings of satisfaction did not come because of a husband. She found satisfaction by serving the Lord.)

Some women put their lives on hold, each waiting for some guy to come riding into her life on a white stallion. They have no china, no decent furniture, and no pictures on the walls—none of the little extras that make a house inviting. They make minimal investment in what they hope is a temporary condition. Their lives reflect a "paper plate" mentality. They cannot comprehend fullness and satisfaction without a man. These precious women have settled for the "generic" version of life. How unlike Jesus' statement in John 10:10, in which He said He came so we might have a more abundant life. Do you believe that the abundant life is only for the married woman? Do you think that a woman with a husband, two children, a nice home, and two insurance policies is more satisfied with life than you are? Life is satisfying only when you diligently serve the Lord, whatever your circumstances.

ENVIABLE SINGLENESS

Singleness is an enviable condition. An unmarried woman has something that a married woman gives up on her wedding day: extra time for Jesus. Too many young women waste valuable years as they wait for life to begin—after marriage. They rarely realize the priceless free time they waste, until it is gone. Have you neglected some mission or ministry opportunities because you feared prolonging your unmarried state?

A young woman heard about this enviable condition and wrote a letter asking Jackie whether she should pursue a doctorate. (She continues to count more birthdays as a single than she had anticipated.) Jackie enthusiastically encouraged her to immediately get her degree. As a single woman, she diligently hit the books without neglecting a mate or a child. Her single state served as the perfect qualification for the pursuit of a doctorate. This is not to say that a woman can't pursue her dreams after she is married, but she will have a much higher price to pay and often the pursued dream turns into a nightmare!

If you love serving Jesus, please do not waste any of the free time you have. Do not consider yourself too unhappy to help anyone else. Self-centeredness will rob you of the joy of serving. Satan, who is effective at distracting you from God's best, wants you to continue dreaming about how "one day" you will get involved in ministry. He wants to sidetrack you from making a lasting investment. Too many women foolishly believe his lies. Therefore, they lose sight of opportunities to get involved in any form of outreach to others. Unsatisfied and unfulfilled, they sink deep into the quicksand of "maybe next year."

Many have embraced the ultimate deception, "Poor me." An excerpt from a single friend's letter exposes this self-pitying lie: "As is usually the case, as soon as I stopped asking what was in it for me and began asking what I was meant to give, things began to improve, beginning with my attitude. I continue to grow and be greatly strengthened in my relationship with God one-on-one and to seek out where I can serve those around me." This single woman is a classic beauty. She has learned how to use her free time for Jesus rather than sit home writing melancholy poetry.

Unrelenting Pursuit

Undistracted and unrelenting describe different facets of the word *diligence*. The Lady of Diligence embodies these terms. A verse that describes her attitude toward ministry and service is First Corinthians 15:58 (NIV): *"Therefore, my dear brothers, stand firm. Let nothing move you. Always give yourselves fully to the work of the Lord, because you know that your labor in the Lord is not in vain."* Do these terms describe your attitude and approach to using your free time for Jesus? Let's examine how diligence affects every aspect of your service and ministry for the Lord.

Diligence and the Ministry of Teaching

Have you been diligently pursuing truth for years, but not giving out as much as you have taken in? Are you involved in a regular Bible study where you give, maybe even teach? Almost as dangerous as neglecting the Word is the habit of taking it in but not putting it into practice. "Impression without expression can lead to depression." Do you keep attending church, Sunday school, Bible studies, seminars, and retreats—taking yet never giving? Take advantage of this time in your life when you can be involved in teaching without so many encumbrances. Maybe you've considered leading a discipleship group. Hesitate no more; go for it! There is no time in your life more perfect than now. Maybe you have toyed with the idea of teaching a Bible study. Do not delay. The future may hold more distractions that would continue to keep you from your goal.

DILIGENCE AND THE MINISTRY OF ENCOURAGEMENT

How many times a week do you find yourself in a position where someone has shared a need with you and you want so much to respond with wisdom and grace? Isaiah 50:4 (NIV) says:

> *The Sovereign Lord has given me an instructed tongue, to know the word that sustains the weary. He wakens me morning by morning, wakens my ear to listen like one being taught.*

Do you have a hard time responding to such an early morning wake-up call? Rising early to develop the tongue of a disciple will open a door of ministry to those who are weary, whether they are at work, at church, or even at the grocery store. Your very words will be a ministry of healing and encouragement. *"The tongue that brings healing is a tree of life, but a deceitful tongue crushes the spirit"* (Prov. 15:4 NIV). Such predawn training will give you the privilege of becoming God's garden hose in a land of many thirsty people.

DILIGENCE AND THE MINISTRY OF PRAYER

Do you have a prayer partner? Or do you only have someone with whom you have regular pity parties? If you do not have a prayer partner, ask the Lord right now for such a gift. A prayer partner can help you pray for others. Of course, this prayer partner needs to be a female, one who can encourage you to keep God's perspective on your commitment to being all God wants you to be, whether married or single.

"A prayer partnership serves as one of the greatest assets for accomplishing the deepest and highest work of the human spirit: prayer."[3] Praying regularly with someone (or a small group) is such a vital part of your service to God. To intercede on behalf of someone else's need is a privilege. When you intercede with a partner, the "duet" of harmony before God can change your world. Matthew 18:19 (NIV) describes this harmonious duet: *"Again, I tell you that if two of you on earth agree about anything you ask for, it will be done for you by My Father in heaven."* That little verb *agree* refers to harmony. Do you have someone with whom you can prayerfully approach God in harmony? Rather than searching for a life partner, look for a prayer partner. Together you can participate in God-given prayer projects. Together you can discover how you can take your concerns for others and turn them into prayer projects.

DILIGENCE AND THE MINISTRY OF SERVICE

It is doubtful that there could ever be a better time to serve Jesus than this "moment" of singleness. Rather than wasting precious moments fantasizing about an earthly lover, take advantage of your free hours each day to serve the Lord of Heaven. If you are frustrated and distracted rather than fruitfully serving Jesus, then ask Him right now to adjust your vision.

As Ruth diligently worked at what she could, God sent her a man to protect and provide for her. God will do the same for you if that is His plan. Is there a ministry opportunity you should be working with? Why not consider a short-term mission trip? Don't worry about that certain guy you have had your eye on for a while. If he is God's best for you, he will be there when you return. Your single state may not be permanent, but it definitely is not to be a comatose state until your Prince Charming arrives and whisks you off to his castle. Single women are not "Sleeping Beauties" waiting for their prince to fight his way through the thorns and past the wicked witch to finally kiss them awake. That is an illusion often used by the enemy to defraud women.

Is there an opportunity of service that you have avoided because you can't give up your "post on the castle wall" looking for your knight in shining armor? Is there an application for a summer ministry waiting for you to fill out? Such a chance may come again next summer, but then it will be even harder to respond to the prospect of serving, for time brings more and more distractions. As you get older, you assume more obligations and responsibilities that demand your time and attention. Such distractions will make serving Jesus even more difficult. Have you given Jesus full reign over your time?

Limitless ministry opportunities exist for the Lady of Diligence. These ministries are available right this moment. They do not demand a Bible college education. The only requirement is a single woman who desires to use her time wisely in ministry.

DILIGENCE AND THE MINISTRY OF WRITING

This ministry requires pen, paper, and a willing heart. Much of the New Testament was originally written as letters to believers. An encouraging letter or postcard can be read and re-read. So often a person will think about writing someone a letter, but the thought never becomes action. You may ignore the inward suggestion because of a busy schedule or a resistance to writing. A personal note, though, serves as oxygen to the soul of the recipient. *"He who refreshes others will himself be refreshed"* (Prov. 11:25b NIV).

If you are not comfortable writing a full letter, or your schedule does not permit such a ministry in writing, then purchase some pre-stamped postcards and try to send them regularly to different people who need a refreshing word. Write an email or send a Facebook message. The Lord wants you to be involved in the lives of those around you, and writing is one of those opportunities.

DILIGENCE AND THE MINISTRY OF LISTENING

A ministry of listening is available right now. When someone is grieving, your presence provides more power than words. When someone is burdened, you may want to just listen and silently pray rather than verbally give the solution to the problem. Being content to listen to someone today is a gift you can give. A listener provides a healing audience for someone who is hurting. When Jackie's sister died, listeners who allowed her to share the loss and cry freely were God's greatest source of comfort. Being content to listen is a gift you can give to someone today.

It may take a gentle touch to minister to the spirit. It also may require just being with the person, whether standing for hours in a hospital hallway or sitting by a sickbed. Sometimes even the greatest songs or truths are not the appropriate thing during a crisis: *"Like one who takes away a garment on a cold day, or like vinegar poured on soda, is one who sings songs to a heavy heart"* (Prov. 25:20 NIV). This ministry requires not seminary training, but a loving, listening heart.

DILIGENCE AND THE MINISTRY OF HOSPITALITY

The ministry of hospitality is not producing a demo for the Parade of Homes or a feast featuring Julia Child. Simply cooking for others is a significant ministry, especially during illness or bereavement. Casseroles and cakes can be such a blessing to a new mother, an elderly neighbor, or someone emotionally devastated by a death in the family. What a way to share the love of Christ with someone who needs to see Christianity in action.

Please do not limit your ministry of hospitality to candlelight dinners for the man of your dreams. Think how a beautiful, candlelight dinner for a group of single women, or even high school girls, could minister to them.

DILIGENCE AND THE MINISTRY OF HELPS

This ministry requires time, but it is invaluable. Helping others with the "dailies" of life is a gift that breaks their exhausting monotony. Helping a friend get her apartment ready for special guests, or helping her move into a new place, leaves the recipient grateful. Mere physical labor may seem so insignificant in comparison to church visitation, but the Word of God speaks clearly to such a misconception. *"Whether, then, you eat or drink or whatever you do, do all to the glory of God"* (1 Cor. 10:31). Maybe a friend needs a ride to the airport during rush hour, or maybe she needs her oven cleaned, or even her laundry done. These duties can all be done unto the Lord. *"Whatever you do, work at it with all your heart, as working for the Lord, not for men"* (Col. 3:23 NIV).

NON-NEWSY WORKS

For those of you who are diligently going after Jesus and the privilege of serving Him, here is a very special reminder. Sometimes you will be called to do some monotonous work that will not make the headlines. It may frustrate you because it doesn't seem very "impressive." Consider the reality of all the non-newsy things Jesus did during the majority of His life (30 years), before He began His formal ministry. What more humbling work could Ruth have done than gathering leftover grain for the survival of her mother-in-law and herself?

Richard Foster brilliantly penned this thought, "If all of our serving is before others, we will be shallow people indeed."[4] Jesus spoke clearly about the constant public display of our service. *"Everything they do is done for men to see..."* (Matt. 23:5 NIV). The next time someone asks you to help out in service that is monotonous and non-newsy, don't hesitate. The King records such works (see Matt. 25:34-35). Teaching Bible studies, going out on evangelism teams, mission trips, and even prayer groups—all these are priceless opportunities to serve, but they are not the only avenues. Serving in the preschool department at church, going to kids' camp, and even cooking in the kitchen for a junior high banquet are all honorable services that the Lady of Diligence can embrace with respect.

Look at your schedule and decide how some of your free time that was wasted yesterday might be redeemed today. Allow no more room in your schedule for "pity parties." Such wise use of your free time will give you the gift of "no regrets." Your future service will be focused and no longer distracted.

Free hours,
Not wasted by me,
Using my free time,
To serve only Thee.
Realizing how temporary free time will be
Never to regret a missed opportunity,
For others to be blest,
Through yielded me.
—JMK

BECOMING A LADY OF DILIGENCE

Determine what may have kept you from being more involved in ministry by seeing which of the following four characters you identify with the most.

Jealous Jenny: Do you focus on the gifts others have been given and, therefore, never find your own niche in ministry? Have you unwisely compared yourself with other women? (See First Corinthians 4:7; 12:7; Romans 12:3.)

Prima Donna Paula: Do you want to serve God on your terms? Do you want to write the script and have the leading role? (See John 4:34; 7:16,18; Matthew 23:5.)

Fearful Frances: Do you fear what others think? Are you afraid of becoming too involved and being labeled a fanatic? Do you hesitate to be a Lady of Diligence because you feel so inadequate? (See Proverbs 29:25; Second Timothy 1:7; First Thessalonians 5:24.)

Doubting Doris: Faith is believing what God says about you. Do you long to become more involved in a number of ministries, but feel your faith will fizzle before you finish? Have you struggled with serving the Lord in the past, so you doubt yourself today? (Part of ministry is learning, so don't let yesterday's struggles prevent future successes.) (See First John 4:4; Second Timothy 1:9; First Timothy 6:12.)

To get involved in any ministry demands a sacrifice. Have you allowed your self-centeredness to dominate your daily schedule? Why not go through your checkbook tonight and see how many checks were written for things concerning others? (See Second Samuel 24:24; Philippians 2:3-4; Matthew 19:29.)

ENDNOTES

1. John Fischer, *A Single Person's Identity* (Discovery Papers, Catalog No. 3154, August 5, 1973), 3.

2. Elisabeth Elliot, *A Chance to Die* (Old Tappan, NJ: Fleming H. Revell Company, 1987), 117.

3. Charles F. Stanley, *Handle With Prayer* (Wheaton, IL: Victory Books, 1982), 15.

4. Richard J. Foster, *Celebration of Discipline* (San Francisco, CA: Harper & Row Publishers, 1978), 117.

Chapter 3

LADY OF FAITH

Faith...
a fruit whose blossoming aroma
inspires one to victory,
and sustains one after loss.
—JMK

If you are spouse-hunting, we have heard that Alaska, Montana, and Florida have an abundance of men. Proportionately, women most outnumber men in the Northeastern states.

Are you panicked because you are residing in one of these male-sparse states? A recent statistic from the National Census Bureau states that the percentage of single men in Palm Beach has increased by 47 percent since 1980. Palm Beach, Florida—where the boys are! (Sounds like an old movie from the 1950s.) Do you suddenly have the urge to relocate? Don't start packing yet.

The Census Bureau in 2000 confirmed the USA's male population being higher than females—with the exception of three states: California, Alaska, and Hawaii. In these three states the female population was higher. An article in *USA Today* stated: "The Census Bureau reports today that for the first time since the early 1900s, the USA's male population grew faster than the female in the 1980s."[1] Are you breathing easier? Such a statistic does not alleviate your need to be a Lady of Faith. The existence of more single men does not mean exemption from the often trying process of waiting for God's best by faith.

One friend assumed that by going to a big Christian college, she would inevitably find Mr. Right. Considering that she was from a very small town where more livestock lived than people, her strategy for finding a spouse seemed quite logical. She completed her four years and returned home without her "MRS" degree. Where do you think she found her mate? You guessed it, back in her very small hometown. Her father invited her to come and watch their church baseball team, and guess who showed up on the opposing team? Mr. Right, a guy she had met at youth camp more than a decade earlier. You know the rest of the story. Her logic did not find Mr. Right. She returned to a hometown barren of many males, and God, who is not limited by our circumstances, delivered her mate from way out in "left field." God did not honor her logic, but He did honor her faith in Him to meet her needs.

Do you presently live in a town or city where you need "eyes of faith" in relation to the prospects of a mate? Do you attend a church where the "pickins are slim"? Let's take a closer look at two contrasting attitudes toward one's circumstances.

WHERE THE BOYS ARE

Think back to how the love story in the Book of Ruth began. Three widows, Naomi with her two daughters-in-law, Orpah and Ruth, have just been through the painful experience of losing the men they loved. Just facing each day without their mates required much faith because of the difficulty in providing for one's own needs. Naomi, being a Jewess, made the decision to leave Moab and return to her hometown in Israel (Bethlehem). Her two daughters-in-law had become young widows, so she encouraged them to return to their families where they each might find another husband. Naomi's suggestion appeared very rational. Naomi knew that they (being Moabites) had a better chance of finding husbands in Moab than in Israel.

> *...Go back, each of you, to your mother's home. May the Lord show kindness to you, as you have shown to your dead and to me. May the Lord grant that each of you will find rest in the home of another husband* (Ruth 1:8-9 NIV).

Would Ruth have ever found a godly husband to be united with if she had also returned to Moab?

Naomi lovingly pointed Orpah and Ruth in the direction of possible prospects. She actually encouraged them to go in a direction where they could *see* how they might each find a husband. Orpah followed Naomi's advice and chose logical sight for future direction. She gave Naomi a kiss good-bye and headed "where the boys are." Such "choices" are often based on logical sight and do not need even a mustard seed of faith.

Many single women spend their free time searching for the same kind of location chosen by Orpah. They attend schools because they can "see" the prospects. They join churches based on apparent ratios of men to women. They go to seminars, retreats, and conferences looking for the man of their dreams, only to demand a refund for the nightmare they often find (the ratio of women to men typically registered at retreats being seven women to every one man).

Some women have changed churches because they were in a "no prospective mate" district. Others avoid churches under-stocked with available men. Can you relate? Some single women serve only one term on a mission field and never return because the ratio of available men to women shrinks even smaller on the mission field than in their home church. A single woman serving as a missionary wrote: "Well, here I am in a no-hope situation. There is only one single man to about fifty single women." On what are these women focusing—on the situation or on the Sovereign One?

CHANCE RENDEZVOUS

A woman who takes the route of Orpah (sensual, logical sight) often invents ways for a "chance rendezvous" with the man of her dreams. You can see her loitering in the very area that Mr. Right regularly frequents, hoping that he might finally notice her and the romance will begin. This sounds more like a Harlequin romance. Such a young woman might sing in the choir, not because she wants to make a joyful noise unto the Lord, but because she wants a weekly chance to sit near the prospect (single man) that her "sensual sight" has focused upon. Such impure motives for such a noble cause! Proverbs 19:14 says, *"House and wealth are an inheritance from fathers, but a prudent wife is from the Lord."*

If the Lord wants to give you a man, He does not need your clever "chance rendezvous." This is not advocating that you avoid men completely and expect the Lord to "UPS" His choice to your front door. You need to participate in activities that involve men and women, but be sensitive to your motives whenever you find yourself in the presence of "available men." Consider this Scripture whenever checking your motives and your pulse! Proverbs 16:2 (NIV) says, *"All a man's ways seem innocent to him, but motives are weighed by the Lord."*

You can prevent disappointing moments if you check your heart whenever you go to a singles' activity. Much preparation (like taking a shower, putting on makeup, styling your hair, doing your nails, and choosing the perfect outfit) precedes one's attending such an activity, yet so little heart preparation does. The gal with sensual sight can become so obsessed with finding her guy that she neglects her inner self. Orpah's style (logical sight) tends to become the norm, but Ruth offers an alternative to this vain search for Mr. Right. She demonstrates what it means to be a Lady of Faith.

EYES OF FAITH

Orpah's example of going after the available men could have influenced Ruth to return to Moab, the home of her parents and the gods of her youth. Ruth, however, remained with Naomi and her God. Ruth certainly must have considered the probability of remaining single if she went with Naomi. Even though it promised no prospects of a husband, she chose to follow Naomi and her God back to Bethlehem. Ruth chose to trust God with her future. She looked not with sensual sight, but through "eyes of faith." Even though Ruth was young in her faith in the God of Israel, she chose to trust with her heart for the future her eyes could not yet see.

The International Children's Bible describes faith in this way: *"Faith means being sure of the things we hope for. And faith means knowing that something is real even if we do not see it"* (Heb. 11:1). This childlike expression of such an abstract quality can become a daily reality in the life of the Lady of Faith. Your hope cannot be put in some dreamed-up future. It must be in the God who knows your past, present, and future, and loves you enough to give you the best.

Are you in what seems like a "no-hope situation"? Maybe you are attending a church that requires you to exercise faith to even open the door and go in, since every man there is either married, engaged, or the age of your baby brother. Instead of becoming fearful during this trying situation, look to the Lord through "eyes of faith." To do so brings God great pleasure. Hebrews 11:6a says, *"And without faith it is impossible to please* [totally satisfy] *Him...."* Your daily use of "eyes of faith" brings Jesus such satisfaction.

Do you long to please Him? Then reconsider your circumstances and realize that what seems to be a hopeless situation (no prospects on the horizon) is just the flip side of the view through "eyes of faith."

Sometimes in an attempt to be a Lady of Faith, one can get side-tracked trying to hurry the "male order delivery" process.

One must admit that it is more likely a woman would find a godly man in a church, at a Christian college, or in a local Bible study. These are obviously good places to find Mr. Right, but the assumption of finding him can result in disillusionment. Hundreds of wonderful single women live and breathe in all the right places, but they remain single.

You may wonder, "How can I be a Lady of Faith when I feel so insecure deep in my heart that God will deliver the goods? What if I have faith in God and end up being 98 and unmarried?" Of course, you would never outright admit that you're not sure you can trust God. That would appear too ungodly! But there's that sneaking fear in the back of your mind: "If I really give up my search and have 'eyes of faith,' God might not give me what I desire, like a husband, a home, and children." God knows when your heart aches for these precious things. But He also knows that these earthly things will not make you secure.

To be sure, your gnawing fears are very common. The enemy knows how common these fears are, and he feeds them by adding a few lies like, "If you give your desire to the Lord, He will send you to outer Bufelia where all the men are three feet tall," or, "If you give all your desires to the Lord, you might get married, but you'll definitely not want to take pictures of your fiancé for your friends to see."

"Can I really trust God with all my hopes and dreams? How will I meet Mr. Right if I have eyes of faith? Doesn't God need any help in developing my dreams? What about needing to be in the right place at the right time? How will I meet Mr. Right if I'm not out and about where he might be? I feel the urge to make a mad dash to the next party or to attend the college with the most available men." Such anxious thoughts are based on fears, not faith. "Faith does not eliminate questions. But faith knows where to take them."[2] You may say you have faith and are just being practical. Are you? What is the opposite of faith? Fear. Who knows that better than the enemy? At the base of his being is the desire to trick you into missing God's best. Satan wants you to believe the lie that cripples faith: God cannot be trusted.

In order to have "eyes of faith," you may have to use a spiritual eye wash to remove the debris that the enemy has dropped into your eyes. The Lady of Faith will have times when her secure eyes of faith begin to blink into an anxious twitch of insecure, sensual sight. She can admit her insecurity to her heavenly Fiancé, and He can calm the twitching eyes. Spending some quality time in the Word is the best "eye wash" for "eyes of faith."

Romans 10:17 says, *"So faith comes from hearing, and hearing by the word of Christ."* A Lady of Faith may have to spend dateless weekends in male-saturated churches. She can only be content in this trying situation if she has her "eyes of faith" properly focused on the ultimate relationship—with her heavenly Bridegroom. Datelessness is a common type of debris that irritates the "eyes of faith," but the eye wash treatment—quality time with Jesus and reading His Word—is always effective.

DIVINE ENCOUNTER

In contrast to the manipulated "chance rendezvous" of the single woman Orpah, Ruth had a divine encounter that affected not only her marital status, but also biblical history. That first morning in Bethlehem, Ruth happened to stop in a field belonging to Boaz. Interestingly enough, the same day, Boaz "just happened" to visit that very same field where Ruth was gathering the leftover grain. Their meeting was neither an accident nor the product of female maneuvering. Instead it was the work of a sovereign God.

God providentially directed Ruth to the field of Boaz. You find this divine encounter in the second chapter of Ruth, verse 3: "...*and she happened to come to the portion of the field belonging to Boaz....*" The verb *happened* in Hebrew means "chanced upon." This leaves no room for manipulation. She had a chance, and her chance transported her into the center of God's will and right to Boaz's field. Boaz was wealthy and available. Ruth did not "have plans" when she chanced upon his field. Ruth's "eyes of faith" led her to the exact spot where she would meet her Mr. Right, Boaz, whose name means "pillar of strength." (Contrast the meaning of his name to that of her first husband, Mahlon, which means "weak and sickly"! God rewarded Ruth's faith with a husband who was a "pillar of strength.")

If Jesus wants you married, He will orchestrate the encounter. You have nothing to fear except getting in His way and trying to "write the script" rather than following His. Jesus does have your best interest at heart. He desires to bless you by giving you the best. Sometimes what you perceive as the best is nothing more than a generic version. Consider His wisdom and love in comparison to your own wisdom and self-love. In whom are you going to trust—all Wisdom and Everlasting Love or little ol' finite you? Ever since the Garden of Eden, women have often felt they could and should know as much as God. Much pain in our world has resulted from dependence on our wisdom rather than on our Father's.

MEETING ACROSS CONTINENTS

A beautiful airline stewardess left her secular job and went to Germany as a missionary. Her "eyes of faith" sometimes twitched as the reality of no prospects, especially English-speaking ones, continued to loom before her while she diligently served the Lord. At a Bible conference, she met a single guy who served the Lord on the other side of the world. He was an unlikely candidate according to sensual sight and basic logic, but a long-distance courtship began, and they eventually married. Today they serve the Lord together in the Philippines.

Your circumstances and geographical location do not threaten God's will and purpose. Just as God brought Eve to Adam, Rebekah to Isaac, Ruth to Boaz, and someday the Bride of Christ to Himself, He will one day bring Mr. Right to you if you are to be married. This is true regardless of your unique situation. Your location or your occupation may not make you very accessible to available godly men, but these roadblocks do not handicap God. Time and time again, we have had the privilege of watching God bring a wonderful, godly guy into the life of a Lady of Faith. He seems to suddenly appear out of nowhere.

One young lady faithfully attended her church for years. Often she needed reminding that "he's just not here yet." God brought her Boaz from across the country to where she was in Florida. This single woman had developed better than 20/20 vision in relation to her "eyes of faith." Many tears of faith had washed away the debris that often caused her to doubt if she would ever get married. She used those times of doubting to grow in faith as she turned to God who orchestrated the future blessing for her.

God brought His best for one woman all the way from Escondido, California, to Kenya, Africa, where she was serving her Lord. She was not anxious about the absence of available men. After a broken engagement and a couple of years of less-than-satisfying dating, Vivian had volunteered to go to Kenya, Africa, to teach missionary kids. Just before she left for Kenya, she attended a Bible study where she met a precious Christian guy named David. Had she not been leaving for Africa that week, they might have had time to become better acquainted. Frustrated by the reality of meeting such a fine Christian guy just before leaving to go halfway around the world, Vivian followed the Lord to Africa with "eyes of faith." Little did she know the script God had written. Halfway through her first term on the field, a construction team arrived from the United States to do some work for the academy where she taught. Guess who was part of the team? You got it: David. He and Vivian not only got acquainted, but they also married right there in Kenya. Just as

Jesus brought David to Vivian, Jesus can bring your life-mate to you, no matter where you live.

The ultimate demonstration of Ladies of Faith are the single women who have lived the ten principles in this book—and who themselves continue in a state of singleness. They have not numbed their longing to be married; instead, they have embraced their Lord so tightly that they face their prolonged singleness with peace, not bitterness.

One woman named DeDe has allowed her heavenly Bridegroom to sustain her through more than 40 years as a single. She has never stopped desiring a husband and children, but they are not the focus of her life. Her focus is on the "daily bundle" God gives her. Her "daily bundles" are specific assignments to love and encourage the people in her world. Instead of having her own baby wrapped in a bundle, the Lord gives her someone else's child to love and encourage (she is the vice-principal of a Christian school). Rather than having a husband to wrap her arms around, she has teachers to give hugs and thoughtful notes to during their demanding and draining days. This Lady of Faith has not only pleased her heavenly Bridegroom, but also been a blessing to the Bride of Christ.

Have you hesitated about taking a new job or even going to a foreign mission field because you might miss Mr. Right? Have you passed up opportunities to serve in another Sunday school department because you might miss meeting the man of your dreams? If you are trying to orchestrate the "divine encounter," you might be setting yourself up for a disappointing crash. Wherever you are, whatever your circumstances may be, whether divorced, widowed, or single and getting older every day, be assured that God has not lost your address or your file. He knows exactly where you are and what you need. Remember, God has already taken care of your greatest need—your salvation—and as Romans 8:32 reminds us, *"He who did not spare His own Son, but delivered Him up for us all, how will He not also with Him freely give us all things?"*

You make the most important decision in life, giving your life to Jesus Christ, "by faith." The second most important decision concerns your life-mate. This decision also demands the element of faith. Waiting for one's life-mate and then saying "I do" to him demands secure faith, like Ruth's faith in the God of Israel.

Before you read any further, if you have been full of doubts and anxiety in reference to your future mate, take a few moments to confess your doubts to God and ask His Spirit to develop in your life this quality of faith. Your faith during the "waiting period" pleases God.

Don't fear or resent the waiting periods in your life. These are the very gardens where the seeds of faith blossom. Whenever circumstances stimulate you to deepen your faith, don't resist them; instead, embrace them willingly. Elisabeth Elliot said in *Passion and Purity* (a must-read for those who are having an anxiety attack during their extended waiting periods):

> I do know that waiting on God requires the willingness to bear uncertainty, to carry within oneself the unanswered question, lifting the heart to God about it whenever it intrudes upon one's thoughts.[3]

Whenever the "unanswered question" captures your mind, or you are overtaken by the restlessness of singleness, take a moment to commit that care where it belongs. As First Peter 5:7 says, *"Casting all your anxiety on Him, because He cares for you."* This intruding anxiety about your lack of a life-mate is not reality, but rather a weakness that the Greater Reality is capable of handling. Just go to Jesus as soon as the intruder arrives. Such a practice will only enhance your life as a Lady of Faith. Many single women have not recognized that the trying, frustrating waiting period is the perfect classroom for the Lady of Faith. Don't skip class! Embrace those dateless nights and, by faith, rest in His faithfulness.

BECOMING A LADY OF FAITH

Go through selected psalms and circle the words *trust* and *rely upon* in red. Notice David's trust in God. This exercise will strengthen your "eyes of faith." What are two other ways to strengthen your faith?

Can you see the parallel between a strong devotional life and the Lady of Faith? Read Romans 10:17.

Can you see a parallel between your own journey of faith and your daily quiet time with God?

Read through Hebrews 11 and underline all the verbs. Then go back through and confess, "By faith I can _____," filling in the blank with the verbs from each verse.

Is there anything you can think of that you can't do by faith?

Can you trust God to sovereignly bring you together with a Boaz?

What causes you to struggle in your walk of faith?

Explain how you tend to manipulate your rendezvous with men and/or how you can allow God to be your heavenly dating service.

Can you see how an extended period of singleness serves as a great opportunity to develop into a Lady of Faith? Explain.

ENDNOTES

1. *USA Today*, April 10, 1990, 4.

2. Elisabeth Elliot, *A Chance to Die* (Old Tappan, NJ: Fleming H. Revell Company, 1987), 117.

3. Elisabeth Elliot, *Passion and Purity* (Old Tappan, NJ: Fleming H. Revell Company, 1984), 59-60.

Chapter 4

LADY OF VIRTUE

Providing lasting pleasure,
potential beyond measure,
the rarest of treasure,
a reputation of virtuous character.
—JMK

*O*ne of life's most costly and beautiful objects is born out of pain and irritation—the pearl. A tiny piece of sand slips into an oyster's shell and begins to rub against the soft tissue, causing irritation. In response to the irritation, the oyster produces a hard substance. This substance eventually develops into one of the world's most beautiful jewels—a lovely luminous pearl. In fact, the greater the irritation, the more valuable the pearl!

Like the oyster, Ruth experienced many irritations or trials in her young life. She grieved the deaths of her father-in-law and husband. She bravely faced the turmoil of change in the direction of her life as well as a move to a foreign land with a bitter mother-in-law. When she arrived in that strange land, the trials did not end. She was immediately thrown into a new working situation among total strangers with new customs. Through all this stress, her new faith began to wrap itself around the painful situations. The by-product was a pearl from the washbasin of Moab.

Many single women view themselves as ugly oyster shells lying on the beaches of life, beset with the trials and problems that come with not being married. To make matters worse, they compare their crusty exterior to all the beautiful seashells around them and wonder how any man could ever give his attention to them.

If you are one of these women, be encouraged. Don't view the trials of singleness as irritating grains of sand to be discarded as quickly as possible. Realize that God has them there to create something beautiful in you. James 1:2-4 says:

> *Consider it all joy, my brethren, when you encounter various trials, knowing that the testing of your faith produces endurance. And let endurance have its perfect result, that you may be perfect and complete, lacking in nothing.*

God is using the sands of singleness to make you perfect and complete. He's developing pearls of character in your life. He knows that whatever you use to "catch" a guy, you must also use to keep him. If you attract a guy with only your looks, then you are headed for trouble, since looks don't last. As time goes on, we all end up looking like oysters. Therefore, what you look like on the inside is far more important than what you look like on the outside.

Consider again our Lady in Waiting. What enabled Ruth to catch Boaz's attention? Was it her gorgeous hair or beautiful eyes? No! The answer is found in Boaz's response to her question in Ruth chapter 2.

> *Then she fell on her face, bowing to the ground and said to him, "Why have I found favor in your sight that you should take notice of me, since I am a foreigner?" Boaz replied to her, "All that you have done for your mother-in-law after the death of your husband has been fully reported to me, and how you left your father and mother and the land of your birth, and came to a people that you did not previously know"* (Ruth 2:10-11).

Boaz was attracted to the virtue and character displayed in Ruth's life. A woman of virtue is irresistible to a godly man.

At a singles conference, one pastor's wife spoke of her life as a child. She grew up with a harsh alcoholic father. He left the family without a penny when she was a young teen. Her outward appearance was very plain, and she could not afford fancy clothing, makeup, or expensive hairstyles. She had very little time to socialize because she had to work to support her family. Instead of feeling bitterness over the rejection she had experienced or frustration over her lack of material possessions and free time, she trusted God to take care of her. She developed a strong prayer life and asked God to make her beautiful. She worked hard and grew strong in faith, believing that God would provide all she needed.

Her testimony was stirring, but the real climax came the next day as her husband spoke. He said, "My wife's character is what caught my attention. Her inner beauty was irresistible. Now, thirty years of marriage and half a dozen children later, I am more attracted to and in love with her than when I first met her." This lady gained her knight's attention with lasting godly character. Today their marriage and ministry remain strong and blessed because of the qualities she allowed God to develop in her while she was single.

An ugly oyster shell is an unlikely place to find a lovely gem, but Isaiah 55:8 says, *"For My thoughts are not your thoughts, nor are your ways My ways...."* You may see an ugly shell, but God sees the beauty He is creating in you. Are the sands of singleness causing you bitterness right now, or are you allowing these trials to change you into a pearl? The Lord wants you to be a Lady of Virtue—a costly, beautiful pearl for all to admire.

THE BODY BEAUTIFUL TRAP

The world has convinced many Christians that the only way to get a man's attention is through a gorgeous body. Hollywood has sold the lie that a woman will never marry the man of her dreams if she is not pretty enough or slim enough or tall enough or if she does not have high enough cheek bones! Most dateless women think their condition is the result of the "reflection in the mirror." Consequently, women spend millions of dollars every year believing the myth that physical beauty is mandatory for marriage.

Proverbs describes how a woman with no character got a man's attention. Some of the descriptives used for her include the following: smooth tongue, captivating eyes, persuasive and seductive speech, a mouth smoother than oil, and flattering speech (see Prov. 5:3; 6:24-25; 7:21). The techniques used today by the modern woman are as old as the first woman who ever snared a man's soul. The whole emphasis is on the superficial, external aspects of a woman—aspects that fade with every passing day. Many women's magazines glorify this woman's techniques rather than expose her bitter end. Marriage based simply on outward beauty can lead to immorality and, ultimately, divorce when an even more attractive body comes along.

The Word of God very clearly warns women not to fall into "the body beautiful trap." *"Your beauty should not come from outward adornment, such as braided hair and the wearing of gold jewelry and fine clothes"* (1 Pet. 3:3 NIV). Although braided hair and gold jewelry are not wrong in and of themselves, real beauty is not found on the outside. This verse does not advocate homeliness as proof of godliness. Some women are under the misguided perception that to be holy, one must look homely. This is not true. Women should seek to look their best. This verse simply challenges you to not devote all your energies toward painting the outside, thus neglecting the enduring qualities that need developing on the inside.

The key to beauty is found in First Peter 3:4 (NIV): *"Instead, it should be that of your inner self, the unfading beauty of a gentle and quiet spirit, which is of great worth in God's sight."* This kind of beauty can only get better the older it gets. As Jackie once said, "If a man chose me for external beauty, his destiny would be hugging a prune. But, if a man chooses me for my internal beauty, his destiny will be unfading beauty even in the twilight years of marriage, because of Jesus."

When you look at the virtuous woman of Proverbs 31:10-31, you will see God's picture of a beautiful woman. There are 20 verses describing her. Only one verse mentions her outward appearance. If you were to spend 1/20 of your time on outward physical beauty and the other 19/20 on developing the other qualities God describes as beautiful, such as wisdom, kindness, and godliness, you would become the excellent woman Proverbs 31:10 says a man should try to find.

Remember what King Solomon said in Proverbs 31:30 (NIV) about the external emphasis of charm and glitz? *"Charm is deceptive, and beauty is fleeting; but a woman who fears the Lord is to be praised."* There are many women who fear pimples, wrinkles, flabby thighs, and crow's feet, but very few women who really fear the Lord. With which are you attractive to men: the snares of Proverbs 5, 6, and 7, or the beauty of First Peter 3:4?

FIT FOR A KING

When you picture the perfect man for you, what is your prince like? Do you see a man devoted to God? A man of character—teachable, loyal, faithful, gentle, and kind? What kind of woman do you think this godly man desires to marry—a shallow woman or a woman full of charm who knows how to dress and capture other men's attention? Is this the one he imagines he will one day want to spend the rest of his life with—the mother of his heirs? No way!

To marry a prince, you must first become a princess. To marry into royalty, you must be appropriately prepared. Even Diana, the Princess of Wales, had to go through a period of "waiting and preparing" before marrying Prince Charles. She had to learn how to properly act, dress, and speak so she would honor the royal family. Is it any wonder that a heavenly princess must prepare inwardly for the calling to which she will give her life? As you set your attention on developing godly character, Christ will change you into the beautiful princess He created you to be.

Ruth is not the only biblical example of a Lady in Waiting who developed into God's virtuous pearl. Consider the story of the lovely Rebekah in Genesis.

> *The girl was very beautiful, a virgin, and no man had had relations with her; and she went down to the spring and filled her jar and came up. Then the servant ran to meet her, and said, "Please let me drink a little water from your jar." And she said, "Drink, my lord"; and she quickly lowered her jar to her hand, and gave him a drink. Now when she had finished giving him a drink, she said, "I will draw also for your camels until they have finished drinking." So she quickly emptied her jar into the trough, and ran back to the well to draw, and she drew for all his camels. Meanwhile, the man was gazing at her in silence, to know whether the Lord had made his journey successful or not. When the camels had finished drinking, the man took a gold ring weighing a half-shekel and two bracelets for her wrists weighing ten shekels in gold, and*

said, *"Whose daughter are you? Please tell me, is there room for us
to lodge in your father's house?" She said to him, "I am the daughter of Bethuel, the son of Milcah, whom she bore to Nahor." Again
she said to him, "We have plenty of both straw and feed, and room
to lodge in"* (Genesis 24:16-25).

The "pickins were slim" in Rebekah's shepherding community. Worse
than that, she worked full time for her father tending sheep! As you read
her story though, there is good indication that Rebekah was doing more
than "just waiting." Look at the endearing qualities she developed for
her unknown knight (Isaac).

Genesis 24:15-16 shows that she was a hard worker with a *"jar on
her shoulder"* serving her dad's sheep. She also was *"a virgin, and no
man had had relations with her."* She had not settled for second best
in her wait. She had been under her father's authority and in her
father's home serving his interests. Her respect for others showed
in her kindness to a stranger in verse 18: *"'Drink, my lord'; and she
quickly lowered her jar to her hand, and gave him a drink."* This was
no slow, lazy woman, but one with the character quality of genuine
care for someone in need. She had character like "Ruby" in Proverbs
31:20: *"She extends her hand to the poor, and she stretches out her hands to
the needy."*

Rebekah did not stop after one act of kindness either! *"...I will
draw also for your camels until they have finished drinking"* (Gen. 24:19).
Rebekah had initiative and served without even being asked. She was
not being manipulative with her service either. This was not a plan
to get a man. She was not initiating service and working with such
gusto for the reward of a young man's attention. She was treating a
smelly old traveler and his dusty cantankerous camels special because
that was her character! She was attentive to the needs of those around
her and sought to meet them. She didn't offer them a sip of water, just
doing a halfway job—she waited until they were finished drinking.
Look at her diligence in verse 20: *"So she quickly emptied her jar into the
trough, and ran back to the well to draw, and she drew for all his camels."*
She was a gracious, giving woman, as Genesis 24:25 says: *"Again she
said to him, 'We have plenty of both straw and feed, and room to lodge in.'"*

The servant had found a wife for his master's son completely on her virtuous character. She wasn't even in Isaac's neighborhood trying to meet him. She was busy with her father's sheep, but God brought them together. When the servant made his intentions known and wanted her to leave with him in Genesis 24:54-57, Rebekah knew she had been in the Lord's school of preparation, and she was ready. Her answer was, *"I will go"* (Gen. 24:58). Are you becoming a virtuous woman that a man may need as a helpmate? Are you using these days to develop godliness in order that, if asked, you will be ready? Whether you marry or not, every woman should seek the virtues of Christlikeness.

Rebekah's story closes with the perfect ending to a love story: *"Isaac… lifted up his eyes…. Rebekah lifted up her eyes, and when she saw Isaac she dismounted…. Then Isaac brought her into his mother Sarah's tent…and she became his wife, and he loved her…"* (Gen. 24:63-64,67). God rewarded this virtuous woman's wait with her dream come true. The wait was worth it. Isaac loved the woman who waited for him.

If Rebekah had not developed godly character, would Isaac have been so attracted to her? Perhaps for a time, but within marriage, the real man and woman comes out. That can be a wonderful or a horrible experience. God desires that every man and woman develop their inner lives so that through the passing years and fading of outward beauty, their love still deepens and grows. Are you developing into a woman who will be able to live "happily ever after"?

TO TELL THE TRUTH

So there are two ways to get a man to notice you. The first way, "the body beautiful trap," is to get his attention by how you look on the outside. This is a snare because looks don't last. They are superficial. The second way is what caused Boaz to notice Ruth and Isaac to be drawn to Rebekah. A Lady of Virtue is noticed because she has gained admiration for her godly character. Be truthful. Which approach best represents you? Take the following test. Check the items in each column that describe you most often. Score each total of qualities on the two lists to see if you are developing inner or outer beauty most diligently.

LADY OF VIRTUE	BODY BEAUTIFUL
A person to whom all people are attracted (friendly)	Nice only to those who can help your dating status
Seeking God first	Seeking a relationship first
Interesting—with goals for yourself personally	"Shopping"—known to be looking for a husband
Becoming the lady God wants you to be	Waiting to be found
Realistic	Living in romantic fantasy
Truly interested in the person you date and his best interests	Looking for your future in the relationship
One who is spiritually challenging	Exciting sensuality
One who gives friendship	One who expects friendship
One who communicates verbally	A wallflower
Committed to trusting God	Clinging to a guy
Prepared for lasting friendships	Playing games
Open to other friendships	Possessive
Secure in the Lord	Insecure without a "dream man"
Building positive qualities in yourself	Wanting him *now*
Trusting God	Trusting in schemes and plans to catch a man
Patiently waiting	On the hunt
Score yourself: (total qualities)	*Score yourself:* (total qualities)

How did you do? Are you allowing the Holy Spirit to use the sands of singleness to create in you priceless pearls of virtuous character?

STRINGING TOGETHER A PEARL NECKLACE

The qualities Ruth and Rebekah displayed do not come from the jewelry store; neither are they activated the day someone places an engagement ring on your finger. Virtue is developed over time as you allow God's Spirit to do a special work in your life.

It is the Holy Spirit, not you, who produces the godly character you seek. These pearls of character are listed in Galatians 5:22-23 as *"...love, joy, peace, patience, kindness, goodness, faithfulness, gentleness, self-control...."* As these qualities develop, your life will become like a beautiful necklace strung with the pearls of godly character.

Galatians 5:19-21, however, describes some "beads" with which many singles choose to adorn their lives instead. They are *"...immorality, impurity, sensuality, idolatry, sorcery, enmities, strife, jealousy, outbursts of anger, disputes, dissensions, factions, envying, drunkenness, carousing, and things like these...."* If you desire to be a Lady of Virtue, these beads cannot belong on your necklace. If you see that you have a bad bead in your strand of pearls, it must be removed and replaced with the character quality that pleases God.

To remove the bad bead, confess the sin that developed this unattractive quality. Be honest with yourself and don't cover over or excuse the sin God shows you. Be specific. For instance, instead of saying, "Forgive me for all my many sins," say, "Lord, I have been envious of __. Forgive me for dwelling on what You have given *her* instead of thanking You for what You have given me." After specifically describing the bead that detracts from your inner beauty, then receive God's forgiveness. His Word says, *"If we confess our sins, He is faithful and righteous to forgive us our sins and to cleanse us from all unrighteousness"* (1 John 1:9). You no longer need to feel condemned or guilty because *"as far as the east is from the west, so far has He removed our transgressions from us"* (Ps. 103:12).

Once you have received God's forgiveness, ask the Lord to cleanse you from whatever caused the sin in the first place. For example, envy often results from comparing yourself to others or from an ungrateful heart. This deeper problem must be changed if envy is to be decisively overcome. If you do not cleanse your heart of these deeper issues, you will find yourself always on your knees asking forgiveness because of a continual struggle with the sin of envy.

One deals with these deeper issues through the power of God's Holy Spirit. He provides the needed power to take care of the deeper issues that produce bad beads. Galatians 5:16 speaks of this when it says, "...*walk by the Spirit, and you will not carry out the desire of the flesh.*" How does one walk by the Spirit and tap into this pearl-producing power? Three portions of Scripture make it clear.

The first, Ephesians 4:30a, says, "*Do not grieve the Holy Spirit of God.*" You grieve or hurt God's Spirit when you choose to think, say, or do something that offends God. To tap into pearl-producing power, you must first decide to live a life that will please your Lord in all respects. From the time you wake in the morning until you go to bed at night, set your heart's desire on exalting Him.

The second verse is found in First Thessalonians 5:19. It says, "*Do not quench the Spirit.*" To "quench" gives the word picture of throwing water on a fire. When God's Spirit prompts you to do something, give expression to that impression. Don't douse it with cold water by ignoring His leadership. For example, He may prompt you to perform an act of kindness, or caution you not to say something you are about to say, or lead you to encourage a friend who may be hurting. Whatever it is, seek to obey the Spirit of God in you on a moment-by-moment basis.

Finally, to tap into pearl-producing power, Ephesians 5:18 says, "...*be filled with the Spirit.*" To be filled, something must first be empty. To be filled by the Spirit you must be empty of yourself and full of God. You give the Holy Spirit complete and total control of your life. When you became a Christian, you received all of the Holy Spirit. To be a virtuous woman, you must let the Holy Spirit have all of you.

There are many imitations of a true pearl, but with years, the shiny pearl paint cracks and wears off and all that is left is an unattractive bead hanging on a string. God's Spirit, however, produces true inner beauty, as you confess your sin, avoid displeasing God's Spirit, obey even the slightest of His promptings, and give the Holy Spirit full control of your life. Pearls of godly character take time to develop, but how blessed is the woman adorned by them!

You can settle for an imitation necklace of fake pearls by trying to simply cover over ungodly character, or you can allow the Holy Spirit to use the sands of singleness to create the real thing. If you want a cheap imitation, a modeling or charm school will be sufficient for what you seek. But if you want genuine pearls, you must allow the Holy Spirit to perform a special work in your life. Determine to string a lovely pearl "necklace of virtue" as a treasure for your Lord.

THE PEARL

In every oyster there lies the ability
to produce something rare.
Truth like a grain of sand will produce
the pearl that is hidden there.
Young woman, you are often mocked and scorned,
and told you never should have been born.
You want to run away, to hide your hurt.
Your heart is wounded, bleeding and torn.
God makes not mistakes:
every life is special,
every life is planned.
Seeds can sprout in sand.
Open yourself up to the Spirit of God,
grow in grace and maturity,
be what He wants you to be.
Your beauty, your strength lies deep within you.
Young woman, young girl,
open yourself up to God.
Allow Him to reveal your pearl.
—SYLVIA HANNAH

BECOMING A LADY OF VIRTUE

Study Rebekah in Genesis 24 and write out all the character qualities you find. Which of these do you need to develop? Pick one of these qualities and describe how you will specifically work on making it real in your life.

What books have you read dealing with the virtues/disciplines of a godly woman? In contrast, how many magazines have you read that deal with external glamour? What good books can you begin to read that will help develop your own personal godliness?

Pick out a picture of a woman who, according to magazines, "has everything." What features do you see? What appeal has been used? What is dangerous about comparing yourself with pictures like that?

Read Proverbs 31. In prayer admit, "Father, You don't choose to zap me into completion. So today I choose to cooperate with the Holy Spirit as You make me a Lady of Virtue. From my Scripture reading, show me one quality from Proverbs 31 that I need to develop." (For example: discipline, thoroughness, graciousness, giving, diligence.) Pray over this quality for a month before moving to something else.

Examine the "necklace" you are stringing by checking it in the light of Galatians 5:16-24. How many bad beads do you see in your necklace? Confess these sins and ask God's Spirit to control you in these areas. Spend time with a godly friend who will pray for you weekly until the bad beads are replaced by quality pearls.

 *Chapter 5*

LADY OF DEVOTION

In the receiving line at her younger sister's wedding, many guests greeted Brenda over and over with teasing remarks. She heard comments such as, "Always a bridesmaid, but never a bride. When is it going to be your turn? The only girl in your dad's home still unmarried!" Though these well-wishers may have been speaking out of fun or even compassion, their speech was not wise. The barrage caused its damage. It is hard enough for a single woman to keep her focus where it should be without friends making insensitive comments. How much better it would be for the Lady in Waiting if she were encouraged to pursue her undistracted devotion to the Lord Jesus Christ, instead of being made to feel like she does not quite measure up. If Jesus had been one of the guests, He would have surely commended her for productively using her single time to its fullest.

Much too often people view a single woman as though she should be pitied rather than envied. Nothing could be further from the truth. A Lady in Waiting has the advantage of being able to develop her love relationship with Christ without the distractions that a husband or family inherently bring to one's heart.

This has been God's plan from the beginning. He tenderly created woman to love Him and to experience the blessedness of fellowship with Him. In those first days, Eve communed with God in indescribable fellowship and oneness. When God came to walk in the cool of the day, there was no fear, only love. Eve had only positive feelings about God.

She loved Him and knew He loved her. She enjoyed Him and devoted herself totally to His pleasure.

God still desires to know and be known by women today. But because sin entered the world, we no longer have a clear picture of the true God. "Satan's first attack upon the human race was his sly effort to destroy Eve's confidence in the kindness of God."[1] Satan lied to Eve about God's character. *"Indeed, has God said...?"* (Gen. 3:1) Satan has continued to lie to Eve's daughters. As a result, fear has often alienated women from the One who loves them as they need to be loved. Deep within a woman's soul remains the longing for the gentle embrace of the God Who Is, not the god that the enemy has craftily devised.

Boaz spoke of Ruth's devotion to God when he said, *"May the Lord reward your work, and your wages be full from the Lord, the God of Israel, under whose wings you have come to seek refuge"* (Ruth 2:12). Ruth chose to cling to Naomi's God as her own even though her mother-in-law had drawn a negative, harsh picture of Him:

> *She said to them, "Do not call me Naomi [pleasant]; call me Mara [bitter], for the Almighty has dealt very bitterly with me. I went out full, but the Lord has brought me back empty. Why do you call me Naomi, since the Lord has witnessed against me and the Almighty has afflicted me?"* (Ruth 1:20-21).

Would you be devoted to a God like Naomi's? In Naomi's bitterness, she no longer referred to God as "the Lord" as she had in verses 8 and 9, but with a title that can cause one to feel alienated and insignificant— "the Almighty." Though Ruth clung to Naomi as a mother, she did not accept her mother-in-law's view of God for herself. "If we think of Him (God) as cold and exacting, we shall find it impossible to love Him, and our lives will be ridden with servile fear."[2]

Your past experiences, present circumstances, or your parents' devotion or lack thereof may cause you to have an incorrect view of God. But nothing and no one can give you a clearer picture of the true God than slipping under His wings and discovering for yourself who God really is, the refuge for which you long. He desires for you to come again "into the garden" and walk with Him in complete fellowship. This is the fullness of devotion.

As a single, you have a wonderful opportunity to use your time to maximize your fellowship with God. When you love someone, you give them your heart, the center of your being. God asks for no less. He desires a totally devoted heart. Deuteronomy 6:5 says that you are to love Him with all your heart (deepest devotion), your soul (what you think and what you feel), and your might (your strength and energy).

Many women today are devoted, all right! They have devoted themselves to developing a love relationship, but not with the Lord. They erroneously seek for love in sensations and promises. The world's version of love is something they want to "fall into." Meanwhile, "true love" escapes them. True love can only be found in undistracted devotion to Jesus Christ.

To love Him like this, you must know Him intimately. Paul expressed the desire to *"know"* God in Philippians 3:10. In Greek, this word *know* means "a knowledge that perfectly united the subject with the object."[3] Paul was desiring to know God intimately. Second Peter 1:3 says that everything pertaining to life and godliness is yours *"through the true knowledge of Him."* Peter and John in Acts 4:13 were identified as uneducated men, but the people observed their confidence and devotion to the Lord and marveled. In the King James Version of Scripture, the people exclaimed that these men "knew" Him, or that *"they had been with Jesus."* This "knowing" has the same depth as the term in Genesis 4:1 when Scripture speaks of the intimate relations Eve had when she *"knew"* or "had been with" her husband. It is a personal, intimate knowledge. Do you have a devotion to God that causes people to marvel at how intimately you know Him? Do you know God in a way that causes Him to be an intimate, personal part of your being as you may desire a husband to one day be?

As a woman, you have been created with a desire to be known—not just in a physical or general way, but deeply known and intimately loved. If you are hoping a man will one day fill your heart's desire for intimacy, you will be disappointed. God knows your deep longings for intimate love. Only He, the Lover of your soul, can fill this need completely.

Your heavenly Father tenderly created you with needs that only God can fully understand and fulfill. As you come to know who He really is, He will meet your needs for love.

Your heavenly Father is incapable of doing evil. He loves you, and forgives and completely forgets confessed sins and grievances. Is this the God you know? You may think you know God, but your responses to God will betray you. If you retract in fear, try to hide things, give excuses when you do something you feel God would not like, then it shows your knowledge of God, like Naomi's, is incorrect. God is not supersensitive, selfish, or temperamental.

Do you ever have a feeling of guilt hanging over your head that you are not doing enough to please God? Do you feel like the scale of expectations is tipping heavily in the negative and you must balance it? Do you feel like you could never do enough to pay for your inability to be perfect? Then your view of God is incorrect. God is not hard to please. He takes delight in His creation and quickly notices every simple effort to please Him (see Ps. 103:11-14).

Do you feel like God requires too much of you? Do you feel like God denies you the things you need most? If you do, then you don't really know God. Psalm 103:8-14 destroys these wrong assumptions about God. Have you lived with lies about God for too long? Get to know Him.

God wants to do you good and not evil. Jeremiah 29:11 says He wants to give you a future and a hope. Has your wrong picture of God been invented by the enemy in order to rob you of a true knowledge and love of God? Do not be deceived as Eve was in the garden. Get to know the One your heart truly desires to love. To love God, you must know Him intimately, personally, and devotedly. This does not require immediate entrance into a convent; you get to know Him by seeking Him.

SEEKING TRUE LOVE

Seeking God is very similar to developing a friendship. You talk a lot, you listen, you write each other letters, you think about each other, you find out what the other likes and does not like, and you try to do things that please that person. The more you spend time together, the more intimately you know your friend. And the more intimately you know your friend, the greater your love will be. It works the same way with your relationship with God.

Jeremiah 29:12-13 promises that a woman who diligently seeks God with all her heart will find Him. Your heart is the key to devotion to God. To find God, you must seek Him with your whole heart. A half-hearted search is not sufficient. This means you cannot seek God while you do your own thing.

Is God demanding too much to require that you seek Him with all your heart? No way! Think of it this way. Mr. Right comes over one day and begins to speak of his devotion to you. He says what you have been waiting to hear: "I love you. I give you my heart completely. For 364 days of every year, I will devote myself to you and you only." But then he adds, "However, *one* day each year I want to date others and see what I have missed. Don't worry; you can have *all* the rest. Will you marry me?"

What would your response be? Would you want this kind of devotion? Would it be selfish of you to deny him his heart just one day a year to give to others? No! Absolutely not. You would want his total love and devotion. You would want his heart all 365 days a year. Similarly, giving Christ your heart means you are not free to give it away to other things or people that come into your life (in idolatry). You can't give a part to relationships that delight you in this world and still seek God with a *whole* heart. You cannot keep a part of your heart for something that may seem better if it comes along. Devotion to the Lord Jesus Christ is giving everything or nothing at all. Your devotion to Christ must be a serious commitment to His Lordship. Christ loves you and is completely committed to you. Wholeheartedly devote yourself to loving and enjoying Him in return, 365 days a year.

If you are to know God intimately, then you must seek Him, not only with a whole heart, but also with a clean heart. When you think of the word *bride*, you probably first imagine a beautiful, clean, pure woman in white. No grime or dirt mars the image of purity. As a Christian you are part of the Bride of Christ. Any grime or dirt of sin will mar your image before Him.

The Lord's fiancé must have a clean heart. You must clean up any blot of sin that may arise between you and your heavenly Sweetheart. Sin causes God to back away from a person. It is disgusting to Him; He will not abide with it. Picture a couple deeply in love. He loves to be near her—so near he can breathe the fresh aroma of her sweet breath! What love! He hates onions, though, especially on his beloved's breath. It really turns him off. What do you think she does before she sees him if she has eaten onions? Well, she wouldn't want the sweetness of their fellowship hindered, so she brushes away what offends him. Not only does she brush, but she also "Scopes, Close-ups, and Gleems." She doesn't want to offend her love! She wants nothing to come between them. Sin is far more repulsive to God than even onion breath is to a sweetheart. If you want your devotion to God to be complete, don't merely brush at sin lightly. Get in there and confess it, clean it up, and clear it out. Be rid of it. If you notice you have spiritual halitosis during the day, take care of it immediately. Let Psalm 51:10 be your prayer: *"Create in me a clean heart, O God...."*

Many seek God, but only for His hand. They don't want God as much as they want something from God, such as a man, happiness, or a family. This impure search for God is limited to what you can get. It is more of a self-love than a God-love. This seeking will end in misery, not in the union of love you desire. God cannot be used like your credit card. He knows your motives. To grow in your knowledge of God, you must seek God correctly, which means you must also seek God with a pure heart.

A woman with a pure heart for God does not focus on what He gives, but delights in who He is. She seeks God's *face*, not just His *hand*. Would you want someone to say he loves you just so you would do something for him? To find God, you must seek Him with pure motives. Seek Him for who He is, not just for what He can do for you.

Have you ever tried to develop an intimate relationship with Jana Jabberbox? She's the gal who has lots to say and loves to hear herself say it. You try to say something when she takes a breath—which isn't often—but she keeps right on talking. She never listens. It's a one-way conversation, and you are left out. Even when someone is very special to you, you do not get too excited with a steady monologue. Listening is an important part of developing a closeness with someone else. If you want to get to know the Lord, you must seek Him not only with a whole, clean, and pure heart, but also with a listening heart.

As you spend time with God during your daily devotional time, learn to listen to Him as you read of His love and thoughts about you in the Bible. Think about what He is saying to you personally. Sit silently and write what impressions come to your listening heart. As you read and study His love letters, the Bible, you begin to see what He really thinks of you and what wonderful plans He has for you. As a result, your devotion grows and grows.

To find God you must seek Him with a whole heart, a pure heart, a clean heart, and a listening heart. Hebrews 11:6 (NIV) says that He *"rewards those who earnestly seek Him."* Does this describe your growing relationship with the Lord?

Singleness does not have to be a curse. Single gals do not have to wear long faces and be pitied until they are finally married. Quite the contrary! Singleness puts you in an advantageous position because, more than likely, you have much more time to seek the Lord now than you will ever have if you marry.

AN ADVANTAGEOUS POSITION

Married women wrestle constantly with having to balance the physical and emotional demands placed on them. All women must learn to balance their priorities, but the single woman's heart is not sent in different directions by the needs of a husband and children.

Before the sun rises, a mother of young children may gingerly creep down the stairs and dig under the pile of unanswered letters and school assignments to find her Bible. "Ahhh! A few moments of undistracted time," she whispers as she opens her Bible. To her chagrin, from the top of the stairs she hears, "Is it morning yet?" She puts her Bible down and whispers for the little early bird to come quietly down. She encourages him to sit with his favorite book, turns to find her Bible, and begins to read (while Junior makes animal noises reading beside her). Suddenly, from upstairs comes the sound of splashing. "Oh no—Mommy! I missed the potty, and it got on me!" Up the stairs she races to free the soggy victim, mop the floor, wake the school-age child, and get breakfast for everyone.

Her husband needs a button on his shirt, help finding his keys, and dinner an hour early. The kids need an arbitrator, a chauffeur, a nurse—and their P.E. clothes to be washed immediately. She sorts her way through piles of unwashed clothes cluttering the bedroom, trips over toys in the hall, and shovels aside newspapers and coloring books to collapse on the couch for a minute, only to be roused by screams from the children as the day's first civil war breaks out. Phone calls and drop-in visits continue to interrupt her day at every turn. It is midnight before she finally gets to the dirty dishes…and where is her undistracted time for devotion? If she was a wise Lady in Waiting and used her singleness to develop her devotional life, she has resources that allow her to commune with God during the wildest of days. A wife/mother may find her day beginning early and ending late, often before she has had any uninterrupted time to seek her heart's True Love. A single woman can choose to cherish the single time instead of feeling unhappy with it.

The Word of God illustrates the advantageous position of the single woman in relation to the affairs of life:

> *An unmarried woman or virgin is concerned about the Lord's affairs: Her aim is to be devoted to the Lord in both body and spirit. But a married woman is concerned about the affairs of this world—how she can please her husband* (1 Corinthians 7:34 NIV).

God says the unmarried woman has the advantage when it comes to her devotion to the Lord. An unmarried woman can give the Lord what a married woman rarely can—undistracted devotion. The time to develop a consistent devotional life cannot wait until you marry. Many single women waste valuable years as they wait "for life to begin"—after marriage. Ask any wife, even without children, and she will tell you her own juggling routine. A married woman struggles to have time alone with herself, much less time alone with God.

Becoming a Lady in Waiting, devoted to loving, knowing, and seeking God, will not come cheaply. You are the one who determines the depth of your relationship with God. He does not have favorites. You must choose to pursue the Lover of your soul—your heavenly Fiancé.

A single woman, one who chose to take advantage of her singleness, wrote the following poem:

THE SINGLE GIFT

How blessed you are, you single one,
Don't talk of care and woes.
You've got too much to be thankful for,
Oh what, you'd like to know.
It's no mistake, no misdirection
Of God's perfect plan
That you've not found your special lady
Or you, that certain man.
God loves you so and has much more
To give than you've ever received.
That He's giving His best to you right now,
You really must believe.
His best is Himself, do you have it in full,
Or only a bit on the side?
No man can meet your needs like God,
Nor can a lovely bride.
If your life's not complete, you know that Jesus is
And your life He will fill
If you'll only put Him first each day
And live to do His will.
He's gifted you for undistracted
Devotion to the Lord.
There should be nothing that can interfere
With Him and prayer and the Word.
Unless you let down the guard of your heart
And let others take His place,
Then you'll lack joy and peace and hope
And not experience His grace.
So give your heart right back to God,

Let Him keep it safe for you.
And when it's better than His best,
He'll make your one into two.
—DONNA L. MIHURA

God has given you a precious, privileged time. Don't waste a day of it! You will never have it again. These days can be treasure-finding days in your Kingly Father's chambers. As you linger at the window ledge searching for a glimmer of your knight's shining armor, don't miss the jewels your Father has for you to adorn yourself. Will you grow cold and bitter at the window sill, or will you hold your royal head high, glowing in your Father's love and attention? The choice remains with you, dear princess. Your Father will not force you to turn from the window, but He longs to fellowship with you. Come into His chambers, delight in His Presence. May you be found in Him—a Lady of Devotion.

BECOMING A LADY OF DEVOTION

Read Deuteronomy 30:11-20. What are the benefits of devotion to Christ? What are the results of living a life not devoted to Christ?

What warnings does God give about your heart in Deuteronomy 11:16 and Deuteronomy 30:17? What gods seek to distract your heart?

How did David seek God in Psalm 63? What was his reward?

How is your heavenly courtship progressing? How can you make it better?

Have you come to a place where your relationship with Jesus is beyond comparison with any earthly love?

Does your daily devotional relationship with Jesus satisfy you from the top of your head to the bottom of your toes?

Are you following hard after Jesus, or every eligible guy?

Read Song of Solomon 6:1. Does your love relationship with Jesus cause your friends to seek after Him as the Shulammite woman's praises did her friends? Why or why not? What can you do differently?

If you have never spent a consistent devotional time with God before now, begin by reading a psalm a day. After reading the psalm, write answers to these three questions in a notebook:

- What does this passage say about me?
- What does this passage say about the Lord?
- How can it apply to me?

ENDNOTES

1. A.W. Tozer, *The Root of the Righteous* (Camp Hill, PA: Christian Publications, 1986), 5.

2. Ibid.

3. W.E. Vine, *Vine's Expository Dictionary of New Testament Words* (Westwood, NJ: Barbour, 1985), 639.

Chapter 6

LADY OF PURITY

*N*o one was surprised when Tim and Susan began dating. They seemed just right for each other. They could talk about anything and had the same ideals for a strong Christian dating relationship. After a year of steady dating, Susan realized how deeply she loved Tim. She wanted to be his wife. She began to show her affection for him in different ways. They began to kiss and touch a little. She felt this was all right. She rationalized that she was in control of the situation and intended to remain pure until they married.

Marriage? Well, Tim had not actually made any kind of commitment, but she felt in her heart that he soon would.

Their little kisses and touches became more involved, but they always quickly asked forgiveness of each other and God when the petting became intense. After several months of these heavy petting sessions, Susan began to feel Tim had become distant. She then began to think that she may not have adequately assured him of her love. Maybe he was having second thoughts about her. She feared she might lose him—but she couldn't! He was the one.

Susan purposed to do whatever it took to keep him. She wondered if she had acted old-fashioned. After all, she just knew they would marry one day. Maybe he just needed to know the depth of her commitment to him.

Gradually, their relationship became more and more physical until one evening, Susan gave Tim the gift she had vowed not to open until her honeymoon night. She had imagined how strong and pure this moment of intimacy would make their love. Certainly this would cement the deep love they had for each other. It didn't.

Tim's face was no longer gentle. Susan felt as if he were a stranger. Her heart died within her. They were together, yet further apart than they had ever been. As he rose to leave, he said nothing. Instead of cementing their love, this one act of physical affection destroyed it. Susan longed to take her treasure back. She longed to start the night over. Unfortunately, the harsh reality had only just begun.

Tim and Susan are fictitious names, but this is a true story—and not just for this one young lady. It is true for hundreds of women who want to do what is right, but who unwisely give away their gift of physical purity too early. The gift is a treasure that can be rewrapped and given again, but never again for the first time.

We live in a day of blatant sexual impurity. A woman who marries, still a virgin, has become the exception, not the rule. Statistics say 80 percent of all unmarried women have given away their virginity by 20 years of age.[1] The Ruth of our biblical story, like us, also lived in a society of rampant moral decay. Ruth's story occurs during a time of year when sexual promiscuity would be at its height in the small farming community of Israel: "Immoral practices at harvest times were by no means uncommon and, indeed appear to have been encouraged by the fertility rites practiced in some religions."[2]

In this promiscuous society Ruth was a Lady of Purity, even in the midst of a potentially compromising situation. Ruth 3:7 says:

> *When Boaz had eaten and drunk and his heart was merry, he went to lie down at the end of the heap of grain; and she came secretly, and uncovered his feet and lay down.*

At a glance, you may read this and picture the beginnings of an X-rated scene in Ruth's story. But you must realize that Ruth was acting according to the customs of the time. She was not slinking into Boaz's bed to seduce him. In obedience to her mother-in-law's instructions, Ruth quietly lay at his feet for him to notice her, thus symbolizing her subjection to Boaz as her nearest of kin. This would give him the opportunity, if he so chose, to take legal action for the well-being of Ruth and her mother-in-law. (A woman had no form of social security and very few rights in that culture without a man.) This was not a brazen act of seduction, but an act of obedience to God's plan for her provision in that day. One thing is certain. When she left to go home, she walked away as a Lady of Purity.

Although the customs of Ruth's day may be difficult to understand, the temptations to compromise physically are not. Unfortunately, many women have been snared by the devil's deceptions and robbed of their innocence. How does today's single woman safeguard this special treasure and, like Ruth, go home at night a Lady of Purity?

DEADLY DECEPTION

Remember how the serpent deceived Eve by causing her to question God? He caused her to believe that God wanted to deny her something good, not provide her with something better. The enemy wants you to believe that if you wait to have sex, you will miss out on some of the delights of life.

Godly women must avoid basing their comprehension of the pleasures of sex on what commercials advertise, magazines glamorize, or books sensationalize. These are all full of the enemy's propaganda. Today's society seeks ultimate pleasure with no pain. But following society's example usually brings just the opposite. Look to your heavenly Father, your Creator, for the truth. God gives true sexual fulfillment to the lady who waits for this gift. God intended for you to enjoy the fulfillment and pleasure of sex within marriage only. The wonder and joy of this intimate act is maximized through purity before marriage.

Ask any woman of God who waited and she will tell you with eyes aglow that it was worth the sacrifice of denying her desires for a time. Look at that woman's marriage. Most likely the romance between her and her spouse still burns in a delightful love affair. Compare this real-life situation to the illusions in just one half-hour of "true life" romance on the television in an episode of "As the Stomach Turns" or "Body Watch." Have those actresses and actors (who, by the way, never scrub a toilet or break a nail and who always seem to be in their evening gown attire) found true fulfillment? They shout, "Ah! Yes—the delights of sex." Do not be deceived. Sex is special! Not sensuous sex, but satisfying sex in your Creator's way and time.

WHY WAIT?

Since sex is desirable, why not have sex? Why would God want to limit your pleasure with someone for whom you feel affection but haven't married? Have you ever been dieting but treated yourself to a huge piece of rich chocolate cake with fudge icing to celebrate some special occasion? Cake is good. Cake is desirable. The more cake, the more pleasure. But cake, in the midst of a strict diet, can really make one sick! The pleasure of a big, luscious piece of cake depends on the right timing, just as the pleasures of sex do.

God wants you to be a Lady of Purity because He wants to protect you from the consequences that sex before marriage brings. These consequences can be physical, emotional, relational, and spiritual. Let's look at these a little more closely.

PHYSICAL

Have you ever secretly opened a Christmas gift before Christmas Day and rewrapped it, putting it back under the tree? How thrilling and exciting it was when you saw the surprise. But what about the "big day" when the gifts were supposed to be opened for the first time? Where was the excitement when you opened your gift? The gift did not seem quite as special because it had already been opened for the first time. Each woman receives one "first time." God desires for your precious gift to be given to a committed lover who will cherish, keep, and protect you in marriage. God wants you and your gift to this man to be treasured and cherished, not trampled and conquered. Song of Solomon 8:4 (NIV) says, "*...Do not arouse or awaken love until it so desires.*" God wants to protect you from losing your virginity.

God also wants to protect you from the sexually transmitted diseases that could affect not only you, but also your future husband. One young single cried the night she discovered that she had contracted genital warts. She grieved over the realization that when her future knight in shining armor proposed to her, she would have to disclose the fact that she carried an infectious disease. This grieved her more than the fact that genital warts are incurable. Not only could you or your husband personally incur irreparable physical damage, but also transmit these infectious diseases to your future children.

God also desires to shield you from an unwanted pregnancy. Although precautions exist, pregnancy always remains a possibility. A rushed marriage, adoption, or abortion only complicates the consequences.

Judy, a wonderful Christian girl with a promising future, looked forward to graduating from high school. To celebrate this special occasion, she went to a party with a great-looking guy. She decided a few drinks that night would be OK. She didn't want to seem "different" in front of her date. His invitation to go off to a secluded room made her feel uncomfortable, but the evening was so special and her date was so kind and tender and romantic.

In the following months, Judy tried to deny the physical changes she was experiencing. Bible College would start soon, so she blamed them on the stress. God had forgiven her for going all the way that night—surely He would not have allowed her to get pregnant. It would ruin all her plans.

Only after her mother noticed her condition did Judy go for a doctor's appointment. Unfortunately, it confirmed the worst of her fears. Judy would soon be a mother. Regardless of how sorry she was and the fact that God had forgiven her, the consequences of that one act changed her life forever. God wanted to protect Judy physically, but He left the choices up to her.

God desires to shield you from the negative physical consequences of premarital sex. He wants to protect you from sinning against your body. First Corinthians 6:18 (NIV) says, *"Flee from sexual immorality. All other sins a* [woman] *commits are outside* [her] *body, but* [she] *who sins sexually sins against* [her] *own body."* "He wants you to be free from an addiction to premarital sex. Passionate physical exchange is a short-lived high. As with drugs, you keep wanting more intense highs."[3]

EMOTIONAL

God intricately and delicately formed women with emotional characteristics that differ from men. A woman cannot separate her emotions from her physical state. If a woman's emotions could be separated from her physical state, she would not struggle with PMS. The man who touches your body also touches your emotions. God made you that way, and He desires to protect your heart from being ripped apart by any man. You cannot make love to a man and remain emotionally untouched, no matter how hard you try. Therefore, if God knows that the man you think you love cannot care for your heart, He does not want you to give him any part of your body. You cannot give one without affecting the other! How your heavenly Father longs to keep your emotions safe and to guard you from feelings that threaten to wreck your emotional well-being!

God wants to protect you from the devastation of condemnation. The devil loves to get you down, to make you feel unworthy, thus making you unable to glorify God or stand before others. He enhances this tactic when he can whisper in your ear, "Some Christian you are. How can you witness to Jane? She may have heard…. You can't be a missionary; you compromised, remember? …Condemned…Condemned… Condemned."

If your emotions lied to you, causing you to give away your treasure to the wrong man, haunting fears may also begin to plague you: *Will he still respect me? Will he still love me? Why is that all he wants from me right now? What if I'm pregnant? Will anyone else find out? What if my parents find out? How can I face them? If we break up, what if the next man I date finds out?* Day and night these fears can play on your mind and emotions. God wants to protect you from these emotional traumas.

After premarital sex, there will usually be some lurking doubts. Would he have loved me without my body? Would he have married me if I hadn't gotten pregnant? Will he be attracted to someone better-looking after we're married? Most overwhelming are the doubts of God's love for you and, possibly, doubts of your salvation or your ability to ever again have a morally pure relationship.

You can be fully forgiven and cleansed by Christ, but damaged emotions take time to heal. The Lord doesn't want you to suffer these hurts. You are precious to Him. That's why He sets loving limits on your physical relationship and emotional attachments.

The spiritual side of sex is often overlooked. Even many Christians are not aware of the profoundly spiritual nature of their sex lives. A person will feel acute spiritual pain and separation from God when engaging in sex outside of marriage, but may not even realize how spiritually beneficial and unifying sex is within marriage.[4]

God does not intend to deny you pleasure. He protects you so you might enjoy physical health, emotional stability, relational intimacy, and spiritual blessings. If you marry, He wants you to grow more in love with your husband with each passing year. He wants you to live in complete trust of one another and spend a lifetime in love instead of the consequences of a fleeting night of uncontrolled lust.

GUARDING THE TREASURE

How then does a Lady in Waiting guard her purity? Once a man has a woman's heart, her body is not far behind. That is one reason Proverbs 4:23 says, *"Watch over your heart with all diligence, for from it flow the springs of life."* To walk in purity, a Lady in Waiting must first guard the key to her heart. This does not imply that your relationships with men are robotic and free from feelings. It means that you focus on growing in friendship, not romance.

Here is how Debby guarded her purity while dating:

> I asked the Lord to help me remember not to take my heart away from Him and give it to a boyfriend too quickly. To keep this commitment, I decided I would pray before accepting any date. Before going out, I would pray again, this time asking that my thoughts and actions during the time together would not center on encouraging him romantically, but building a friendship and encouraging his love for the Lord. At times, when I felt flutters of romance rising and my heart trembling, I would ask the Lord to renew my strength and reset my focus; I would picture myself kneeling in new commitment.
>
> I enjoyed friendship-building "dating" more after deciding to let God protect my heart. The only man who was given the key

to my heart was the man I married. When we were engaged, I gave him a small red velvet box with an antique key inside to symbolize that I was giving him my heart to care for and cherish as the Lord had done before I met him. I am grateful that now Bill cherishes me as a priceless treasure and views the key to my heart as a privileged possession. An added bonus is that marriage is full of the "extra special" romances that I denied myself before I met my husband.

Don't let your heart be given away too easily. If a man says he loves you, you don't have to echo the phrase. To men these three words can mean all kinds of things, like "I lust for you," or "I want you to kiss me." Or maybe he just can't think of anything else to say at the moment! But what did that "I love you" do to your heartstrings? Gradually those "I love yous" can trap you emotionally and lead you on physically. To guard the key to your heart, make a commitment to say you love someone only if you love him with a committed love, not a casual love feeling. You will remain much more in control of your friendship. Real love will have time to blossom and grow without those three words. Guard and save them to be whispered when God reveals it is time. What a gift to tell your fiancé, "You are the first person I have ever said this to: 'I love you.'" Give meaning to those precious words, and you may use them and hear them with fondness through many happy years of marriage.

There's a second step you can take to guard your purity. It's a radical statement, but save all your kisses for your future husband. One woman who made this decision said, "Early in my dating, I tired of giving a kiss at the door for a hamburger, coke, and fries. What would I have to give next for a steak dinner or a night on the town? After I was married, I realized the decision not to give my kisses freely to my dates had an added bonus. For every kiss I denied dates at the door, the man I married received my kisses 'with interest' in our years of marriage. It was worth waiting for kisses—so they would be full of meaning—for years."

A woman's kiss or embrace is not just another way of saying thank you! A kiss should say something more intimate. If so, do you want to say intimate things to every guy you date? All the kisses you give before marriage and all the kisses you give after marriage express the love that belongs to one person: your knight.

If you remember to whom your kisses belong, you won't be so quick to give them away. If you think you may be dating Mr. Right, give your friendship time to grow before you give the "fringe benefits." He will appreciate them and respect you much more if you wait.

Realize that a kiss starts physical contact and once you get started it's hard to turn back from passion. Determine what you mean with a kiss. Let it reveal your heart, not "rev up" your hormones. One lady put it this way when asked why "friends" have trouble becoming friends again once they start dating: "Once you start having sex, that's about the only thing you have in common."

A third practical step is to make your decisions and choices about what you will and will not do with a date *before* things become hot and heavy. Here are some examples of "dating standards" that many godly women have made. They will help you resist the pressure to "open the gift" too early. (You can find more in Chapter 9.)

- I will date only growing Christian men. (You will most likely marry a man you date. This is important!)
- I will concentrate on the friendship—not romance. (Don't be tricked!)
- I will not spend time with him at home when we are alone.
- I will not give kisses and hugs freely.
- I will not lie down beside a man.

Don't set standards "as you go." Emotions can be tricky. You must make wise choices before the "flutters" and "heartthrobs" become so loud you cannot hear yourself think. Write them down and read them often! Commit them to God regularly in prayer.

During a Bible study, one Lady in Waiting made this point about "dating":

Before Jesus became Lord of my relationships, I accepted our society's idea of dating as the time for a man and woman to be alone together. This time usually was devoted to romance and involved a measure of physical involvement—gradually accelerating if the dating continued. As I became closer to the Lord, I began to see dating from His perspective as a time for friendship-building without a need for promises of love or giving physical affection. As I spend time in group situations instead of one-to-one dating, I can really see the character of the guy friends I am spending time with. Doing things with groups also guards our purity, but doesn't limit our friendship-building and communication. When I do spend time with a guy, I don't refer to it as dating any longer. I talk about "friendship-building" founded on Christ—the One who holds my heart and guides the friendship.

Too many women think that if they give a man what he is longing for in terms of physical satisfaction, they will inevitably win his love forever. Hundreds of women have lowered their standards sexually and gone further than they knew the Lord wanted in hopes of hanging onto the guy they were spending time with. It's a lie. Don't believe it!

Women are easily turned on by words. Most men know this. Another way to protect your purity is to stand on guard when you hear "sweet talk." Don't let any of these lines cause you to surrender.

- If you love me...
- I have never felt such love before...
- Just try it once...
- I won't get you pregnant...
- I want to spend the rest of my life with you...
- Since we're going to be married anyway...
- Nobody is still a virgin at your age...
- What we do in private is no one else's business...
- If we only go so far and not all the way, it's OK...
- They are doing it, and they are Christians...
- If you won't prove your love, I'll find someone who will...

- You are too old-fashioned...
- Do it now so we will be prepared for marriage...
- It will never happen to us...

You can't believe any of these. They have been said before, the gift has been opened, and the lady left in an emotional heap labeled "conquered." These words have trapped many ladies—beware! When you catch yourself rationalizing what you are doing and assuring yourself you are in control, make a second check. You'll be glad you did. A godly man will not pressure a woman verbally, but will cherish her with his declarations of love and take her home before they have to regret any violation of their purity.

WHAT IF IT'S TOO LATE?

You do not have to make the same mistakes many have made. But if you are reading this "after the fact" and are dealing with the guilt of the lost gift, do not be discouraged. Although it is true that there is only one first time, God is the God of the first-time experience. Let Him heal your broken heart through forgiveness. Agree with God that you have sinned and leave the sin before Him. Then guard yourself from entering into that sin pattern again. Learn a valuable lesson, but do not continue to beat yourself with condemnation. Jesus paid for those sins at Calvary. Do not continue to allow yourself or the enemy to defeat you with remembering a sin once you have confessed it to God and those you have offended. There may be consequences of your sin, but you do not have to live with the guilt of it.

God is the God who forgives and forgets. Jeremiah 31:34 says, "*...for I will forgive their iniquity, and their sin I will remember no more.*" One of God's greatest abilities is that He forgets the sins of those who belong to Christ Jesus, "*I, even I, am the One who wipes out your transgressions for My own sake; and I will not remember your sins*" (Is. 43:25). Let this be your motto:

> *...but one thing I do: forgetting what lies behind [as God does] and reaching forward to what lies ahead, I press on toward the goal for*

the prize of the upward call of God in Christ Jesus (Philippians 3:13-14).

Even though you have been freed from the guilt by confession, do not use it as an opportunity to continue in sin or to leave yourself open to temptation. Continue to choose freedom over sin's mastery. Lay aside every encumbrance and the sin that so easily entangles you and run with endurance the race set before you (see Heb. 12:1). How? Fix your eyes on Jesus (not on your sin, the past, or even yourself). Jesus is the Author and Perfecter of your faith (see Heb. 12:2).

There is one last response that brings complete freedom. You must forgive and forget the sins of those who sinned against you. Jesus is very clear in Matthew 5:21-24 about what to do with anger toward a brother. But how do you do it? First choose to forgive your brother with your heart, and then God will help you work through the emotions that may remain. You will not be free of the hurt if you harbor bitterness. A quick way to ruin a beautiful complexion is to hold on to an unforgiving, bitter attitude.

If you have opened your gift too soon, do not be kept from beginning new again. Accept God's forgiveness and refuse to feel like damaged goods. God has better in store for you. You, dear Lady in Waiting, are a treasure. The enemy attempts to deceive you when he offers to delight you by his ways and means. Don't lose sight of the value of what you have or of who you are. Don't allow the flickering pleasures of an evening of "making love" destroy a lifetime of "lasting love."

BECOMING A LADY OF PURITY

Second Samuel 13:1-19 is a painful story of rape, but note the reaction of the man who got what he wanted. After his sexual thirst was quenched, what was his response toward the woman for whom he lusted? How did he feel toward the woman? Why?

How can a young woman stay pure? (See Psalm 119:9,11.)

How do friendships affect your purity? (See First Corinthians 15:33.)

Write out a specific list of ways you will guard your purity as you build relationships with the opposite sex.

Is striving to be pure too hard? (See First Corinthians 10:13.) List some of the ways of escape God has given you.

Write out what a kiss means to you. What are you wanting to say when you kiss a man? Is there any other way to say this? How could adding physical affection to a friendship limit communication-building?

ENDNOTES

1. Nadine Joseph, "The New Rules of Courtship," *Newsweek Magazine*, Special Edition, Summer/Fall (1990): 27.

2. Arthur E. Cundall and Leon Morris, *Judges and Ruth, an Introduction and Commentary* (Chicago, IL: InterVarsity Press, 1968), 287.

3. Tim Stanford, "The Best of Sex," *Campus Life Magazine* (February. 1992): 25-26.

4. Ibid.

Chapter 7

LADY OF SECURITY

"*I* still can't believe it!" one friend exclaimed. "I had a date with the perfect guy! I spent days searching for and finding a gorgeous outfit, I had my nails done, and my hair looked better than it ever has. I took a whole day off work to get ready and left in plenty of time to get there. The 150-mile drive to pick him up was nothing. I could have flown I was so excited. I tried to calm myself down the whole drive, but could not help thinking how right we were for each other, how beautiful our relationship and future would be. We went to a very romantic setting. I can't believe it! I was ready, willing, available. Everything was perfect, except for one problem. It turned out that he was gay."

This single woman diligently and faithfully "went after her man," only to find disappointment and pain. Ruth, our epitome of a Lady in Waiting, had a totally different approach.

> *Then he [Boaz] said, "May you be blessed of the Lord, my daughter. You have shown your last kindness to be better than the first by not going after young men, whether poor or rich. Now, my daughter, do not fear. I will do for you whatever you ask, for all my people in the city know that you are a woman of excellence"* (Ruth 3:10-11).

Ruth—single, young, and widowed—must have experienced the lonely longings for the warmth of a husband. But she lived in victory over the desire to "man hunt." Instead of "going after the boys," she sat still and let God bring her prince to her. She was a Lady of Security.

FEELINGS OF INSECURITY

Why do women tend to "go after the guys"? Why do women experience difficulty being still and waiting for the man to initiate and develop the relationship? You find the answer in one word: insecurity. An insecure woman has her world centered on something (marriage) or someone (Mr. Right) that can be lost or taken away. Insecurity keeps a woman from experiencing consistent joy even within a relationship because a man cannot provide security, only God can.

Insecurity causes you to cling to a relationship. You feel a lack of confidence unless you have a man. When he is not with you, you fear he will not come back or call again. You want him to make a commitment so you will not lose him. You want all his time and attention. All your dreams, plans, and goals revolve around him. Insecurity in a relationship can cause jealousy and bickering. It makes you lose your confidence when he looks at another woman. You want to know his plans and with whom he spends his time. You don't want him to be around other interesting or attractive women; you feel threatened when he is.

Insecurity can cause you to be demanding and have unrealistic expectations of your relationship. When he hurts or disappoints you, you can be upset for days. You live with the fear of doing the wrong thing and losing him. You constantly feel the need to "define" your relationship and talk about your love for each other. You feel that you must show your love for him in greater and greater ways.

Insecurity fills the relationship with frustration and worry. You think, "I can't live with or without him!" You find yourself scheming to keep him.

Lisa even told her boyfriend she was pregnant so he would make a commitment to marry her. Her well-devised plan backfired as she had to go deeper and deeper into the lie when her new husband discovered she was not. She felt she would experience happiness and security only when he was hers. Instead her scheming caused guilt, making her feel alienated from him. His anger toward her for being married before he felt ready resulted in great difficulty in their relationship.

BELIEVING A LIE

Why do women feel they have to go after men? Many women have believed a lie. They think, "I must get the best for myself because God may not give it to me." What do you think would have been the outcome of Ruth's life if she had chosen to believe this lie? Would she have returned home with Orpah and married one of the local guys? Would she have followed Naomi to a new land, but taken control of her own destiny in choosing a mate to care for herself and her mother-in-law? With these poor choices, her life of blessing and joy found in Boaz would not have happened, and we would have missed the blessing of a book such as Ruth.

Ladies, God gives you the choice between His plans and yours. In the midst of her circumstances, Ruth could not have possibly seen that a man like Boaz would one day be her prince. Neither can you with your limited perspective see who or where your prince will be. Only God has all things in view. Are you trying to control your own life? Are you making plans for your life that only God should make? Don't settle for less than God's best. Surrender the terrible burden of always needing life on your terms. Don't look back one day and regret that you made your "life-mate" choice from a limited perspective because you longed for the security of a relationship. God can and will give you His best if you wait for it.

SECURE LOVE

Women tend to struggle with insecurity because of the unique way God created them. God made every little girl with the need to love and be loved by her earthly father. God designed His world with a picture of a family as the theme. The father protects, loves, and cares for his wife and their children. The ideal earthly father models the gentle, nurturing love of the heavenly Father. Many young women in our society did not have a father who followed God's design. This God-given need for a father's love caused a deficit in their lives.

Karen described it this way:

> I never really felt loved the way I needed to be. I wanted someone
> I could love and who would love me in the deepest way. I met

and dated a wonderful man. He was a Christian, good-looking, popular, and best of all, he loved me. A deep wonderful friendship with him flourished for almost two years. I wanted to be his wife, but he was not making any move toward a commitment. I was a 21-year-old virgin. I wanted to keep him so badly that I knew I was willing to do anything. I did not intentionally plan to compromise my high standards, but I felt if I were intimate with him, it would show my deep commitment to him, and I would be able to keep him.

As a child I wanted my dad to really love me, but I never seemed to gain his love. I thought this man could fill that need for love that I felt. I was wrong. I lost both my virginity and my closest friend with one act. I believe if I had dealt with the insecurity in my life, I would have seen clearly that no man could meet the heartfelt need for secure love I wanted.

As a little girl, you may remember feeling the desire to be cherished, loved, and accepted by your daddy. If he failed to show that love to you in God's way, perhaps you continued to search for a man who would. No man, not even a husband, can fill the need you have for secure love. Only Jesus, who *"is the same yesterday and today and forever,"* will never disappoint or fail you (Heb. 13:8).

Turn to your heavenly Father now. Pour out to Him your heart's longing to be loved. See His arms open wide and His empty lap ready to embrace and hold you near. He considers you dear. He longs to give you satisfying love. Perhaps He does desire to give you a man to love also. But the man you marry cannot meet your need for security. Only God's love brings security.

MANIPULATION AND MANEUVERING

When you see a woman going after the guys, you probably don't immediately say, "Yes, I see that she really is insecure!" Insecurity dwells in the heart. What you see outwardly is a woman's age-old ability to manipulate and maneuver. When a woman manipulates a situation, she feels personal satisfaction because she believes she is in control.

At one college, a new student arrived who was one of the most attractive guys ever to arrive on campus. In fact, whenever he walked by, the air would move because of all the gasping women. When he walked into the dining hall, the females would suddenly stop talking. (That alone was a miracle!)

Linda, who worked in the Dean of Men's office, had a myriad of females ask for his class schedule. Why would his class schedule be significant? Such information offered a chance for a "life-changing" experience. These silly women would find out his daily schedule and, as soon as their classes ended, would *run* to wherever he would most likely be walking, and "just happen" to be standing on the corner as he passed. Daily, these committed manipulators "just happened" to see him after English literature and then "just happened" to see him after World Civics. Such a schedule definitely kept these gals in peak aerobic condition as daily they frantically tried to arrive in his personal hemisphere.

Manipulation and maneuvering can also take the form of serving as a "surrogate (substitute) helpmeet." Many women want to marry as badly as they want to go to Heaven. They long to care for a man, so they run around trying to find at least a "generic" version of the real thing. These precious (but deceived) women constantly look for a man with a need and pounce on that need in hopes of eventually winning the affection of the man. Any male in need irresistibly attracts them.

Once, a single man at a conference mentioned his need for some name tags, and a mob of women scurried to get tags for him. It was like a race, or a spring sale at the mall! One typical surrogate overheard that a man needed his house cleaned because his parents were coming for a visit. The young man had little time to do it himself because he had been so busy helping at his church, so he made his need known. This "Martha" decided to help the needy man, but didn't check her motive. She assumed that he would appreciate her help so much that he would repay her with some extra attention, perhaps even a date. At the same time, she knew that one of her female friends at the church also had a need, yet Martha would not lift a finger to help her catch up domestically.

What is the difference? Women may find more pleasure doing for a man than a woman because the potential "payoff" seems more valuable.

She envisions surrendering her "surrogate" apron for an engagement ring. A wise woman once said, "Do not do for a brother that which you would not do for a sister." Brownies often are baked for the best-looking and most desirable guys, but seldom for the average Joe. (How all these guys stay slim is a miracle—except for their constant running from all the aggressive, manipulative women.)

A "manipulator" may hear of a female friend who needs help and callously allow her to do without it. But if one handsome guy even slightly alludes to his desire for something to drink, she may "crawl across broken glass" to get him a cool drink, all the while quoting Scripture about giving a cup of cool water to him who is thirsty. Allow God to use you to minister to brothers and sisters equally with no ulterior motives. In the beginning, Ruth ministered not to a desirable man, but to a bitter widow—her mother-in-law, at that!

Another form of maneuvering is to become the guy's "mom." Insecure females all too often deceive themselves into thinking that because they do so much for a particular young man, they will surely win his love. *Wrong!* It is easy for a man, whether he is young or old, to let a woman sacrifice for him. Why? Most men are used to the sacrifices of a woman. Good ol' mom has been sacrificing for him since the womb. Sure, the young man will say, "Thanks," but young men do not marry their mothers! When a woman does something really nice for a certain guy, he usually does not spend the rest of the day thinking about her unselfish service (he may be accustomed to receiving). The woman may begin to feel used.

Some women prepare meals, sew on buttons, and wash the guy's clothes—all the things a mom would do—assuming all this is practice for their future together. Inevitably, the man she has served so unselfishly may fall for a girl who can't bake or sew and thinks you take all clothes to the dry cleaners that "fluff and fold."

Elisabeth Elliot says she is often asked the question, "What can I do to get him to notice me?" Note carefully the advice she gives:

> My answer is "nothing." That is, nothing toward the man.
>
> Don't call him. Don't write a little note with a smiley face or a flower or fish under the signature and put it in his campus

mailbox. Don't slide up to him in the hall and gasp, "I've just got to talk to you!" Don't look woebegone, don't ignore him, don't pursue him, don't do him favors, don't talk about him to nine carefully selected listeners.

There is one thing you can do: turn the whole business over to God. If he's the man God has for you, *"No good thing does He withhold from those who walk uprightly"* (Ps. 84:11). Direct your energies to obedience, not to nailing the man. God has His own methods of getting the two of you together. He doesn't need any help or advice from you.[1]

Notice the word *nothing*. Maybe this little dose of reality will help you constantly check your motives whenever relating to a guy.

MOTIVE CHECK

This is not to say that you cannot do nice things for a man; it is simply a warning to check your motives. A woman with selfish motivation mentally plots the next maneuver to capture the attention of the man of her dreams. Before you go to another activity to spend time with the available guys, as you check your hair and makeup and teeth, give yourself a thorough "heart flossing." Ask the Lord to reveal any impure motive that resides in your heart. Before you bake one more thing for a brother or purchase one more book or meaningful card, be very careful to check your motive and honestly respond to whatever the Lord shows you. You can save yourself many tears and much frustration if you are just willing to do a regular "motive check" on your heart.

To keep your motives pure, check them daily. Proverbs 16:2 (NIV) says, *"All a man's [woman's] ways seem innocent to him [her], but motives are weighed by the Lord."*

Manipulation and maneuvering can be deadly. If you maneuver to get a man, you will have to maneuver to keep him! This is not implying that there is no work involved in a good relationship, but there is a huge difference between working and maneuvering. You recognize the difference between the two by discerning your motive. Refuse to be a member of the M/M (Manipulation and Maneuvering) Team!

QUITTING THE HUNT

To quit the hunt and stop "going after the guys," you must first avoid maneuvering and manipulating. Ruth did, and God can give you the grace to do it too. Believe that God will take care of you regardless of your circumstances. Don't put your own devices to work. You can only see the outward man from today's perspective. God sees men's hearts from the perspective of eternity. With His perspective, He can see much better what you need. Trust Him and let Him show you His dependable love for you.

Second, you must put your security in Christ. He longs for you to be secure in His love. He wants to protect, lead, and love you. To develop security, give your heart and emotions to the Lord. Debby remembers a specific time in her life when she pictured herself before the Lord. In her mind's eye she imagined His loving, kind, Father's face. She pictured herself bringing her broken, lonely heart to her heavenly Father after yet another love bubble had been burst. Debby specifically gave the Lord her love life that day. She prayed:

Father, my heart is fragile and delicate and easily broken. I have tried to find one who will cherish me, without Your view. My heart has been broken and my emotions bruised. I ask You to take and guard my heart. I will choose not to entertain thoughts and emotions of love which cause me to give my heart away too readily. I will come quickly to You when I start feeling like I am in love. Please hold the key to my heart and emotions until a day I can give it to the man You have prepared for me.

Debby has often said what a difficult turning point this was for her. She wanted to trust the Lord with this precious area of her life, but had nagging feelings that she might never again have the giddy, delightful feelings of love. As she dated, she spent time in prayer before and after dates to make sure her heart and emotions were still in the Father's hands. Many times she feared she would never feel those "heart leaps of love," but instead would just marry one of the "nice" guys she had dated.

One day, as she was praying, she realized she had come to really care for a man named Bill in a special way. They had been dating for several months, and the temptations to let her emotions run wild were very real. Instead, she wrote this in her journal:

I feel as though I really care for Bill in a deep way. You know what is best for me, Father. I have given my heart to You and my emotions, too. I will wait for a clearer indication that he is my knight in shining armor than just how I feel. You will not allow my heart to be broken again if I leave it with You. I trust You to keep me calm and waiting on Your best timing.

A formula she wrote in her prayer journal to help her keep perspective was this: *With Jesus first and my boyfriend second, I will have lasting peace and security.*

All this may sound like a good idea, but how do you begin? To build security into your life, spend time in God's Word. Proverbs 1:33 says to listen to God and live securely. As you do, you will find out what God is really like—what His character is—not just what you think or have heard He is like. You will be surprised at how differently He sees you than what you have thought. Read through the Psalms and write down the many promises He has made to you if you are a believer. Psalm 16:11 (KJV) says, *"Thou wilt shew me the path of life* [married or not]; *in Thy presence is fulness of joy* [His presence, not marriage, brings joy]; *at Thy right hand there are pleasures for evermore."* (What more could a girl ask for?)

By spending time in God's Word, you will also learn what God thinks of you. In First Peter 2:4, God says you are choice and precious to Him. He calls you precious, honored, loved, and His redeemed one in Isaiah 43:1-6. Isaiah 43:7 says you were created for His glory. You are very special to God—so special that He has plans for you: *"plans for* [your] *welfare and not for calamity to give you a future and a hope"* (Jer. 29:11b).

The New Testament is also full of God's thoughts of you. You are accepted (see Rom. 15:7); you are not condemned (see Rom. 8:1); and you are His child (see John 1:12). (By the way, the female child of a King is a *princess.* Act like the valuable princess you are, and plan to be treated as royalty.) You also are the temple of God (see 1 Cor. 3:17). He is your adequacy (see 2 Cor. 3:5), and He leads you in His triumph (see 2 Cor. 2:14). His love letter to you, the Bible, is full of all the wonderful things He says about you.

Do not allow insecurity to motivate you to maneuver or manipulate your relationships. Instead of hunting for a husband or boyfriend, concentrate on becoming a woman of excellence (see Ruth 3:11). As a Lady of Security, wait for your heavenly Father to bring about His perfect plans for you.

> *Learning to sit still,*
> *Resting in His will,*
> *Confident to abide,*
> *With Him by my side,*
> *Resisting manipulation,*
> *Waiting only for His stipulations.*
> —JMK

BECOMING A LADY OF SECURITY

Look at the things most important to you, the things on which you spend the most of your time and energy (e.g., appearance, money, career, family, friendships, dates). If these were taken away, how would you be affected? Security is basing one's life on that which cannot be taken away. Are you building your life on what makes you secure or insecure?

Do you find yourself manipulating for friendships with guys? Proverbs 4:23 exhorts you to watch over your heart. Write out ways you can respond when the temptation to "scheme" for a date comes your way.

Meditate on Colossians 3:1-3. How could these verses help you the next time you feel insecure and want to take future matters into your own hands?

What can a Lady in Waiting do with her feelings while she waits? List them from Psalm 37:3-7.

In your journal confess any times you sought to manipulate a person or situation. Seek to put your security in your King and ask His Holy Spirit for help.

How would having your security in the Lord and not in whom you are dating affect you if the dating relationship ended? Could you be grateful for a friendship even without the promise of a future? Being secure in God's forever love (see Heb. 13:5) allows a woman to build relationships for friendship, not merely romance for a future.

ENDNOTE

1. Elisabeth Elliot, *Passion and Purity* (Old Tappan, NJ: Fleming H. Revell Company, 1984), 59-60.

Chapter 8

LADY OF CONTENTMENT

*Y*ou have just returned home from a great singles' retreat where you once again surrendered your frustrations as a single in exchange for God's peace and contentment. As you listen to your answering machine, you hear a certain voice. The most sought-after bachelor you know asks you for a date next weekend. Do you remain calm and give your expectations to the Lord? Or do you jump back in your car and head to the mall to register your china and look at some wedding gowns? Would the prospect of a date with the most eligible bachelor in town cause you to experience the "Pre-romantic Stress Disorder"? Or would you surrender your expectations to Jesus?

For a single woman to experience genuine contentment while soloing in a "couples' world," she must avoid the ditches of discontentment. She needs to learn the mystery of contentment and its power over the restless torture of desire.

THE TORTURE OF DESIRE

It has been said that suffering is having what you do not want (singleness), and wanting what you do not have (a husband). As a single woman, you would probably scream "Amen" to such a description of suffering. You know what it is like to get up each day knowing that you do not have what you want—a husband. How do you cope with such a longing?

Longing for what you do not have is a universal condition. It is not limited to singles. It is true that the longing for a husband can be satisfied on your wedding day, but that longing is soon replaced by desires and expectations about the marriage relationship that may not be satisfied in a thousand lifetimes. If you are presently discontent as a single woman, you can count on being dissatisfied as a married woman in the future.

The mystery of contentment often seems to escape the understanding of the single woman. She assumes that her circumstances justify her condition and give her permission to remain dissatisfied with her life assignment. Not having learned how to lay down the terrible burden of always wanting life to be on her terms, she continues to struggle with the torture of her desires. The restlessness caused by her desire for what she does not have makes waiting seem an impossible task. In fact, to the discontented woman, the word *wait* probably compares to a cuss word in her mind. A Lady in Waiting finds her capacity to wait for God's best to be rooted in contentment.

THE CAPACITY TO WAIT

Circumstantially, Ruth had the perfect excuse to be discontented. Widowed at a young age, her circumstances provided the perfect breeding ground for self-pity and bitterness. In fact, her mother-in-law changed her own name from *Naomi* (pleasant) to *Mara* (bitter) to signify her discontentment. Yet Ruth chose to cling to the God of Israel, whom she found to be trustworthy even in difficult circumstances.

Contentedly facing each day's task, Ruth received the attention and blessing of the most eligible bachelor in town. Then Naomi told her that Boaz was a candidate for being their kinsman-redeemer (see the levirate law in Deuteronomy 25:5-10). This simply meant that the Mosaic Law allowed Boaz, as the closest kin, to redeem the childless widow and keep the family name alive. The law could even require that Boaz marry Ruth. Can you imagine finding the most eligible bachelor and saying to him, "The law requires you to marry me before my thirtieth birthday"?

Naomi instructs Ruth to approach Boaz and ask him if he would be their kinsman-redeemer. This episode is covered in chapter 3 of the Book of Ruth. Boaz's response to Ruth's request is precious: *"And now, my daughter, don't be afraid. I will do for you all you ask. All my fellow townsmen know that you are a woman of noble character"* (Ruth 3:11 NIV).

Can you imagine any man saying to you, "I will do for you all you ask"? His willingness was directly related to the character he had noticed in her responses to life and God.

Ruth returns home with the good news. Naomi, however, does not immediately respond by taking her daughter-in-law to the mall to look for a wedding gown. An anxious and discontented woman would think that a willing and interested bachelor is enough motivation for ordering wedding invitations. But for the Lady of Contentment, this would be inappropriate behavior.

Naomi's response to Boaz's willingness may have put a damper on most single women's racing heartbeat: *"Then Naomi said, 'Wait, my daughter, until you find out what happens. For the man will not rest until the matter is settled today'"* (Ruth 3:18 NIV). Who has to *wait?* The woman must wait. Who is the one who will not rest? The man, Boaz, will not rest.

WAIT

Such an assignment is not to cause suffering, but to prevent it. Women experience so much needless pain when they run ahead of God's format. Naomi knew that there may exist an even closer kinsman who would qualify to redeem her and Ruth. (In fact, there was a kinsman closer than Boaz whom she did not know about, but he would be disqualified by a former pledge.) Naomi did not want Ruth's heart to race ahead into disappointment in case the circumstances did not go as assumed.

DITCHES OF DISCONTENTMENT

Being single can be difficult enough for a woman, but the heartbreak from being "led on" by a man can dangerously lead to a ditch of discontentment. Some women are so emotionally scarred from falling into such a ditch that it literally takes them years to recover and rediscover the capacity to trust any male in their lives.

Why some males are unaware of their capacity to defraud is still a mystery. *"And that no man transgress and defraud his brother* [sister] *in the matter because the Lord is the avenger in all these things..."* (1 Thess. 4:6). To defraud is to excite physical or emotional desires that cannot be righteously fulfilled. Since many men do not realize how their actions defraud their sisters in Christ, single women need to be aware of common situations where a guy might lead a woman on. When aware of such techniques, a single woman can avoid unnecessary heartbreak and more effectively keep a rein on her emotions.

One way a guy may lead a woman on is by the unwise things he may say or do. A wonderful single guy started a letter one day with the words *Dear Sunshine*. When asked who this "Dear Sunshine" was, he said it was his nickname for a girl at college. He came up with this affectionate nickname for her one evening while they stood on a hill overlooking the school as the sun was setting. When asked if they were dating, he replied, "Oh, no, we are just friends, and there isn't any future for our relationship." He was encouraged to stop calling her Sunshine because it would defraud her emotionally. But, like many men, he had a hard time understanding that calling her Sunshine might cause her to dream about being the "sunshine" in his future after they graduate.

A second way a man might defraud a woman is by ascribing to an unwritten code that has been distributed by Hollywood and swallowed by most of Christianity: friendships with the opposite sex must be romantic and must not establish any emotional boundaries. What Hollywood advocates is like body surfing on the crest of an emotional wave. To establish boundaries seems like an attack on love. Ironically, limits protect real love and leave no room for painful defrauding.

Ken and Jackie established some specific guidelines for their dating relationship in the areas of leadership, communication, and purity. Classmates (even Christians) thought their goals and guidelines would prevent their friendship from blossoming and surviving. Contrary to popular opinion, they have been building on those guidelines for the past 20 years—and romance thrives in their relationship.

In a McDonald's commercial, a guy presented clear guidelines for him and his date. Just before the couple gets to the car, the guy makes one last remark, "I want you to realize that this is just a date, not a commitment and not a proposal." The girl just smiles and continues toward the car, en route to McDonald's and a movie. Now, you may feel his style is just too honest, but such clear communication prevents much misunderstanding between a man's actions and a woman's interpretation of his behavior.

Another way a guy may defraud a woman is by emphasizing the future potential of the relationship rather than focusing on the present opportunities for the friendship to grow. This way of defrauding incites feelings in a woman that cannot be properly fulfilled at that time. This creates emotional turmoil for many women, making it difficult to wait with contentment. Postpone talk of a future together, marriage, or what kind of home you want until engagement. Do not encourage talk of things that "might be," but rather encourage words and actions that develop the present friendship.

THE ELEVENTH COMMANDMENT

Keeping in mind these common ways that women can be defrauded by men, realize that a single woman can sabotage her own contentment by defrauding herself. A single woman can defraud herself as effectively as can her male counterpart. Protect your contentment by adopting this "Eleventh Commandment": Thou shalt not defraud thyself.

Women defraud themselves by confusing ministry with matrimony. A guy tries to help a girl grow spiritually, and she sees his care and interest as leading inevitably to marriage. Another guy and girl work on a ministry team together and their spiritual intimacy is confused in her mind with romantic intentions.

Misread intentions between males and females put them on a collision course. The crash can be avoided if the Lady of Contentment would keep in mind that her emotions must be submitted to the facts: ministering together is a privilege as a believer, not an automatic marriage opportunity. Daily, throughout the world, women's hearts are broken because they allow their emotions to run ahead of commitments. Women, young and old, seem to resist controlling their emotions. As a result, they end up emotional cripples, angry at the men who failed to live up to their emotional fantasies.

A most innocent gesture can produce the most elaborate fantasy. A man sends a single woman a thank-you card for her vital help in some project or ministry. What is her response to this kind gesture? She laminates the card, anticipates a future with him, and allows her expectations to run rampant.

Counselors are constantly helping men and women properly interpret their relationships. Nancy had been in counseling for more than a year because her heart had been broken and her emotions devastated through defrauding. She told her counselor how she had deceived herself in her relationships with men.

As a new Christian, Nancy joined a large singles ministry where she became very attentive to the various needs of the singles director. She did all the special things that a "mom" often does for her son, or a woman does for her boyfriend. Not only did she attend to his practical needs, but she also was an inspiration to him as she grew by leaps and bounds in the Lord. She unselfishly gave him every spare moment she had, helping him with the many needs he had as the leader of such a huge singles group. If he needed someone to counsel a woman, he always called on her. If a speaker needed a ride to the airport, he called on her. She was a 24-hour crisis line at his disposal. To the undiscerning eye, it all seemed innocent—a very dedicated new Christian enthusiastically serving her singles director. But the lack of discretion on the part of the minister, coupled with her own spiritual immaturity, made a deadly combination. She confused ministry with matrimony and defrauded herself.

After a Christmas trip together where they shared many deep emotions, she went to Israel for a month. When she returned, he greeted her with the shocking news that he had become engaged while she was away. Did he ask the woman who had worked faithfully by his side to share his life and ministry? No. He proposed to a sweet, but less-involved member of the singles group. Needless to say, this devastated Nancy. This is not an isolated incident. The number of single women defrauding themselves seems to have grown to epidemic proportions.

To heed the Eleventh Commandment, you must consciously resist doing another good deed for a man in your life until you know the motive behind your "unselfish" gesture. How many gifts have you already given to some guy in your life because you sensed that the relationship had future dating potential? How many ministries have you participated in because of the chance to be seen by him? How many times have you volunteered to help a brother when you knew you would not be so willing to help a sister in Christ?

The easiest way to break the Eleventh Commandment is to play the "surrogate wife or mother" in relation to a brother in Christ. You pick a worthy recipient of your time and attention, then you tend to any special needs you find out about in the guise of unselfish giving. There are single women who wash the guy's clothes and clean his apartment, but haven't even been on their first date with him. You might as well wash his car also. What this single woman does not know is that doing good deeds for a man does not win his love. Why? Most of the time, he is used to a woman waiting on him. Remember good ol' mom?

A dedicated Christian should do good deeds, but when you limit your service to the men in your group, it will ultimately backfire. You can end up feeling bruised by your own self-defrauding when you realize the man has taken your special gestures of service for granted.

One summer, as a member of a traveling drama team, a single woman gave herself unselfishly to a particular guy in the group. For ten weeks, during every free minute, she helped him study to pass his ordination exam, which required pages of memorization. At first, all the help she gave him really impressed the other team members. But as time went on, it became obvious to everyone, except him, that her feelings for him had changed from sisterly love to romantic affection. Was anyone to blame for the pain that came at the end of the summer? If both had more discernment, maybe they could have acted more wisely in their friendship so she would not have been defrauded.

When the tour was over and everyone went their own way, he gave her a hearty hug and big "thank you"—and off he went to his ordination, which was followed by his marriage to a girl from back home. What happened to the one left behind with the big "thank you"? She learned a hard lesson, but she was emotionally devastated. She carelessly allowed herself to give her heart away. She gave hours to someone in the hope of reciprocation, but she ended up empty-handed with only a painful memory of giving so much and getting so little. Her motive was wrong. She defrauded herself through unchecked emotions.

PRENUPTIAL FANTASIES

An important method of limiting your own self-defrauding is through daily discipline over "prenuptial fantasies." Such fantasies may provide you an escape from monotonous reality, but these moments are dangerous. They will aggravate your struggle for contentment because they are not innocent daydreams, but an attack on your godly contentment. You may be so used to daily fantasies that you might not even realize when you begin daydreaming again about your prince.

Often a single woman's struggle with contentment can be traced back to her fantasies more than to her frustrating circumstances. Just think for a moment about three words from Second Corinthians 10:5 (KJV): *"Casting down imaginations."* Fantasizing about a future with a guy you have been watching in Sunday school or at work is nothing more than your very active imagination. What should you do when you start daydreaming about a guy you've never dated or even formally met? You must take your thoughts to Jesus and leave them in His capable hands. This daily discipline of taking your fantasies to Jesus is the foundation for your future as a contented woman, whether you are married or single. Right now they are just prenuptial fantasies, but when you are married, those fantasies about other men could continue.

Lack of discipline in the area of "casting down imaginations" may result in self-defrauding and needless discontentment. Sally did not develop this discipline and was hurt needlessly. She went as a counselor to a national youth convention and met a sharp Christian guy from her home state. They enjoyed chatting between seminars, and after she returned home, he began calling her long distance. After each phone call, she would dream and talk to her friends about their potential together. She thought about his being younger, but refused to let her fantasy be spoiled by something as insignificant as age. She allowed the fantasy to move into vivid living color after every long distance phone call. Then her dreams turned into a nightmare. During one of their delightful conversations, he asked her a favor. "Would you mind if I come and visit you during spring break?" That sounded exciting to her, but then he asked the second part of his favor. "Would you mind if I bring two friends?" She assumed he meant two guys he had been discipling, but to her surprise their names were not Bill and John but Sarah and Becky.

After she picked herself up off the floor, she very politely told him that such a plan would not work. When she hung up the phone, she felt angry and betrayed that he apparently wanted to use her home (three blocks from the beach) as a vacation spot. Maybe the guy was insensitive to her, but her hurt was multiplied because she had chosen to spend the preceding days and nights daydreaming about their potential relationship. Her pain and anger could have been reduced if she had exercised some discipline in relation to prenuptial fantasizing about this guy.

Friends too often participate in the development of one's prenuptial fantasies. After only one date with a wonderful man, a girl will share the details of the evening, and her friends will not only share her joy, but also foster excessive imaginings by asking questions like, "Do you think this is the one? Could this be the Boaz you have been waiting so long for?" We not only need the discipline of monitoring our own fantasies, but we also need friends who will remind us not to run ahead of God's timing. Such monitoring of our emotions and accountability between friends is so helpful for the Christian single woman.

Spiritual Monitor

When a friend excitedly calls to tell you about the evening she has just spent with a special man, you often know before she gets two paragraphs into telling of the evening where she is going—fantasy land. As she begins to tell you that he is a friend from her past who recently became a Christian and is suddenly back in her life, be careful. As she rattles on at 100 miles an hour, it would be easy to say, "Maybe your Boaz is finally here"—but don't. Remember wise Naomi and avoid defrauding your friend. By enthusiastically building false hope in a situation that could be here today but gone before her next paycheck, you can easily help a friend to defraud herself. To help her monitor her reactions, point out that one long distance phone call from a male friend is not reason enough to take him home to meet her parents. Encourage your friend, instead, to wait until she sees how the friendship develops.

Your monitoring may not be appreciated at first, but the fruit of such counsel will be sweet. This is not to suggest that you cannot share a friend's joy about a wonderful date with a godly man. But a gift greater than simply sharing her joy is to encourage your friend not to run ahead of the relationship through prenuptial fantasies. Many tears have been shed over relationships that never materialized except in one's dreams.

At a girls' night out, a single woman shared how she used to resent spiritual monitoring from her mom in relation to her fantasies. She used to dread her mother's calm and reserved response to her dramatic presentation of the date she had with the man of her dreams. Her mom, a vivacious woman, seemed so restrained and even a little cynical when responding to her daughter's "bubbly babbling" about Mr. Right. How could such an outgoing, positive, and uplifting mom be so reserved when responding to the dreamy-eyed chatter about the arrival of the man worth waiting for? Did her mom have information of which the daughter was unaware? Had she hired a detective to follow the man of her daughter's dreams and find incriminating information? Of course not! This mom, like Naomi, was extremely wise in monitoring her own response so her daughter would not get excited and distracted by a prospect who might never become a reality.

How refreshing to hear about a wise mom who helped her daughter not to deceive (defraud) herself. Too often moms innocently focus on the famine their daughters face in relation to dating. Instead of encouraging her daughter to use her free time for Jesus (i.e., to be a Lady of Diligence), mom and daughter analyze and re-analyze her dateless state and head for the mall to soothe the emptiness. Not everyone has been blessed with a "spiritual monitor" in a mother, but we can learn from this one's example, and we can be spiritual monitors to the single women in our lives.

How can you begin to be a spiritual monitor? The next time a friend is bubbling over with joy after a date with a wonderful guy, pray for your capacity to share her joy; then pray for the courage to speak the truth about surrendering her dreams to the Lord and not running ahead of Him in her expectations. The spiritual monitor knows the importance of surrendering her own expectations to the only One who can be trusted with her desires and dreams. She can encourage others to surrender their own prenuptial fantasies in exchange for the truth in Psalm 62:5 (KJV): *"My soul, wait thou only upon God; for my expectation is from Him."*

Did you expect to be married by now? Or did you expect to be married forever, and now you are divorced? These expectations mean that you need God's tender loving care and the encouragement of a spiritual monitor who will regularly remind you not to run ahead of the Lord in your relationships with men.

Two women took the challenge to be spiritual monitors to their dearest friend, who was dating Mr. Wonderful. These friends had to consistently resist fanning the fire of their friend's enthusiasm. They monitored their responses and limited their reactions to what was reality and not hopeful fantasy. Because this single woman had waited quite a long time for her Boaz, it would have been easy for her to run with the simplest amount of attention received. But since her best friends monitored their lips, she was free to respond properly to her boyfriend. Unmonitored chatting can lead to major defrauding.

Ironically, the same close friends who help to accelerate the prenuptial fantasy may be the ones who must comfort the lone lovebird when Mr. Right asks another girl out and no more history is to be made with him. Her disappointment will be in direct proportion to the degree that she and her friends responded prematurely to a relationship that will last only in her memory. The next time a friend shares the details of an exciting evening with such a hunk of a guy, don't overreact. Instead, say to her, "I am thrilled that you had a great time. I am so glad you shared your excitement with me. Now do yourself a favor and before you close your eyes to dream tonight, prayerfully commit Mr. Wonderful to Jesus." You will be a true friend and a spiritual monitor for her.

Thousands of needless tears,
Produced by careless cheers,
Assuming that Boaz is finally here,
When the arrival of her prince is not even near....
—JMK

If you do not have a spiritual monitor in a close friend, then ask the Lord to help you find such a friend.

THE MYSTERY OF CONTENTMENT

Whether married or single, in prison or shopping at the mall, the key to enjoying this moment rests with your inner contentment. When your happiness in life is based on "your terms," it is a terrible limitation that will result in a hollow gladness. Singleness does not produce lack of contentment any more than marriage provides contentment. Lack of contentment is the result of the terrible burden of wanting life on your terms.

Married women complain about their lack of contentment as often as single women do, if not more. Both groups of women need to develop the quality of contentment. Paul the apostle, while living in a dark, damp dungeon, wrote of the mystery of contentment that does not depend on circumstances. He described the secret as a "learning process" to which he willingly submitted rather than resisting the conditions:

> *Not that I speak from want, for I have learned to be content in whatever circumstances I am. I know how to get along with humble means, and I also know how to live in prosperity; in any and every circumstance I have learned the secret of being filled and going hungry, both of having abundance and suffering need. I can do all things through Him who strengthens me* (Philippians 4:11-13).

Whether married or single, one must learn that it is Jesus who strengthens you to walk in the most dismal or delightful of circumstances. True contentment is learned. You are not born with it, and you cannot buy it at one of Kmart's blue-light specials. Your classroom for learning is your daily life. Every shattered dream or unfulfilled expectation serves as a perfect opportunity to learn contentment. These circumstances are your classroom assignments for learning the mystery of contentment. Learning contentment will require complete dependence upon Jesus, for difficult circumstances without the strength of Jesus can rob you of potential contentment. Do not be deceived into thinking you do not need Jesus' strength to face the good circumstances as well as the bad. When the sun is shining with no clouds in sight, you may assume that you can securely bask in the sunshine without any prospect of rain; however, this full feeling can easily breed a tendency to ignore Jesus: *"Otherwise, I may have too much and disown You and say, 'Who is the Lord?'"* (Prov. 30:9a NIV).

STOP ARGUING WITH THE UMPIRE

Do you now see the incompatibility of anxiety-filled singleness and contented godliness? Are you ready to rid yourself of the ditches of discontentment that have robbed you of so much peace and joy?

Defrauding by a man, a friend, or even oneself will aggravate your lack of contentment; however, the source of your lack is not defrauding or even frustrating circumstances. Your lack of contentment is because of *pride*. Pride can be described as an excessively high opinion of what one deserves. When a single's life is not moving in the direction she wants (husband, career, children, house, etc.) the arguing often begins. With whom is the single woman arguing? It is none other than the umpire, the arbitrator: Jesus. *"Let the peace of Christ rule* [arbitrate, umpire] *in your hearts..."* (Col. 3:15).

The struggle with the Umpire is not limited to the single women up to bat! Every woman who has descended from Eve must learn to trust the call of her heavenly Umpire. The trouble from the beginning was a woman not listening to the Umpire, but reaching out for a life on "her terms." Why would a woman argue with such an all-wise Umpire? *"Pride only breeds quarrels"* (Prov. 13:10a NIV).

Consider a very poignant verse that brilliantly reveals the war in all of us. *"What causes fights and quarrels among you? Don't they come from your desires that battle within you? You want something but don't get it"* (James 4:1-2 NIV). Honestly face any struggle you may have with your pride-driven desire to have life on your terms. Exchange your pride for Jesus' strength so you may accept whatever assignment the Umpire has for you from this moment forward. Dating is not a reward or a prize for living for Jesus. A Friday night without a date is often a night of "being spared" by an all-wise Umpire.

My soul finds rest in God alone (Psalm 62:1 NIV).

BECOMING A LADY OF CONTENTMENT

Do you have a spiritual monitor? Are you a spiritual monitor? (Read Proverbs 28:23 and Hebrews 3:13.) Are you intimidated by the prospect of this role in a friend's life? Why?

Review the methods of defrauding by a guy and by yourself. (Read First Thessalonians 4:6.)

A contented woman has the ability to lay down the terrible burden of always needing life on her terms. Are you a contented woman? (Read Judges 21:25; Luke 1:38; Matthew 26:39.)

Pride is an excessively high opinion of what one deserves. Do you struggle with pride's control of your desires? (Read Proverbs 13:10, 16:18, 29:23; Jeremiah 5:3; James 4:1-2.)

Does toe-tapping, nail-biting, "I'm a quarter past 30 years old" thinking rob you of contentment? What limits God from acting on your behalf? (Read Matthew 6:27; Isaiah 30:18; Isaiah 64:4.)

Chapter 9

LADY OF CONVICTION

On the eve of her wedding day, Cindy, a Lady of Conviction, wrote the following poem to her bridegroom:

> Dear Sweetheart,
>
> For many years I sought to find my most perfect mate, but all that ever resulted from my search were shattered dreams, a broken heart, and what seemed to be an endless wait. I wanted to find God's very best, but first He had to teach me that in His loving hands, I must solely rest.
>
> So, one evening I prayed "God, just as You put Adam to sleep until the perfect one for him, he was ready to meet; so put me and my desires to sleep until I too am ready to know the one You have chosen for me."
>
> From that time forward, God gave me a peace. And although others came into my life, God protected my heart and spared me from more strife. Then when God knew that in His hands I had placed my heart, He brought you into my life, and I was history from the start.
>
> My dear friends who know me well perhaps see tomorrow as a miraculous day. For they have known me and all my picky ways. Once while in the dorm, A.M. came into my room and asked me just exactly what I was looking for in a man. I ran to my diary and pulled out a list of 30 qualities I was looking for and on which I would insist.

As I read each trait one by one, dear A.M. looked at me; she was very stunned. After pondering the list she said with a nod, "Well, Cindy, looks like you'll have to marry God." Well, God you are not, but my heaven on earth you are. God heard my prayers and answered them in the most perfect way with you.

I have no unanswered questions, no doubts, no hesitations, no reservations. You are my Prince Charming, my knight in shining armor, my gift from the sea, my gift from God. — Cindy Jordan Feldewerth

Does it seem too unrealistic for today's woman to set her sights on a knight in shining armor? Was Cindy just an idealist who got lucky and found a man who satisfied her list of "30 traits"? A single friend (a modern Ruth) wrote a letter in which she admitted that her high ideals often made her feel like the "Lone Ranger." She said, "So often I meet women who don't want to go the deeper, more radical route of separation from our culture in seeking after God's standards." Do we lower our standards because we seem out of step with all our peers? Does the woman in Proverbs 31 seem obsolete? Maybe for the "cosmopolitan" woman she is obsolete, but not for the Lady of Conviction. God has the best in hand for those who seek Him.

Ruth's choice to wait for God's best resulted in her union with a Boaz rather than a Bozo. Ruth not only married a man who was a "pillar of strength" (Boaz), but she also was blessed by the privilege of bearing a son (Obed) who would be part of the lineage of Jesus Christ. Ruth's wise choices resulted in her experiencing God's overwhelming goodness.

DAMAGED GOODS

Ruth did not allow the past influences of a heathen culture to keep her from setting new standards and making wise choices for her life that would honor God. Ruth could have allowed herself to remain within a destructive family cycle that moved against God's standards. She could have given up on a godly lifestyle by assuming she was doomed as "damaged goods." But she didn't. She chose, instead, to break her family's sin cycle and establish a new godly cycle.

After becoming a Christian, Jackie found herself ashamed of her lack of a proper upbringing. She says this:

> I knew I had been forgiven for the past, but I often wrestled with the feelings of being damaged goods. I found myself envying other girls who were from godly homes and great heritages, spiritually. Whenever I would be introduced to a wonderful Christian guy, I would immediately think, "I'm not good enough."
>
> This was exactly how I felt when I first met my husband. He had asked Jesus to take control of his life at the young age of eleven. He went to church faithfully; he never smoked, drank, or fooled around sexually. His high standards were very intimidating to me. Throughout the years of our friendship, I knew he would never date me because of my imperfect past and ungodly family. Was I in for a surprise! As I continued to make choices to break the ungodly influences of my past, the Lord was working on bringing Ken and me together as a team for His glory. Like David, I thought, *"Who am I, O Sovereign Lord, and what is my family, that You have brought me this far?"* (2 Sam. 7:18b NIV).

Ungodly cycles can be broken. Your destiny is not something that is left to chance or fate; it is the product of wise choices.

DESTINY—CHANCE OR CHOICE?

Do you think your ideals and standards are too high? Do you feel the pressure to compromise and settle for the generic version of life? Ruth lived in an era that was exactly like modern America. Judges 21:25 describes the era in which she lived: *"In those days there was no king in Israel; everyone did what was right in his own eyes."* We too live in a culture where it seems that no one fears God and people just "do their own thing."

You, like Ruth, will be greatly affected by your choices. Ruth's wise choices allowed her to break a godless family cycle and begin a new cycle that the Word of God triumphantly records. God has not changed—and neither have men. The high standards in God's Word are not irrelevant, but completely applicable to finding God's best for your life. Choices, guided by your convictions rather than by chance, determine your destiny. How wise have your decisions been in the past in regard to relating to and dating men? Have you made some poor choices that you can see were the result of your own lack of proper convictions in the areas of love, sex, and dating? Your present choices will affect the rest of your life in this delicate area that is often a collision course—male/female relating.

You cannot make good choices without proper, biblical convictions. Don't carelessly leave your dating/relating standards to chance. Too much depends on your decisions in this area. A stanza from the song "Guard Your Heart" by Jon Mohr captures this warning:

The human heart is easily swayed
and often betrayed
at the hand of emotion.
We dare not leave the outcome to chance;
we must choose in advance
or live in agony,
such needless tragedy.

From the beginning of time, God has shown His own people exactly what course they should take to avoid needless tragedy. A passage of Scripture that clearly states the reality of our own choices of happiness or misery is Deuteronomy 30:15-20. Remember that the media, music, literature, teachers, and peers often oppose the godly choices that you might want to make.

STANDARD-BEARER

May we go back to the basics for just a moment? What is a conviction, and how does one develop biblical convictions? A conviction is a standard that serves as a springboard for your choices. Consider where your standards, in the area of relating and dating, originated. Are your standards based more on Hollywood's terms of love and romance, or have you allowed God's Holy Word to shape your perspective?

The Lady of Conviction gives the Lord permission to renew her mind on a daily basis. She spends time searching the Word of God for standards that will guide her safely to God's best. She has made a significant choice as a godly woman. She has surrendered her mind to a new persuasion: God's perspective on love and romance. The convictions that she establishes, based on the Word, allow her to resist being squeezed into the mold of this world. She is a non-conformist in a biblical sense, as in Romans 12:2 (NIV) which says,

> *Do not conform any longer to the pattern of this world, but be transformed by the renewing of your mind. Then you will be able to test and approve what God's will is—His good, pleasing and perfect will.*

Notice the words *test* and *approve;* your convictions (whether Hollywood-based or Bible-based) gauge your ability to "test and approve" the relationships you've had or will have.

If you want to live by God's standards for love, sex, and dating, you must prepare yourself for the inevitable resistance that "standard-bearers" face. When you live by your convictions, many of your friends will consider you unrealistic. Some of your girlfriends may even think you are stubbornly opinionated. Facing such opposition from the people you love is not easy, but the Lord will give you the grace to refuse to compromise. A true standard-bearer wants to be a vanguard in a movement. Through Jesus' strength, you can stand firm, unwavering, as you wait for His best. The woman without the high ideals that the Word of God sets forth leaves her choices to chance. She will tend to end up with a Bozo rather than a Boaz because she cannot measure accurately the man behind the "makeup."

Since most biblical convictions are in opposition to all the propaganda from Hollywood, relatively few, even among Christians, hold to these standards. This harsh reality is revealed throughout the Word:

> *You are like unfaithful wives, flirting with the glamour of this world, and never realizing that to be the world's lover means becoming the enemy of God! Anyone who deliberately chooses to love the world is thereby making himself God's enemy. Or do*

you think what the scriptures have to say about this is a mere formality? (James 4:4-5 PNT)

When you pass up dates with certain guys because you know they do not measure up to God's standards, then you have taken seriously your commitment not to oppose God. If your friends pressure and oppose you, ask the Lord for the strength to be more concerned with being His friend and not His enemy through compromising standards.

In America, government agencies regulate the standards of the food that you consume on a daily basis. For example, meat is subject to federal regulation of its grade, weight, and quality. How much more significant than ground beef (even prime rib) is the man with whom you hope to share the rest of your life? Such consideration and evaluation cannot be obtained through a glance or chance encounter at the "meet" counter. A lifelong relationship demands the highest standards of regulation. There are men breathing on this planet today who can handle such scrutiny and be found "worth waiting for."

AVOIDING BOZOS

What is a Bozo? A Bozo is a guy whose outward appearance is a façade. It is hard to discern who he really is because of the "makeup and costume" he wears. What he appears to be physically, socially, and even spiritually is just a performance. A Bozo is a counterfeit of a Boaz.

It is possible to avoid such a clown. Your standards and convictions will help you recognize the difference. The remainder of this chapter will accentuate the genuine Boaz. Concentrating on the real thing will make the Bozos more apparent.

Before any girl accepts her first date, she should have established in her heart and mind a biblical alternative to Hollywood's dating style. As a prerequisite to every date, you should examine your motive (elaborated in the chapter on contentment). Are you going out with this guy because you haven't had a date in years? Are you going out with someone who may not really be a Christian because you think a date—even with a Bozo—is better than no date at all? Many women spend time with guys who do not really care for them. They would rather waste an evening with a Bozo than face another lonely night in a dateless condition. Some women even give up their biblical convictions in order to get a date with a certain guy. Do you feel as though you allow your dating schedule to determine your personal worth? Many single women are prisoners of the world's dating syndrome. They equate their self-worth with how many dates they had last month.

Have you dated more Bozos than Boazs? If your answer is yes, you may need to develop higher ideals. A very attractive and popular high school girl was challenged to develop a list of biblical dating standards and to put them into practice. She carried a copy of those standards in her wallet for five years. Thus she dated more Boazs than Bozos because her convictions helped her clearly see the type of guys with whom she was relating and ultimately dating. Do you carry God's standards for dating in your heart as well as in your wallet?

One Auburn University graduate left school with not only a diploma but also a very specific list of the qualities she was looking for in a future mate. See if her list contains any of the qualities you are looking for in Mr. Right:

- Spirit-controlled Christian (see Eph. 5:18).
- Jesus is #1 in his life, not just an ornament (see Mark 12:30).
- Broken; understands how to rely totally upon Jesus (see Phil. 4:13).
- Ministry-minded; wherever he is, he is available (see 1 Cor. 4:2 NIV).
- Motivator; man of vision, concerned about lost souls (see Rom. 10:14).
- Sensitive spirit; in tune to the needs of others (see Gal. 6:2).
- Understands the awesome responsibility of a husband to his wife (see Eph. 5:25-31).
- Humble enough to be a disciple (teachable) and able to disciple others (see Matt. 28:19-20).
- Man of prayer; he knows the key to success is his private time with God (see Col. 4:2).

- Family man; he desires to have children and raise them properly for God's glory (see Prov. 22:6).

Clear standards for dating and relating will guard you against compromise and making wrong choices out of sudden emotion rather than a God-directed will. These guidelines for your dating friendships will keep God as your focus rather than allowing the guy to become the focus (idol). Clear standards coupled with accountability to a sister in Christ will help you walk in the convictions you establish. To guard you against haphazard meetings or just the "WFs" (weird feelings) in your heart, you need standards for which you will be accountable.

A disclaimer (or an additional note) that we would like to include at this point is not to simplify the reason so many women are attracted to Bozos. The issue of standards is most relevant, but may seem simplistic. We acknowledge that some women find it difficult to raise their standards and change their patterns because they are still entangled with the past. Unresolved conflicts with a father, a brother, or an ex-boyfriend may overshadow and control the attraction to Bozos. In this case, we suggest a possible date fast, a period of time during which you refrain from accepting another date until you can sort out some of the unresolved conflicts from the past. This method has been used by many single women who have been entangled with old dating patterns. During the "date fast," they find time to search for new ways of relating and dating biblically.

If you have already spent time with the Lord establishing dating/relating standards, then you will receive affirmation through the following material. If you have been letting your dating routine be controlled by chance rather than biblical choice, consider not accepting another date until you have nailed down your convictions. Too much is at stake.

Once you have set dating standards and understand the significance of a constant motive check (daily bringing the flutters in your heart to the Lord), you are ready to consider other guidelines for successful dating and relating.

WEDDING DAY CHAINS

"Here comes the bride all dressed in...chains!" Hey, wasn't that supposed to be "all dressed in white"? The last word in the chorus was changed to "chains," not because the bride is marrying a member of a motorcycle gang, but because she made the unwise choice of marrying an unbeliever. The chains symbolize what she has to look forward to as a believer married to an unbeliever. The Word of God speaks clearly about a partnership with an unbeliever. A common verse used for this conviction is Second Corinthians 6:14-17, but you find a more poignant message for the one who wavers in this conviction in Joshua.

> *But if you turn away and ally yourselves with the survivors of these nations that remain among you and if you intermarry with them and associate with them, then you may be sure that the Lord your God will no longer drive out these nations before you. Instead, they will become snares and traps for you, whips on your backs and thorns in your eyes, until you perish from this good land, which the Lord your God has given you* (Joshua 23:12-13 NIV).

One would be foolish to disobey God in the area of marrying an unbeliever.

When a single woman experiences a prolonged period of datelessness, loneliness tempts her to compromise her conviction concerning dating a growing Christian. Her dateless state may pressure her to surrender to the temptation of dating an unbeliever. She may justify such a date in the guise of being a witness for Jesus. Many single women have been trapped emotionally with an unbeliever when it all began with "missionary dating." Ponder this: every unbelieving marriage partner arrived as an unbeliever on the first date. As trite as it may seem, every date is a potential mate. Avoid dating an unbeliever.

Many women want so desperately to date that the only qualification they have for the guy is that he goes to church. Every Sunday, churches have people attending to appease God or to satisfy a religious urge. You must set a higher standard and resist dating a guy who is not growing in his intimacy with Christ.

THE MAN WORTH WAITING FOR

How would you describe the ideal man? A group of sharp women were asked to describe a "Man Worth Waiting For," and all of them immediately replied: spiritual leader. One woman expounded on this quality in her unique way: "I want a guy who enjoys talking about Jesus in such a way that it reveals his obvious, bursting love for Him." Too many guys want to talk about Jesus for 60 seconds and their car or job or latest toy for the rest of the evening. One woman shared a verse that she thought his life should reflect: Psalm 73:25: *"Whom have I in heaven but You* [the Lord]? *And besides You, I desire nothing on earth."* Do such spiritual men exist? Yes, but they are exceptions and not the rule. Their appearance requires waiting on the part of the recipient.

Before considering the specific qualities found in a Boaz, one should deal with certain physical stereotypes. Whether you have been looking for a guy who is a bronzed, blue-eyed blond ("B.B.B.") or is tall, dark, and handsome ("T.D.H."), you need to surrender your desires to the Lord. Everyone has certain preferences. But such a mindset needs to be given to Jesus. Too many single women have missed wonderful treasures in godly guys because the treasure was not encased in a B.B.B. or T.D.H. The Lord will probably not require you to date a guy who repulses you physically. But you need to be open to guys who do not fit your desired stereotype. Too often a guy may satisfy your eyesight, but leave your heart empty and still longing. Remember, after a few years that bronzed, blue-eyed blond can be transformed into a pale, bald guy with bifocals on those gorgeous eyes.

A famous actress told a Christian psychologist that her five husbands had all been attractive outside (they were all B.B.B.s or T.D.H.s), but rotten on the inside. How many women, after the honeymoon is over, feel like they married a stranger? How many newlyweds are disillusioned by their mate's behavior within a few months of marriage? Most marriage counseling problems have their roots in personality problems—not physiques.

The Book of Ruth gives not only the story of a Lady in Waiting, but also the profile of a Knight in Shining Armor. From the first mention of this man Boaz, you begin to notice special qualities that distinguish a Boaz from a Bozo.

You want to marry someone for the qualities he possesses now, not for the qualities you hope he will develop. The most common mistake made by marriage partners is marrying someone they intend to change. Since it is nearly impossible to change a person, you will want to set standards of dating, or of building friendships, with men who are characterized by the qualities below. A single woman can sidestep a lifetime of tragedy by seriously considering these characteristics in a prospective steady date.

Puts the needs of others ahead of his own. This man accepts people just the way they are, loving others even when his love is not returned. He will continue to love someone because of his commitment to that person, not because of how he feels.

> *Do nothing from selfishness or empty conceit, but with humility of mind regard one another as more important than yourselves; do not merely look out for your own personal interests, but also for the interests of others* (Philippians 2:3-4).

Rejoices in his relationship with Christ. You don't have to ask this man if he is a Christian. His joy in the Lord is evident in his life.

> *These things I have spoken to you so that My joy may be in you, and that your joy may be made full* (John 15:11).

Maintains proper relationships. This man seeks a good relationship with everyone—from his friends to his parents. He listens to differing perspectives without feeling threatened. He has the strength to back off from a fight. He works to forgive wrongs done to him and seeks to make his own offenses right. He will not hold a grudge.

> *Pursue peace with all men...* (Hebrews 12:14).

Refuses to jump ahead of God's timing. He is not so eager to be something, do something, or have something that he cannot wait on God's timing. He chooses against impulsiveness so he may be in the exact center of God's will.

> *Rest in the Lord and wait patiently for Him...* (Psalm 37:7).

Seeks to meet the practical needs of others. He is not so self-absorbed that he cannot make time for the needy. He is interested in the welfare of others and is willing to give his time, money, and energy for their benefit.

> *Be kind to one another, tender-hearted...* (Ephesians 4:32).

Stands for what is right. He hates anything contrary to God's holy character. He is known as a man of integrity by those with whom he works.

There will be...glory and honor and peace to everyone who does good... (Romans 2:9-10).

Follows through on his God-given responsibilities. He uses the talents God has given him and realizes that "he + Jesus = adequacy for any God-given job." He is neither overconfident nor absorbed with feelings of inferiority. He is not a dreamer, wishing for more ability, but a diligent steward of the talents he has been given. This man is dependable and stays with even a difficult task until it is completed.

Now it is required that those who have been given a trust must prove faithful (1 Corinthians 4:2 NIV).

Understands the importance of feelings and emotions. Some women may find themselves attracted to a demanding man, assuming that his dominance will be their security. Other women may marry a doormat they can dominate, but inevitably end up despising the man's weakness. A gentle man is the best of both; he takes the initiative to lead but tempers it with gentle responses toward the other's feelings.

So, as those who have been chosen of God, holy and beloved, put on a heart of compassion, kindness, humility, gentleness and patience (Colossians 3:12).

Flees temptations to compromise. This man refuses to be in situations that are sensual, immoral, or impure. He does not entertain friendships that lead to drunkenness or carousing. He avoids talk that could cause strife or jealousy. This man does not allow a temper to control him or anger to destroy him.

Like a city that is broken into and without walls is a man who has no control over his spirit (Proverbs 25:28).

These qualities are not unrealistic ideals. When a man follows Jesus, the Holy Spirit works these into his life. In fact, you can read this list again and match the fruit of the Spirit with the appropriate characteristic: *"But the fruit of the Spirit is love, joy, peace, patience, kindness, goodness, faithfulness, gentleness, self-control; against such things there is no law"* (Gal. 5:22-23).

None of the men you date will have all these qualities perfected. All of us are at differing levels of maturity. A man of God is one who works toward being conformed to the character of Christ. But be careful when a quality of God's Spirit is completely missing in a man's life and he is unwilling to deal with it before marriage. Realize that if character is absent before the wedding ceremony, it will be missing after the wedding ceremony and cause considerable problems during marriage.

Was Boaz, Ruth's knight, the last man of godly character, or was he just one of many? We are convinced that God still grooms Boazs for His daughters today. This does not mean a guy has to be perfect in order for you to go out with him. It does mean that he needs to be growing in Christlikeness by the enabling power of the Holy Spirit before you start to date him.

Do you want to marry a knight in shining armor? Then set your standards high. To be married to a man who loves the Lord and wants to serve Him is one of life's highest privileges. It is worth whatever wait, whatever cost. Nail down your convictions and refuse to compromise by dating men who are not controlled by God's Holy Spirit. These standards will stand guard over the castle of your heart. Proverbs 4:23 (NIV) says, *"Above all else, guard your heart, for it is the wellspring of life."*

BECOMING A LADY OF CONVICTION

Write out your convictions for the kind of guys you will date and the Scriptures where you found those qualities. Why did you select these particular convictions?

What is the problem with just dating guys who are good, but who are not Christians? What is the difference between a good man who goes to church and a growing Christian man? What difference would it make in marriage?

If the wait becomes hard and you meet someone who loves you, but has a glaring character flaw, what do you sacrifice if you marry him? Look through each of the characteristics found in the Man Worth Waiting For section and determine what would be lost in your marriage if that quality was missing in your husband and the father of your children.

Put a check beside each of the following characteristics that *you* can change in your husband after marriage:

____ Unwillingness to communicate (see Prov. 14:10)

____ Dominating ego (see Rom. 12:3)

____ Bad temper (see James 1:19-20)

____ Argumentative tendencies (see Prov. 20:3)

____ Difficulty in apologizing (see Eph. 4:32)

____ Bad language (see Eph. 5:4)

____ Unwillingness to be involved with church (see Heb. 10:24-25)

____ Inability to keep a job (see 1 Tim. 5:8)

____ Jealousy (see 1 Cor. 13:4)

____ Self-centeredness (see 2 Cor. 5:15)

____ Depression (see 2 Cor. 4:16)

____ Unwillingness to give (see 2 Cor. 9:7)

____ Always "going with the guys" (see 1 Cor. 15:33)

____ Wandering eyes (see 1 Thess. 4:2-7)

____ Lying (see Eph. 4:25)

____ Immaturity (see Eph. 4:15)

____ Workaholic tendencies (see 1 Tim. 6:7-11)

What does the Bible say about these qualities in reference to godliness?

LADY OF PATIENCE

*J*anis and Linda were longtime friends and roommates. Inside their hall closet hung two sizes of every color of bridesmaid's dress imaginable. "Well," they would say, with a laugh, "we have been bridesmaids at the weddings of many friends, but we are still here, holding out for the man God has for each of us!" Linda often added, "One thing I do know, when I walk down that aisle in white I want 'Great Is Thy Faithfulness' to be the procession song."

Although their ability to joke in the midst of their prolonged singleness is admirable, one has to wonder how an older woman can be patient when there appears to be no end to the waiting in sight. Waiting isn't easy when you are young, and it can be terribly hard as you get older.

God demonstrated His faithfulness in a special way to these two close single friends who chose to wait for His best, whether they married or not. He allowed each of their princes to appear within weeks of each other. Linda and Janis rejoiced in the faithfulness of God as they planned their weddings and then participated in each other's wedding ceremony. They witnessed God's faithfulness in marriage as in singleness because they waited on His perfect timing for their future.

Was the wait easy? No. Was the wait worth it? Many years of marriage and six children later, the two friends answer with a resounding, "Praise God. Yes, the wait was worth it!"

Take courage, single friend. You are not alone in your wait; neither are you alone in the feelings and struggles you encounter. Many godly women have waited and won. Many women have lost hope and compromised.

Wait patiently and win triumphantly the future your Father has planned for you. It will always be designed with you in mind and is worth being patient to discover.

Ruth was a wonderful example of a Lady of Patience. Ruth did not allow her circumstances or lack of male companionship to cause her to be impatient. Instead she concentrated on developing companionship with her heavenly Father and chose to let Him bring a husband to her if He saw fit. Concern over the ticking of her "biological clock" did not make her fearful of the future. Instead she concentrated on being a lady of character, not on getting a man. She took one day at a time, knowing that God was not bound by circumstances nor her age. She used the wait to become the woman God wanted her to be. At the end of this personal preparation God chose to provide her with a husband. In Ruth 4:13, we see the end to their love story: *"So Boaz took Ruth, and she became his wife...."*

WHY IS WAITING SO HARD?

If God is faithful, why is it so easy to lose patience? Why is it so hard to wait? Why is it easier to settle for less than God's best? Fear is a huge hindrance to waiting. You may fear that your biological clock is ticking away and God has not noticed. You may fear, with every wedding you attend, that soon you will no longer have any single friends. You might feel that you better marry this "OK fella" who just proposed because he's pretty good and you fear you may not find another. Or possibly you fear loneliness and a lifetime of eating by yourself and of going to a church filled with people, only to sit alone.

Fear is an internal pressure. There are external pressures as well. Society pushes single women to grab for marriage because of a male shortage. Your parents want grandchildren, and your cousins want to know, "What's wrong with you?" You feel like you don't fit in with the youth any longer, but you can't very well go to the young marrieds' functions at church (where your friends now attend). If that isn't enough, a knowledge of statistics on singleness can finish you off:

> Marriage patterns in the United States revealed: white college educated women born in the mid-50s who are still single at

thirty have a 20% chance of marrying. By the age of 35, the odds drop to 5%. Forty year olds are more likely to be killed by a terrorist than the minuscule 2.6% probability of tying the knot.[1]

How encouraging! The world is attacking a single woman's confidence as the enemy discourages her hopes through fear. These pressures often provoke single women to take more initiative rather than patiently wait for God's best.

CONSEQUENCES OF IMPATIENCE

There are grave consequences for the single woman who does not choose to develop patience and wait on God's timing. Society is full of heartbreaking examples. Some end in divorce; others end in an emotional separation that causes the husband and wife to merely live under the same roof. Some leave precious children damaged by the insecurity and fear that an unhealthy marriage produces. The personal loneliness and hurt that these lifestyles bring can be indescribably painful. God did not intend a woman to have to live like that.

Impatience to find a man can cause a woman to argue about her "right" to date a man who is not godly, maybe not even a Christian. In Joshua 23:12-14, the Lord warns His people not to marry unbelievers. God knows that an ungodly husband will end up being *"snares and traps for you, whips on your backs and thorns in your eyes..."* (Josh. 23:13 NIV). Many young women argue that they are just dating, not marrying, an unbeliever. But remember—in our society, does anyone ever marry someone he or she never dated? Every date is a potential mate.

Marriage to a non-Christian brings pain to the believing wife. As women, we long to be known and loved for all we are. A man who is spiritually dead can never know the very intimate spiritual part of you that is your heart. He would be blind to much of what you would try to share with him. He could never know and understand you fully.

Be careful when you begin to think that you are "in love" and you "just can't live without him." Think again. Think of the loneliness you will feel when your husband will not attend church with you. Think of the angry bickering that may take place between the two of you because he can never understand the depths of your spiritual awareness and, consequently, your convictions. If you do not think about this now, you may one day think, "Before, I couldn't live without him; now I can hardly live with him." Second Corinthians 6:14-15 is very clear:

> *Do not be bound together with unbelievers; for what partnership have righteousness and lawlessness, or what fellowship has light with darkness? Or what harmony has Christ with Belial, or what has a believer in common with an unbeliever?*

Please consider a greater consequence than being unhappily married to a man who does not know your Lord. Will you be able to handle the pain of watching your children live with possible rejection by their father, day in and day out? Will you think it is worth the cost when you are the only one who gets up on Sunday mornings to take your dear children to church? Will it be worth the compromise when your children look up at you and ask why daddy doesn't love Jesus? They could even reject the Lord for eternity and live a miserable, ill-chosen lifestyle because of the choice you made to marry a wonderful, but lost, man. Children will often follow their father's example—good or bad. Exodus 34:7 gives a warning you cannot ignore: "*...He will by no means leave the guilty unpunished, visiting the iniquity of fathers on the children and on the grandchildren to the third and fourth generations.*" You are not just marrying a husband, but choosing a father for your children.

When you marry, you do not choose blessings or curses for you alone; you choose for the generations after you. If you choose to wait patiently for your knight in shining armor, you will be blessed by the heritage that a prince brings. If you choose to run eagerly ahead of God's plan and marry a man with no conscience toward God, you will reap the life's course he follows, but not alone. Your children's and grandchildren's lives will be directly affected by the man you marry.

Consider the following Scriptures:

> *All these blessings will come upon you and overtake you if you will obey the Lord your God* (Deuteronomy 28:2).

*But it shall come about, if you do not obey the Lord your God...
all these curses shall come upon you and overtake you* (Deuteronomy 28:15).

God warned His people in Deuteronomy of the long-term effect of
their choices. Today other countries may not take our children, but there
are many bondages in our wicked generation that could hold them.

*Your sons and your daughters shall be given to another people,
while your eyes look on and yearn for them continually; but there
will be nothing you can do* (Deuteronomy 28:32).

Have you seen the yearning eyes of a mother as she sees her son on
drugs or her daughter living on the streets? There is nothing she can do
but look on in pain.

These verses in Deuteronomy show that God has always desired to
bless His people, but He will not force them to do what is best. In His
Word He has often warned us to wait, to be careful, and to trust Him.
He will not make us wait. His heart of love begs us to listen and obey so
He may bless us and the dear ones who will one day look to and follow
us. The words He gave to the children of Israel in Deuteronomy 30:15-
20 show the love and concern He has for the choices you make.

*...So choose life in order that you may live, you and your descen-
dants, by loving the Lord your God, by obeying His voice, and by
holding fast to Him...* (Deuteronomy 30:19-20).

You must choose to wait patiently for God's best. If you have seen
patterns in your life that show a lack of patience, commit yourself right
now to waiting for God's best.

You may pray something like this:

*Lord, You are my sovereign God. You know all about me and love
me more than anyone else ever could. You know how I feel, what
I need, and what my future is. I confess that I have taken matters
into my own hands. I confess to being afraid of totally trusting
You. Today I commit myself to focus on You and Your love for me.
Today I commit to look to You for my future—not to my outward*

circumstances. Thank You for knowing how weak I feel, but being strong for me and in me. I love You. I choose to trust You.

You may have to repeat this prayer, or one like it, many times when you feel afraid. But Psalm 103:13-14 assures us that He understands and has compassion on us:

Just as a father has compassion on his children, so the Lord has compassion on those who fear Him. For He Himself knows our frame; He is mindful that we are but dust (Psalm 103:13-14).

DEVELOPING PATIENCE

Kimmy expressed that her focus was set and patience began in a real way in her life when, during her late twenties, she surrendered her life to Jesus. She said, "I remember telling the Lord, 'I don't care if I ever get married, I just want to love You, please You, and know You.' From that time I had a new peace and power. I got involved by ministering to the youth in my church and found joy in serving others. One girl told me her mother thought I was absolutely crazy, being as old as I was, to spend my time with the youth instead of trying to find a husband."

Kimmy served the Lord faithfully and contentedly alone until years later when Lynn recognized her as the lady God had for him. They were soon married because they had patiently used their waiting time to get ready. Kimmy said, "God didn't supply all my wants when I was single. He changed my wants and supplied all my needs, better than I could have imagined."

One older single woman struggling to be a Lady in Waiting cried out to the Lord as to why He was delaying the coming of her knight. She searched her heart, thinking there must be something horribly amiss in her life for God to spend so many extra years developing her into a princess suitable for her knight-to-be. Her self-image began to suffer as she mentally blamed herself for the delays. Tenderly the Father gave her a verse she could cling to: *"Dwell in the land and cultivate faithfulness"* (Ps. 37:3b).

She didn't really understand all that it meant, but chose to believe she was being all she should be before the Lord. As she began to dwell upon the positive things the Lord said about her in His Word, like *"the King's daughter is all glorious within"* (Ps. 45:13a), she was able to reject negative, condemning thoughts and feelings, and choose to be the woman He wanted her to be as a single.

Little did she know that God needed those days to perfect her Boaz. We, as women, are not the only ones who need the days of waiting in order to be perfected for a future life-mate. Her knight had not been a Christian long, and in his spiritual immaturity would not have been a proper spiritual leader. He needed time to be grounded in the Word and to experience complete freedom over the sins of his past.

When the two of them were finally introduced, she understood why she had to wait. While she cultivated faithfulness before God, her knight had been slaying a few dragons and shining his armor. God did not leave her waiting any longer than necessary. She desired a knight, but patiently waited on God's timing. The two of them now glorify God in a ministry to drug and alcohol abusers.

Wait patiently. Perhaps you are giving God time to prepare, not yourself, but your beloved. Let your heavenly Father accomplish His work thoroughly while your single man is undistracted. Issues settled in a person's life while single limit unnecessary stress and difficulty later in a marriage. Psalm 37:7 says, *"Rest in the Lord and wait patiently for Him...."* Wait not for a man or a preconceived perfect future, but for Him. Verses 3, 4, and 5 of Psalm 37 give some great action words for the Lady of Patience to follow in order to wait before Him.

Realizing that marriage is not a dream but real life can also help you to wait more patiently. Instead of merely being envious, get with a godly married woman and see the extra load she carries. Look at all she cannot do, instead of the fact that she has a man in her house. Understand that in reality, married life is not constant communication, daily roses, hugs and kisses, breakfast in bed, and sheer bliss. Marriage is every bit as much work as it is wonderful, even in God's way and time. It is good, but don't be deceived into mistaking it for Heaven.

Since no spouse is perfect, learning to live "as one" is not without its tears. Marriage alone is not a cure-all or answer to every heartfelt need. If you think it is, you had better just keep waiting, for that kind of marriage doesn't exist. Although there is a romantic inside every one of us, you must be realistic regarding marriage, or the shock could be devastating.

"Another thing that helped me wait patiently," Kimmy wrote, "was a sense of humor. Laugh about 'always a bridesmaid but never a bride.' Joke about opening your own attendant shop because you have so many bridesmaid's dresses. Talk about being single with others in a fun way, not with a 'woe is me' attitude."

Find other single girls and plan activities. Don't just sit at home on Friday night. Go out to eat, or to the movies, and become involved working with children, young people, or senior adults. There are many things you can do to stay busy and keep from becoming impatient.

Developing patience is hard. Getting married ahead of God's timing is worse. God may not work according to your time schedule, but He does have your best interests in mind. One single said, "As a teenager, I had my life all planned out. I would meet my husband at age 19, marry at 21, and start my family at 23. These were my plans, but evidently not God's plans for my life. I am 41 now, but enjoy a wonderful single life."

You don't know what tomorrow holds, but you do know who holds tomorrow. Say this with the psalmist:

> *O Lord, my heart is not proud, nor my eyes haughty; nor do I involve myself in great matters, or in things too difficult for me. Surely I have composed and quieted my soul; like a weaned child rests against his mother, my soul is like a weaned child within me. O [substitute your name], hope in the Lord from this time forth and forever* (Psalm 131).

The place of rest that the psalmist found was a result of the choice he made. This quietness of soul did not come naturally to him. He actively chose to take himself out of involvement and quiet his soul (his mind, will, and emotions). He chose to put his hope in God. Are you trying to involve yourself in matters that are too great for you? Can you see into a man's heart? Can you know the future? You know Someone who does know men's hearts and the future. Patiently rest against His chest. He will bring you the peace you need. This attitude of patience is not something that will just happen. By an act of your will you must choose to trust God regardless of what happens. Patiently wait for His best.

Every single woman must at some point come to grips with the fact that not all women will marry. Marriage is not a need, though God chooses to let marriage meet some needs a woman may have. Marriage is not a right, though God chooses to plan marriage for the majority of women. Marriage does not complete a person, though women who properly marry find that marriage rounds out some of their weaknesses. If marriage were a need, right, or completion for women, then all godly women would marry. There are many examples of true, God-honoring women who had no earthly mate but were still Ladies of Patience.

One Lady in Waiting wrote this:

> I believe part of being a Lady of Patience is honestly facing the future. For me that was realizing that I might not ever get married.
>
> I could handle the thoughts of "waiting on the Lord," but to face the reality that it may not be His desire for me to marry was hard to cope with. As I read my Bible, I found Isaiah 54:5. The verse said I was already married to Him. He was my Husband! I was His bride. He wanted me to know Him, my Husband. He wanted me to see myself as His bride, to know His love for me. He wanted to be intimate with me. So I began my walk with my Husband, the Lord Jesus.
>
> I still desire to get married; in fact, many times I have longed for a husband and even cried for one. There have been times when I thought I had met "the one for me," then was terribly disappointed. But I always knew I could go back to my Husband who understood my desire and my hurts. He would encourage me by showing me His love in even deeper ways.

Another single woman named Beverly developed the following Bible study to calm the impatience of her heart.

Why Do I Want to Get Married?	How Can God Meet Those Needs in My Life?
By Beverly Seward Brandon	
I want to be loved.	"…I have loved you with an everlasting love…" (Jer. 31:3).
I want someone to adore me.	The King has brought me into His chambers to adore me. My lover is outstanding among 10,000 (see Song 1:4; 5:10).
I want someone to hold my hand.	"…I will uphold you with My righteous right hand" (Isa. 41:10).
I want to be accepted and valued.	I am accepted in the Beloved (see Eph. 1:6 KJV).
I want a "place," a nesting place that is my own to create and use.	We can rest in the shadow of the Almighty (see Ps. 91:1).
I want help in my days of trouble.	"Call upon Me in the day of trouble; I shall rescue you…" (Ps. 50:15).
I want to share my life—the joys and the struggles—with one person (intimacy).	God will share with me the treasures of darkness and hidden riches (see Isa. 45:3).
I want a champion of my causes—one who is willing to fight for me.	"The Lord will fight for you…" (Exod. 14:14).
I want someone to meet my needs.	God is meeting all my needs (see Phil. 4:19).
I want intimacy.	The Lord is intimate with the upright (see Ps. 140:13).
I want someone to help me in my life.	There is no one like God who rides the heavens to help you (see Deut. 33:26).
I want to walk through life sustained and carried. I don't want the whole load of life.	Even to my old age, God will sustain me, carry me, and rescue me (see Isa. 46:4).
I want a companion for this life.	God invites us to humbly walk with Him (see Mic. 6:8).
I desire children.	God gives us spiritual children like the numberless grains of sand if we invest in lives (see Isa. 48:19).

Beverly's response to this study is "the Lord, my Maker, is my Husband. Only He can meet the deepest needs of my heart. No man can ever come through for me fully. Only He can. He is what I long for. Only God is enough."

Regardless of what you see or what you feel, God is in full control of your situation. You, Lady in Waiting, can walk in victory by choosing to be patient in your wait.

Don't let your impatient longings rob you of the life God wants to bless you with as a single. Realize you do not need marriage for happiness or a full life. If you are holding onto marriage as a right, relinquish this right so it will not keep you from God's fullest blessings. God knows what is best for you. His timing is perfect, and He will take care of His Lady of Patience.

BECOMING A LADY OF PATIENCE

Write out the things that make you lose patience. Which of these cause your Sovereign God concern? Give these concerns to Him and ask Him to help you trust while you wait. "I will trust while I wait, for my God is never late" is a good motto.

Read Deuteronomy 28:1-48. Write on one side of a piece of paper the blessings God wanted the nation of Israel to have as His children. Write on the other side what He asked them to do. What does He require of you?

Read Deuteronomy 28:1-48 again. Write the curses that came from choosing to be disobedient to God. Confess any ways that you have chosen to disobey God's will for your life.

Read Deuteronomy 30 and write down all the tender ways God spoke to His children, trying to help them choose what was best. How can you commit today to remain true to your loving Father and patiently wait? Look at the way He understands how His children feel in verses 11-14.

Make Psalm 27 your prayer and commit it, or another passage, to memory to use on those hard days.

ENDNOTE

1. Eloise Salholz, "Too Late for Prince Charming?" *Newsweek,* June 2, 1986.

PART II

Lady in Waiting
Study Guide

DEAREST LADY,

It is our prayer that the Meditation Journal and Study Guide will help you apply the thoughts and principles in *Lady in Waiting* to your personal life, thus helping you to succeed in your search for life's best.

You can use this Study Guide as an individual or in a group of any size. We recommend that after you read *Lady in Waiting* through once, you then go through it again, chapter by chapter, with this Study Guide.

The questions in this Study Guide are very personal. Thus, when you answer them, this book actually becomes another sort of journal. If you are using this Study Guide in a group setting, then you may or may not want to share your answers, but honest interaction in a group setting is of great benefit to everyone involved.

May the true King draw you ever closer to His heart.

—JACKIE KENDALL and DEBBY JONES

LADY IN WAITING

is not about finding the right man,
but becoming the right woman.
The Lady in Waiting
recklessly abandons herself
to the Lordship of Christ,
diligently uses her single days,
trusts God with unwavering faith,
demonstrates virtue in daily life,
loves God with undistracted devotion,
stands for physical and emotional purity,
lives in security,
responds to life in contentment,
makes choices based on her convictions,
and waits patiently for God to meet her needs.

Chapter 1

RUTH'S RECKLESS ABANDONMENT

*I*n the Book of Ruth, a young widow made a critical decision to turn her back on her people, her country, and her gods because her thirsty soul had tasted of the God of Israel. With just a "taste," she recklessly abandoned herself to the only true God. She willingly broke her alabaster box and followed the Lord wherever He would lead her.

> But Ruth said, "Do not urge me to leave you or turn back from following you; for where you go, I will go, and where you lodge, I will lodge. Your people shall be my people, and your God, my God" (Ruth 1:16).

Ruth had a determined heart, and the Lord honored her faith in moving away from all that was familiar and taking a journey toward the completely unknown. Ruth did not allow her friends, her old surroundings, or her culture's dead faith to keep her from running hard after God. She did not use the excuse of a dark past to keep her from a bright future that began with her first critical choice: reckless abandonment to the Lord God.

LADY OF RECKLESS ABANDONMENT

I. Read Ruth chapter 1.

    1.   What is happening in these two women's lives?

    2.   How do the women feel?

    3.   How do they respond to this time of crisis in their lives?

4. What are their choices?
   * their plans?
   * their hopes?
5. What are their dreams for the future?
6. How do they respond to each other?
7. What do you identify with?
8. How can Ruth remain strong during such hardship?

II. "Ruth moved from a false religion into the only true and eternal relationship. Too many women have been involved in a form of religious worship, but have never had a vital, growing relationship with Jesus."

1. What is the difference between religion and a relationship?
2. Read Isaiah 29:13 (NIV). Does this verse describe your religious experience? Why or why not?
3. Read John 3:16. How can one enter into a personal relationship with God?
4. Describe how you entered into a personal relationship with the Lord. (If you are unsure that you have already done so or wish to make that choice, turn to page 28 for the good news of how you can trade religion for a vital relationship with God.)
5. Which would make hard circumstances easier to live with: a religion of works or a relationship with a God who cares and helps? Why?
6. How do you know from chapter 1 of the Book of Ruth that Ruth's response to God was personal? What verses support your answer?

No one, not even the man you will marry one day, can make you happy—only Jesus can.

III. "Too many Christian women think that the inner longings of their hearts relate only to love, marriage, and motherhood or career."

1. What do you think about this statement?

2. Do women long for something constant, something that will satisfy deep heart longings? Why? What are some examples?

3. Discuss how each of the following can or cannot satisfy a woman's deepest needs.

   * Possessions:

   * Positions:

   * People:

4. Have you assumed that your ultimate fulfillment would be found in things? a position? a relationship? marriage? children? Explain.

5. Why can these never completely satisfy you?

You were not created to complete another, but to complement. Completion is Jesus' responsibility, and complementing is a woman's privilege. A woman not complete in Jesus will be a drain on her husband. Such a woman will expect her husband to fill the gap that only Jesus can fill.

IV. Read Luke 7:36-50. As explained in *Lady in Waiting*, the family of a young woman of marriageable age would give her an alabaster box filled with precious ointment as part of her dowry. The size of the box and the value of the ointment related to the family's wealth. When a young man came to ask for her in marriage, she would take the box and break it at his feet to show him honor.

1. Describe the past of the woman who broke the alabaster box in Luke 7.

2. What was her situation in the present?

3. Explain her hope for the future.

4. What was she sacrificing?

5. What was her reward?

6. Is there something your heart clings to that is too valuable to give to Jesus? What?

7. Are you afraid to be without something or someone? What or who is it, and why?

Think about this: Could this "holding on" to something possibly be keeping you from having open hands to receive something better from the Lord?

The woman in Luke 7 wisely broke her alabaster box in the presence of the only One who can make a woman's dreams come true. What is in your alabaster box? Take your box, with your body, soul, and dreams, and entrust them to Jesus. Write here your prayer of release to His Lordship.

Mary, the mother of Jesus, said, "I belong to the Lord, body and soul...let it happen as you say..." (LUKE 1:38 PNT).

V. Right now, choose to put mediocrity behind you. Determine to pursue Jesus with everything in you—heart, mind, will, and emotions. Whether you are single or married, now is the perfect time to establish a radical relationship with Jesus and to remove any "tokenism" from your Christian walk.

1. Is there anything holding you back from taking this step?

2. What mediocrity is in your life that you can get rid of?

3. Is what you are hanging on to taking your life where you want it to go? Explain.

4. What can you do to make God more real in your life right now?

5. How will you do this? List at least three practical steps you can take.

It will require a determined heart and more than a little courage to wrench ourselves loose from the grip of our times and return to Biblical ways. —A.W. **Tozer**

Write your prayer of commitment.

Incompleteness is not the result of being
single, but of not being full of Jesus.

PRAYER

Dear Jesus,

Thank You for always being there for me. Lord, I want to enter into a deeper relationship with You. I know that You are the One who paid the price for this relationship, who guaranteed it by dying on the cross for me. Yet, I have continued to sin. Now, I repent of all my wrongdoing. Forgive me. Make me a clean vessel, ready to receive all that You have for me. Fill my cup to overflowing. You are my Lord, my Savior—and my best friend. I can depend on You totally to meet all my needs. I belong to You. Today, I come to You in totality.
In Your name, Lord Jesus.
Amen.

Day: _____ Date: _____ Scripture: _____

What does this Scripture say about me?

_____

_____

What does it say about God?

_____

_____

How will this change my attitude and action?

_____

_____

Prayer:

_____

_____

_____

Day: _____ Date: _____ Scripture: _____

What does this Scripture say about me?

_____

_____

What does it say about God?

_____

_____

How will this change my attitude and action?

_____

_____

Prayer:

_____

_____

_____

Day: _____ Date: _____ Scripture: _____

What does this Scripture say about me?

_____

_____

What does it say about God?

_____

_____

How will this change my attitude and action?

_____

_____

Prayer:

_____

_____

_____

Chapter 2

RUTH'S DILIGENCE

*U*nderstanding God's promised provision for widows, Naomi sent Ruth to gather grain in the field of a kinsman. Ruth was willing to use her life to work diligently at whatever her Lord called her to do. She would not be paralyzed by her lack of a husband.

> *And Ruth the Moabitess said to Naomi, "Please let me go to the field and glean among the ears of grain after one in whose sight I may find favor." And she said to her, "Go, my daughter"* (Ruth 2:2).

When she and Naomi moved back to Bethlehem, Ruth did not waste a moment in feeling sorry for herself. She went right to work. Instead of being drained by her discouraging circumstances, she took advantage of them and diligently embraced each day.

What more humbling work could Ruth have done than to gather grain for the survival of her mother-in-law and herself?

LADY OF DILIGENCE

I. Read Ruth chapter 2.

1. Describe what is happening in Ruth's and Naomi's lives.

2. What are they choosing to do with their time?

3. What is Ruth's strength?

4. Did God provide for them? How?

5. What was Ruth's attitude?

II. "Rather than staying home worrying about another 'dateless' Saturday night, realize how much valuable time has been entrusted to you at this point in your life. Rather than resent your many single hours, embrace them as a gift from God—a package that contains opportunities to serve Him that are limited only by your own self-pity and lack of obedience."

1. What do you think about this quote? Explain.

2. In what ways is it true or not true about your life now?

3. What would happen with your singles group or church if each person was constantly serving instead of waiting to be served?

Serving the Lord brings such inexpressible joy.

III. One single woman learned that she did not have to wait for a husband to enjoy beauty in her private life. She could unpack her china and crystal that were tucked away in a hope chest and use them for herself. Through this "full place setting" lesson, the Lord taught her to find satisfaction in serving Him.

1. What do you think about this "full place setting" philosophy?

2. How have you seen the "hope chest" principle keep others from living life to its fullest?

3. Name one way you can begin to be all the woman God desires you to be now.

For those of you who are diligently going after Jesus and the privilege of serving Him, here is a very special reminder: sometimes you will be called to do some monotonous work that will not make the headlines.

IV. Some view their lack of a mate as God's way of setting them apart for a more "noble" task, or for a cross to bear. We tend to selfishly focus on what we don't have rather than on what we do have—like free time—that can be used to help others as well as ourselves.

1. Is there any area in your life that you have put on hold for something you want but haven't seen yet? What?

2. What are some reasons you have given to not spend time serving?

3. In what capacity do you presently serve the Lord?

> *Is your life on hold until you have someone to hold?*
> *Do you have an excuse for not serving Jesus?*

V. Read Matthew 6:21,33.

1. How does the use of our time show where our heart is?

2. List some ministry opportunities that exist where you live.

3. Star the opportunities you listed that you will spend time doing.

> *If all of our serving is before others, we will be*
> *shallow people indeed.* —RICHARD FOSTER

Write a love letter responding to what God has shown you about being a Lady of Diligence. Remember, He doesn't want you to be perfect, just to have a perfect heart toward Him and all that He asks you to do.

Day: _____ Date: _____ Scripture: _____

What does this Scripture say about me?

_____

_____

What does it say about God?

_____

_____

_____

How will this change my attitude and action?

_____

_____

_____

Prayer:

_____

_____

Day: _____ Date: _____ Scripture: _____

What does this Scripture say about me?

_____

What does it say about God?

_____

How will this change my attitude and action?

_____

Prayer:

_____

_____

Day: _____ Date: _____ Scripture: _____

What does this Scripture say about me?

_____

What does it say about God?

_____

How will this change my attitude and action?

_____

Prayer:

_____

_____

Chapter 3

RUTH'S FAITH

*R*uth certainly must have considered the probability of remaining single if she went with Naomi. Even though it promised no prospects of a husband, she chose to follow Naomi and Naomi's God back to Bethlehem. Ruth chose to trust God with her future. She looked not with sensual sight, but through "eyes of faith."

She chose to trust with her heart for the future that her eyes could not yet see.

God providentially directed Ruth to the field of Boaz. You'll find this divine encounter in chapter 2 of the Book of Ruth: *"...and she happened to come to the portion of the field belonging to Boaz..."* (Ruth 2:3).

This leaves no room for manipulation. Ruth's "eyes of faith" led her to the exact spot where she would meet Mr. Right, Boaz, whose name means "pillar of strength." God rewarded Ruth's faith with a husband who was a pillar of strength.

LADY OF FAITH

I. Read Psalm 34:8-11.

1. What do these verses say?

2. What do they mean to you?

3. Are they true?

4. Can God provide for those who seek Him? Why or why not?

5. What is the good thing that you desire most?

6. If it is good for you, will it come? How?

7. What do you need to do while it is coming?

---

*Faith does not eliminate questions. But faith knows
where to take them.* —ELISABETH ELLIOT

II. "How can I be a Lady of Faith when I feel so insecure deep in my heart that God will deliver the goods? What if I have faith in God and end up being 98 and unmarried?" God knows what your heart aches for. But He also knows that earthly things will not make you secure.

1. Are you in what seems to be a "no-hope situation"?

2. What were the situations Ruth and Naomi faced in Ruth chapter 1?

3. How would you react if you have faith in God and still end up being 48 or 58 and unmarried?

4. Is it sometimes hard to trust God for a future that you cannot see? Why?

5. Will worry and fret help or hinder your future? How?

6. How would you feel when, after making plans for God with your limited sight, you find out that you have delayed the perfect plan He had designed from His eternal perspective?

---

*A Lady of Faith has not numbed her longing to be married;
instead, she has embraced her Lord so tightly that she faces
her prolonged singleness with peace, not bitterness.*

III. Read Psalm 138:8, Psalm 139, and Romans 8:32.

1. Who created you with the longings of your heart? How do you know?

2. Who knows the future? Include a Scripture reference that backs up your answer.

3. Who wants you to have the very best? How do you know?

4. What should you do to cooperate with His plan? Include a Scripture reference.

5. Can you really trust God with all your hopes and dreams? Why or why not? List some practical steps you can take to show your trust in God.

6. How will you ever meet Mr. Right if you have "eyes of faith" and don't work at finding him?

IV. Don't fear or resent the waiting periods that appear in your life. Rather, think of them as gardens where the seeds of faith blossom. Whenever circumstances stimulate you to deepen your faith, embrace them willingly (see Heb. 11:6).

> *I do know that waiting on God requires the willingness to bear uncertainty, to carry within oneself the unanswered question, lifting the heart to God about it whenever it intrudes upon one's thoughts.* —ELISABETH ELLIOT

1. How do you feel about waiting on God?

2. What do you think about why God is making you wait?

3. What is true about the reasons He may have for you to wait?

4. Do unanswered questions capture your mind? How and when?

5. Are you overtaken by the restlessness of singleness? When?

6. What do you do when you feel restless?

> *If I work, God will wait. If I wait, God will work.*

For from days of old they have not heard nor perceived by ear, neither has the eye seen a God besides You, who acts on behalf of the one who waits for Him (Isaiah 64:4).

7. What does this verse say to you?

V. "You make the most important decision in life, giving your life to Jesus Christ, 'by faith.' The second most important decision concerns your life-mate. This decision also demands the element of faith. Waiting for one's life-mate and then saying 'I do' to him demands secure faith, like Ruth's faith in the God of Israel."

Only fear ("I'm afraid I missed, will miss, will never...") will block faith. Romans 10:17 shows one how to develop faith. If you have been full of fears, doubts, and anxiety about your future, take a few moments to confess these things to God and ask Him to develop faith in your life. ("I will, I can, I must wait and trust a God who sees, knows, and cares about my future.")

> *Your faith during the "waiting period" pleases God.*
> *Don't fear or resent the waiting periods in your life.*

Day: _____ Date: _____ Scripture: _____

What does this Scripture say about me?

_____

_____

What does it say about God?

_____

_____

How will this change my attitude and action?

_____

_____

Prayer:

_____

_____

_____

_____

_____

_____

Day: _____ Date: _____ Scripture: _____

What does this Scripture say about me?

_____

_____

What does it say about God?

_____

_____

How will this change my attitude and action?

_____

_____

Prayer:

_____

_____

_____

_____

Day: _____ Date: _____ Scripture: _____

What does this Scripture say about me?

_____

_____

What does it say about God?

_____

_____

How will this change my attitude and action?

_____

_____

Prayer:

_____

_____

_____

RUTH'S VIRTUE

$\mathscr{O}$ne of life's most costly and beautiful objects is born out of pain and irritation—the pearl. Like the oyster, Ruth experienced many irritations and trials in her young life. She grieved the deaths of her father-in-law, brother-in-law, and husband. She bravely faced the turmoil of change in the direction of her life as well as a move to a foreign land with a bitter mother-in-law. When she arrived in that strange land, the trials did not end. She was immediately thrown into a new working situation among total strangers with new customs. Through all this stress, her new faith began to wrap itself around the painful situations. The by-product was a pearl.

What enabled Ruth to catch Boaz's attention? Was it her gorgeous hair or beautiful eyes? No! The answer is found in Boaz's response to her question in Ruth chapter 2.

> *Then she fell on her face, bowing to the ground and said to him, "Why have I found favor in your sight that you should take notice of me, since I am a foreigner?" And Boaz answered and said to her, "All that you have done for your mother-in-law after the death of your husband has been fully reported to me, and how you left your father and your mother and the land of your birth, and came to a people that you did not previously know"* (Ruth 2:10-11).

Boaz was attracted to the virtue and character displayed in Ruth's life. A woman of virtue is irresistible to a godly man.

LADY OF VIRTUE

I. Read Ruth chapter 3.

1. Write out every description of Ruth's outward appearance. Include the Scripture references that support your description.

2. Write out every description of Ruth from other people's perspectives. Include the Scripture references that support your description.

3. What two things about Ruth attracted Boaz?

A woman of virtue is irresistible to a godly man.

For the lips of an adulteress drip honey and smoother than oil is her speech (Proverbs 5:3).

To keep you from the evil woman, from the smooth tongue of the adulteress. Do not desire her beauty in your heart, nor let her catch you with her eyelids (Proverbs 6:24-25).

With her many persuasions she entices him; with her flattering lips she seduces him (Proverbs 7:21).

4. What do these verses describe?

5. Do you see these techniques in magazines and ads? Explain.

Most dateless women think their condition is the result of the "reflection in the mirror." Consequently, women spend millions of dollars every year believing the myth that physical beauty is mandatory for marriage.

---

6. What do you think about this statement?

My wife's character is what caught my attention. Her inner beauty was irresistible. Now, thirty years of marriage and half a dozen children later, I am more attracted to and in love with her than when I first met her. —P. Lord

But let it be the hidden person of the heart, with the imperishable quality of a gentle and quiet spirit, which is precious in the sight of God (1 Peter 3:4).

II. Read Proverbs 31:10-31.

1. List every reference to outward beauty.

2. List every reference to inward beauty.

3. Which of these listed are most valuable?

4. Of those listed, which ones get better with age?

As Jackie once said, "If a man chose me for external beauty, his destiny would be hugging a prune. But, if a man chooses me for my internal beauty, his destiny will be unfading beauty even in the twilight years of marriage, because of Jesus."

A pastor once said, "Ladies, how you catch 'em is how you keep 'em."

III. Take the virtue test on page 64 of *Lady in Waiting*.

1. How did you do? In which of the columns did you score the highest? Why?

2. Are you using your single days to be the woman God created you to be? Explain how.

3. Name one negative quality that you have discovered in yourself. How can you change it?

4. What can you do to develop virtue?

IV. To marry a prince, you must first become a princess. A Lady of Virtue attracts admiration for qualities within instead of attention for actions without.

1. When you envision your perfect man, what are the qualities you see in him?

2. Do you have those same wonderful qualities? Explain.

3. Do you think that your perfect man is hoping for a woman whose only beauty is outward and whose skill is in attracting the attention of men? What do you think he is looking for? Explain.

4. Are you seeking admiration or attention from the men around you?

5. Describe the difference.

6. Are you a woman worth waiting for? Explain.

> *A man who has given you his attention can be easily distracted when a more attractive body passes by, but a man's admiration is for a lifetime.*

V. Read Ephesians 5:18. How does a woman tap into "pearl-producing power"? In order for something to be filled, it must first be empty. To be filled by the Spirit means that you must be empty of yourself. Instead, you're full of God. You give the Holy Spirit complete and total control of your life. "When you became a Christian, you received all of the Holy Spirit. To be a virtuous woman, you must let the Holy Spirit have all of you."

1. Do you have the Holy Spirit's filling in your life? Explain.

2. Read Galatians 5:19-23. Which of these are displayed in your life?

But I say, walk by the Spirit, and you will not carry out the desire of the flesh (Galatians 5:16).

> *...If you want genuine pearls, you must allow the Holy Spirit to perform a special work in your life. Determine to string a lovely pearl "necklace of virtue" as a treasure for your Lord.*

Write a prayer of commitment right now to walk by the power of the Holy Spirit instead of by your own flesh. This includes a daily practice of confessing your sin and asking God to fill your life with His power.

You can begin now and watch the beautiful work of God take place in your life.

"Pearls of character" are listed in Galatians
5:22-23 as love, joy, peace, patience, kindness,
goodness, faithfulness, gentleness, and self-control.

Day: _____ Date: _____ Scripture: _____

What does this Scripture say about me?

_____

_____

What does it say about God?

_____

_____

How will this change my attitude and action?

_____

_____

Prayer:

_____

_____

_____

_____

Day: _____ Date: _____ Scripture: _____

What does this Scripture say about me?

_____

_____

What does it say about God?

_____

_____

How will this change my attitude and action?

_____

_____

Prayer:

_____
_____
_____
_____

Day: _____ Date: _____ Scripture: _____

What does this Scripture say about me?

_____
_____

What does it say about God?

_____
_____

How will this change my attitude and action?

_____
_____

Prayer:

_____
_____
_____
_____

Chapter 5

RUTH'S DEVOTION

$\mathcal{B}$oaz spoke of Ruth's devotion to God when he said,

> *May the Lord reward your work, and your wages be full from the Lord, the God of Israel, under whose wings you have come to seek refuge* (Ruth 2:12).

Ruth chose to cling to her mother-in-law's God as her own even though Naomi had drawn a negative, harsh picture of Him.

> *She said to them, "Do not call me Naomi; call me Mara, for the Almighty has dealt very bitterly with me. I went out full, but the Lord has brought me back empty. Why do you call me Naomi, since the Lord has witnessed against me and the Almighty has afflicted me?"* (Ruth 1:20-21)

Would you be devoted to a God like Naomi's? Though Ruth clung to her as a mother, she did not accept Naomi's view of God for herself.

If we think of Him [God] as cold and exacting, we shall find it impossible to love Him, and our lives will be ridden with servile fear. —A.W. TOZER

LADY OF DEVOTION

I. Read First Corinthians 7:34-35.

   1.   Paraphrase these verses in your own words.

   2.   What does this passage mean to you?

3. Compare your life with someone you know who is married and has a job and small children. Who has the most time to call her own?

4. What does "undistracted devotion to God" mean to you?

Singles have a wonderful opportunity to maximize their fellowship with God.

II. Too often people view a single woman through eyes of pity rather than envy. A Lady in Waiting actually has the advantage of being able to develop her love relationship with Christ without the distractions that a husband or family inherently bring to a woman's heart.

1. List some advantages of your life as a single.

2. How often do you think of these advantages? Explain.

3. List some advantages that a married woman has.

4. Do you also have some of these as a single? Explain.

5. A woman can spend her entire single life wishing to get married, and then her entire married life wishing to be single. How can you avoid this scenario?

III. Read Jeremiah 29:12-13. Seeking God is like developing a friendship. Friends talk a lot, listen to each other, write letters, and think about each other. Friends find out what the other does and does not like, and do things that please that person. The more time friends spend together getting to know each other, the greater their love and friendship will be. Your relationship with God works the same way.

1. What are the elements of a dating relationship that help you get to know the other person?

2. Which of these can be used in your relationship with your heavenly Fiancé?

IV. Read Jeremiah 29:11.

1. List what God wants for you as expressed in this verse.

2. In that list, circle what you want.

3. What does a woman need to do to have what both she and God want? (Look at Jeremiah 29:12.)

Do you think God demands too much in requiring you to seek Him with all your heart? Suppose Mr. Right comes one day and begins to speak of his devotion to you. His words are what you've always waited to hear: "I love you. I give you my heart completely. For 364 days of every year, I will devote myself to you and you only." Then he adds, "However, one day of each year I want to date others and see what I have missed. Don't worry; you can have all the rest. Will you marry me?"

4. What would your response be?

5. Would you want this kind of devotion? Explain.

6. Is it selfish of you to deny him his heart just one day a year to give to others?

7. If you would not accept a proposal like this, is it wrong for God to want whole-hearted love?

V. Read Psalm 16:11.

1. Where does this verse say joy and pleasures are found?

2. Where have you been looking for pleasures and joy?

3. How can you be at His right hand?

VI. Your days of singleness are a precious, privileged time. Don't waste a single one! You will never have them again. Let them be treasure-finding days in your Father's Kingdom.

1. How can you fall in love with God?

2. When will your first date with Him be?

3. What will you do on your dates with Him?

4. Read Hebrews 13:5-6,8. What does this say about God's love for you?

It takes 21 days to develop a habit. Will you take the 21-day test? Spend 21 consistent days dating our First Love, and you will fall so in love with Him that you'll want 21 weeks, then 21 months, then 21 years. What a love life you will enjoy with Someone who will never leave you, who will never change, who will always love you just the same!

FALLING IN LOVE WITH MY HEAVENLY FIANCÉ

Each morning I will "date" my Lord. If I hit the snooze one too many times, I will set a lunch or afternoon "date." Before I go to bed at night I will make sure that I have spent at least 5 minutes falling in love with Him.

Beginning with 5 minutes for 21 days in a row:

Minute 1

(30 sec.) I will praise Him and tell Him that I am glad to have this time with Him.

(30 sec.) I will ask Him if there is anything wrong between us and apologize (or confess) any sin that He shows me.

Minute 2

I will read His love letters until they say something to my life. (Start with Psalms and read a few verses each day.)

Minute 3

I will write down in my love letter journal what I have found in His love letter:

A. Something it says about me.

B. Something it says about Him.

C. Something He likes me to do or not do.

Minute 4

I will "listen" or meditate on what I have read and written. (A date is no fun when only one person talks; each must listen to fall in love.)

Minute 5

I will tell Him my concerns and ask Him to help me please Him. We continue this conversation all day.

Your Father will not force you...but He longs to fellowship with you. Come into His chambers delight in His Presence. May you be found in Him—a Lady of Devotion.

Write a prayer of commitment to spend at least five minutes each day dating Him and reading His Word.

Day: _____ Date: _____ Scripture: _____

What does this Scripture say about me?

_____

_____

What does it say about God?

_____

_____

How will this change my attitude and action?

_____

_____

Prayer:

_____

_____

_____

_____

_____

Day: _____ Date: _____ Scripture: _____

What does this Scripture say about me?

_____

_____

What does it say about God?

_____

_____

How will this change my attitude and action?

_____
_____

Prayer:

_____
_____
_____
_____

Day: _____ Date: _____ Scripture: _____

What does this Scripture say about me?

_____
_____

What does it say about God?

_____
_____

How will this change my attitude and action?

_____
_____

Prayer:

_____
_____
_____
_____

Chapter 6

RUTH'S PURITY

When Boaz had eaten and drunk and his heart was merry, he went to lie down at the end of the heap of grain; and she came secretly, and uncovered his feet and lay down (Ruth 3:7).

*Y*ou may read this at a glance and picture the beginnings of an X-rated scene in Ruth's story. But remember that Ruth was acting according to the customs of the time. She was not slinking into Boaz's bed to seduce him. In obedience to her mother-in-law's instructions, Ruth quietly lay at his feet for him to notice her, thus symbolizing her subjection to Boaz as her nearest of kin.

By doing this, Ruth gave him the opportunity, if he so chose, to take legal action for the well-being of herself and her mother-in-law. (A woman had no form of social security and very few rights in that culture without a man.)

So this was not a brazen act of seduction, but an act of obedience to God's plan for her provision in that day. One thing is certain. When she left to go home, she walked away as a Lady of Purity.

LADY OF PURITY

I. Read Ruth chapter 3 again.

1.   What did Naomi ask Ruth to do? Why?

2.   What was Ruth's response?

3.   Do you think Naomi's request may have caused Ruth to wonder? (Remember, she was a foreigner and had not been raised with these customs.)

4. What does Ruth's obedience say about her character?

5. Would you have obeyed your mother (or mother-in-law) even if her request seemed foreign to anything you had ever thought or heard about? Why or why not?

6. What are the verses in Ruth chapters 1 and 2 that show Naomi had consistently tried to do what was best for her daughter-in-law?

7. Do you think Ruth had to remind herself of this?

8. Consider Boaz. What was happening in his life before he went to bed that night?

9. What was his response to a woman in his bed?

10. What does his response tell you about his reputation as a single man?

11. Consider the place where Ruth was lying. Was she seductive or pure in her behavior? (Include Scripture to support your answer.)

12. Why did Boaz ask her to stay the night?

13. Whose reputation was he most concerned with?

14. Do the men whom you spend time with care more for their reputation and needs or for the women of excellence whom they date?

15. Would the guys you date be surprised to find a woman in their beds after a party one night?

16. What difference do these questions make to one's purity?

II. Debby has said, "Early in my dating, I tired of giving a kiss at the door for a hamburger, coke, and fries. What would I have to give next for a steak dinner or a night on the town? After I was married I realized the decision not to give my kisses freely to my dates had an added bonus. For every kiss I denied dates at the door, the man I married received my kisses 'with interest' in our years of marriage. It was worth waiting for kisses before marriage—so they would be full of meaning—for years to come within marriage."

1. Do you think that women today should have to say yes to their dates in the sexual realm, just because he paid for the evening's activities? Explain.

2. How about a simple smile and "Thank you"? Is this not enough?

If a woman wants to say "Thank you for a wonderful evening," she can say it with her words rather than with a kiss.

III. "Lack of self-control before marriage is fornication. Lack of self-control after marriage is adultery. The seeds for adultery are planted in the 'hotbeds' of fornication. A woman subconsciously wonders, 'If he did not exhibit self-control with me before marriage, how can I be sure that he will not give in to temptation during marriage when an attractive younger woman comes along?' A young man who cannot control himself before marriage does not suddenly become a man of self-control because he wears a wedding band!"

1. Explain what this quotation means to you.

2. How does sexual impurity undermine not only one's dating relationship, but also one's future marriage intimacy?

3. Are you encouraging romance (that changes with the tide of emotion) or a relationship (that stands the test of time)?

4. How can you change from romance to relationship?

IV. "Today's society seeks ultimate pleasure with no pain. But following society's example usually brings just the opposite. Look to your heavenly Father, your Creator, for the truth. God gives true sexual fulfillment to the lady who waits for this gift."

1. Read the following verses. What does each say about relating to the opposite sex and the area of sexual purity?

   * Proverbs 4:23

   * Song of Solomon 8:4

   * First Corinthians 6:18-20

- First Corinthians 15:33
- First Thessalonians 4:3-8

2. What do you lose when you wait for a physical display of affection in a friendship?

3. What do you gain if you wait to begin physical affection in a friendship?

4. Many women have said, "We were such good friends until we started dating." What did they do differently or add to their "friendship" when they began to "date"?

"If you encourage your date to play with the bow on your package, he will want to untie the ribbon and unwrap the gift. Don't distract him with the bow. Allowing sex to enter into a relationship before marriage will almost always result in the loss of an intimate friendship with the one you desire to know you for you."

V. "Although it is true that there is only one first time, God is the God of the first-time experience."

1. What if it is too late? What if the gift of purity has already been given away? Read the following Scriptures and write their responses to these questions.
   - Isaiah 43:25
   - Jeremiah 31:34
   - Philippians 3:13-14
   - First John 1:9

2. Briefly, what do these verses say about God's response to your sin when it is confessed?

3. Will you now confess that sin and commit to live a life of physical, emotional, and spiritual purity before God? Write your prayer of confession and commitment.

One girl has been quoted as saying, "There is no condom which protects a woman's heart, mind, and self-esteem."

VI. "Each woman receives one 'first time.' God desires for your precious gift to be given to a committed lover who will cherish, keep, and protect you in marriage. God wants you and your gift to this man to be treasured and cherished, not trampled and conquered."

1. Why is it important for a Lady of Purity to have dating standards or boundaries established before dating rather than creating them as she goes?

2. Write out and pray over the dating standards you feel that God wants for you. (Try to be specific in your areas of known weakness.)

God wants you to have the joy of saying to your knight on that special wedding night, "Here I am, clean and pure, emotionally and physically. No one has touched the treasure of my love. I kept myself for you."

Day: _____ Date: _____ Scripture: _____

What does this Scripture say about me?

_____

_____

What does it say about God?

_____

_____

How will this change my attitude and action?

_____

_____

Prayer:

_____

_____

_____

_____

Day: _____ Date: _____ Scripture: _____

What does this Scripture say about me?

_____

_____

What does it say about God?

_____

_____

How will this change my attitude and action?

_____

_____

Prayer:

_____

_____

_____

_____

Day: _____ Date: _____ Scripture: _____

What does this Scripture say about me?

_____

_____

What does it say about God?

_____

_____

How will this change my attitude and action?

_____

_____

Prayer:

_____

_____

_____

_____

Chapter 7

RUTH'S SECURITY

Then he [Boaz] said, "May you be blessed of the Lord, my daughter. You have shown your last kindness to be better than the first by not going after young men, whether poor or rich. And now, my daughter, do not fear. I will do for you whatever you ask, for all my people in the city know that you are a woman of excellence" (Ruth 3:10-11).

*R*uth, as a single, young, widowed woman, must have experienced the lonely longings for the warmth of a husband. But she lived in victory over the desire to "man hunt." Instead of "going after the boys," she sat still and let God bring her prince to her. She was a Lady of Security.

In the midst of her circumstances, Ruth could not possibly have seen that a man like Boaz would one day be her prince. Neither can you with your limited perspective see who or where your prince will be. Only God has all things in view.

Surrender to God the terrible burden of always needing life on your terms. God can and will give you His best if you wait for it.

LADY OF SECURITY

I. Read Hebrews 13:4-8; Ruth 3:10-11; and Proverbs 1:33.

1. What does Hebrews say about marriage, money, and power—and their ability to provide security?

2. What did Ruth refuse to look to in order to make her feel secure?

3. According to Proverbs, how does a woman live securely?

Security is building your life around something that cannot be lost, destroyed, or taken away.

4. Considering this definition for security, why can the following areas not make a person secure?

   • Positions (who I am and what people think of me):

   • Possessions (what I have):

   • People (someone who will always be there for me, always understand, always love me without change):

5. Read Romans 8:38-39. What is the one position we can have that never changes? Who is the one Person whose love will never vary or change, who can never be lost, stolen, or taken away?

6. Write your own thoughts and feelings about Romans 8:38-39.

II. One reason that relationships have a hard time lasting is because they don't include true love.

1. Why would a single woman work so hard to have a relationship with a man?

2. What is the need that "drives" a woman?

3. How do women manipulate and maneuver to attract a partner?

4. What tactics are successful?

5. Compare some of the tactics listed above with love as described in First Corinthians 13.

III. Did you know that manipulating is a propensity that originated with a curse on the first woman? (See Genesis 3:16. In the Hebrew, desire means to "stretch out after, to run over.") The temptation to maneuver and control is common for all Evettes.

1. Have you ever played the role of the "surrogate mom" when trying to manipulate a guy's attention?

2. What should a single woman do to get the attention of a particular male?

3. Re-read the advice given by Elisabeth Elliot on pages 102-103 of Lady in Waiting. Do you agree with the quotation? Where do you disagree?

4. Who should you be serving when single? (See First Corinthians 7:34-35.)

5. How can manipulation be a form of self-deception?

6. Instead of her "knight in shining armor," who should the single woman be thirsting for?

IV. Some single women are tempted to manipulate the opposite sex because of the "dry and weary desert of singleness." They may hope a relationship with a man will meet their heart's desires.

1. Read these verses and write what they say to your heart.
   * Psalm 39:7
   * Psalm 40:1-3
   * Psalm 62:5
   * Isaiah 64:3-5
   * James 1:17

2. Why is it harder to wait for God than to do things for ourselves?

Oh God, you are my God; I earnestly search for You. My soul thirsts for You; my whole body longs for You in this parched and weary land where there is no water (Psalm 63:1 NLT).

V. Manipulation can be deadly. You can save yourself many tears if you will do a regular "heart check."

1. Take a moment now to do a thorough motive check of your heart. What are you finding?

2. Write a prayer confessing any wrong motives for relationships, and asking God for motives that are founded on having security in Him first.

The man you marry cannot meet your need for security. Only God's love brings security.

3. Can you give to the Lord the key to your love life? Can you allow Him to be your security and not the things that change in life? Write the desires of your heart here. Confess any attitudes of demanding life on your agenda.

No good thing does He withhold from those who walk uprightly (Psalm 84:11b).

Day: _____ Date: _____ Scripture: _____

What does this Scripture say about me?

_____

_____

What does it say about God?

_____

_____

How will this change my attitude and action?

_____

_____

Prayer:

_____

_____

_____

Day: _____ Date: _____ Scripture: _____

What does this Scripture say about me?

_____

_____

What does it say about God?

_____

_____

How will this change my attitude and action?

_____

_____

Prayer:

_____

_____

_____

_____

Day: _____ Date: _____ Scripture: _____

What does this Scripture say about me?

_____

_____

What does it say about God?

_____

_____

How will this change my attitude and action?

_____

_____

Prayer:

_____

_____

_____

_____

Chapter 8

RUTH'S CONTENTMENT

*I*f you consider the circumstances, Ruth had the perfect excuse to be discontented. Ruth's circumstances—widowhood at a young age—provided the perfect breeding ground for self-pity and bitterness.

Yet Ruth chose to cling to the God of Israel, whom she found to be trustworthy even in difficult circumstances.

Contentedly facing each day's task, Ruth received the attention of the most eligible bachelor in town.

> *Then Naomi said, "Wait, my daughter, until you find out what happens. For the man will not rest until the matter is settled today"* (Ruth 3:18 NIV).

Wait. Such an assignment is not to cause suffering, but to prevent it. Women experience so much needless pain when they run ahead of God's format.

Naomi did not want Ruth's heart to race ahead into disappointment in case the circumstances did not go as they expected.

LADY OF CONTENTMENT

I. Psalm 16:11 says, *"You will make known to me the path of life* [married or not]; *in Your presence is fulness of joy* [His presence, not marriage, brings joy]; *in Your right hand there are pleasures forever."* What more could a girl ask for?

1.   Read these verses and write out what they mean to you.

- Psalm 84:11

- Isaiah 30:18

- Isaiah 64:4

2. Is God's Word true?

3. Can God do what He says He will?

4. Why would He make us wait if it is in His power to do a thing that we have asked for and waited for, and we are tired of waiting?

5. When He makes us wait, does it mean that He is angry with us or trying to hurt us or doesn't love us?

6. How can we be sure?

7. What verses do you know that back up what is true regardless of how our feelings receive the assignment to wait?

II. "It has been said that suffering is having what you do not want (singleness), and wanting what you do not have (a husband)."

1. Do most single women think that the ache and empty feeling inside come from the lack of a man to love?

If I find in myself a desire which no experience in this world can satisfy, the most probable explanation is that I was made for another world. —C.S. Lewis

2. Consider what C.S. Lewis said about that ache inside all people (not just singles). What are your thoughts?

3. Can a single woman learn to be content? Consider the reply of a famous single: Read Philippians 4:11-12.

4. Discuss the meaning of the words content and contentment (Greek: "sail away"). Can you trust the sails of your singleness to the wind of God (see John 3:8)?

III. The new "Eleventh Commandment" is "Thou shalt not defraud thyself." Misread intentions between males and females put them on a collision course. An innocent gesture on the part of a male friend can produce the most elaborate fantasy in a woman's mind.

1. How can a discontent single woman be easily defraud-ed by single men? List again the ways women can be de-frauded; see pages 111-113 of *Lady in Waiting.*

2. Do single women defraud themselves more frequently than they are defrauded by single guys?

3. Read Second Corinthians 10:5. How can you discipline prenuptial fantasies (which intensify discontentment)?

IV. Do you have an accountability partner? Naomi encouraged Ruth to be calm and wait (see Ruth 3:18).

1. Every single woman needs an accountability partner ("spiritual monitor") to help her control fantasy and self-defrauding. Who is your spiritual monitor? How specifi-cally has she helped you?

2. List some ways in which you can act as a spiritual monitor.

*Too often it is our friends who accelerate
our prenuptial fantasies!*

V. Read Psalm 55.

1. What can you do when you are discontent?

2. What can you do when you feel afraid?

3. What can you do when you face hard situations?

*A discontent single who gets married becomes
a discontent wife. Marital status does not
remove discontentment from a heart.*

4. Take your discontented feelings to Jesus and leave them in His capable hands. Write a prayer of commitment here to

daily discipline yourself to take your fantasies to Jesus and to begin enjoying contentment in His arms.

And the peace of God, which surpasses all understanding, will guard your hearts and minds through Christ Jesus (Philippians 4:7 NKJV).

Day: _____ Date: _____ Scripture: _____

What does this Scripture say about me?

_____

_____

What does it say about God?

_____

_____

How will this change my attitude and action?

_____

_____

Prayer:

_____

_____

_____

Day: Date: Scripture:

What does this Scripture say about me?

_____

_____

What does it say about God?

_____

_____

How will this change my attitude and action?

_____

_____

Prayer:

_____

_____

_____

_____

Day: _____ Date: _____ Scripture: _____

What does this Scripture say about me?

_____

_____

What does it say about God?

_____

_____

How will this change my attitude and action?

_____

_____

Prayer:

_____

_____

_____

_____

Chapter 9

RUTH'S CONVICTIONS

The Book of Ruth gives not only the story of a Lady in Waiting, but also the profile of a Knight in Shining Armor.

Ruth's choice to wait for God's best resulted in her union with a Boaz rather than a Bozo. Not only did Ruth marry a man who was a "pillar of strength," but she also was blessed by the privilege of bearing a son who would be part of the lineage of Jesus Christ.

Ruth's wise choices resulted in her experiencing God's overwhelming goodness.

Ruth did not allow the past influences of a heathen culture to keep her from setting new standards and making wise choices that would honor God. She chose to break her family's sin cycle and establish a new godly cycle.

Have you dated more Bozos than Boazs? If your answer is yes, then you may need to develop higher ideals.

LADY OF CONVICTION

I. Read the following verses and compare a *Bozo* with a *Boaz* (works of the flesh versus fruit of the Spirit). What convictions do you have on whom to date and marry?

1. Proverbs 16:32. A *Bozo* is controlled by his emotions (lust, anger, etc.); a *Boaz* is able to control his emotions (patience).

2. Romans 8:28,32. A *Bozo* is angered when he doesn't get his way; a *Boaz* can rise above disappointment (faith, peace).

3. First Corinthians 13:4. A *Bozo* doesn't notice the needs of others and is often rude; a *Boaz* is courteous toward others, not just trying to impress them (kindness).

4. Colossians 3:12-14. A *Bozo* is very critical of others, and often intolerant; a *Boaz* is tolerant of imperfection (he has a clear view of himself) (love).

5. Philippians 2:3-4. A *Bozo* is self-centered, always wanting life on his terms. (Amnon is a classic example—he never heard Tamar's pleading); a *Boaz* is others-centered, looking out for the interests of others (meekness).

6. Second Timothy 2:24-25. A *Bozo* is rigid, and his viewpoint is the only right conclusion; a *Boaz* is teachable (ultimate meekness) and has an open heart and mind (patience/meekness).

7. Colossians 3:23. A *Bozo* always has excuses for not doing a task well; a *Boaz* strives to do his work to the best of his ability and to the glory of Jesus (faithfulness).

8. Ruth 3:13-14. A *Bozo* lacks integrity and good character traits; a *Boaz* displays kindness and integrity (goodness).

Because Ruth waited on God, she was showered with blessings through His vessel: Boaz.

II. "You want to marry someone for the qualities he possesses now, not for qualities you hope he will develop. The most common mistake made by marriage partners is marrying someone they intend to change."

1. Are the men you find yourself befriending Bozos or Boazs? Why or why not?

2. List some characteristics you want to find in your Boaz.

III. Before Ruth found her Mr. Right, she broke an ungodly family cycle (see Ruth 1:16).

1. What was her past?

2. What did she choose to do in order to break it?

3. Is there a family cycle you need to break?

4. What can you do to break it?

> *Your destiny is not something that is left to chance*
> *or fate; it is the product of wise choices.*

IV. When you concentrate on the real thing, the Bozos become more apparent.

1. Briefly describe the difference between a Boaz and a Bozo.

2. How many dates would it take for you to discern if the guy was a Boaz or a Bozo? (See Matthew 12:34.)

3. Are the qualities listed on page 129-130 of Lady in Waiting too high for a Mr. Right in this generation?

> *It's not how much you know…but how much*
> *you live that makes the difference.*

V. "Do you want to marry a knight in shining armor? Then set your standards high. To be married to a man who loves the Lord and wants to serve Him is one of life's highest privileges. It is worth whatever wait, whatever cost."

Write a prayer to the Lord committing yourself to only spend time with men of convictions and standards like yours. Tell the Lord what changes you are willing to make in your life to be a Lady of Conviction.

> *…the female child of a king is a princess. Act like the valuable*
> *princess you are, and expect to be treated as royalty.*

Day: _____ Date: _____ Scripture: _____

What does this Scripture say about me?

_____

_____

What does it say about God?

_____

_____

How will this change my attitude and action?

_____

_____

Prayer:

_____

_____

_____

_____

Day: _____ Date: _____ Scripture: _____

What does this Scripture say about me?

_____

_____

What does it say about God?

_____

_____

How will this change my attitude and action?

_____

_____

Prayer:

_____

_____

_____

_____

Day: _____ Date: _____ Scripture: _____

What does this Scripture say about me?

_____

_____

What does it say about God?

_____

_____

How will this change my attitude and action?

_____

_____

Prayer:

_____

_____

_____

_____

RUTH'S PATIENCE

$\mathcal{R}$uth was a wonderful example of patience. Ruth did not allow her circumstances or lack of male companionship to cause her to be impatient. Instead she concentrated on developing companionship with her heavenly Father and chose to let Him bring a husband to her if He saw fit.

Concern over the ticking of her "biological clock" did not make her fearful of the future. Instead she concentrated on being a lady of character, not on getting a man.

She took one day at a time, knowing that God was not bound by circumstances or her age.

She used the wait to become the woman God wanted her to be.

LADY OF PATIENCE

I. Read Psalm 46:10 and Isaiah 40:31.

1. Do you think that single women struggle the most in the area of being patient?

2. Does waiting renew your strength or drain it?

3. If God is faithful, why is it so easy to lose patience, so hard to wait? Why is it easier to settle for less than God's best? Expound.

II. Read Deuteronomy 30:19.

1. What is the blessing God longs to give, described in chapter 10 of *Lady in Waiting*?

2. What is the "curse" He longs to protect us from?

3. Have you ever been tempted to date a non-believer because of a long season of datelessness? What do Second Corinthians 6:14 and Joshua 23:12-13 say concerning this?

III. "Marriage teaches us that even the most intimate human companionship cannot satisfy the deepest places of the heart. Our hearts are lonely 'til they rest in Him." —Elisabeth Elliot

1. Does loneliness hinder the development of your patience?

2. What develops patience besides prolonged singleness?

3. Consider this source of patience:

We can rejoice, too, when we run into problems and trials, for we know that they are good for us—they help us learn to endure. And endurance develops strength of character in us, and character strengthens our confident expectation of salvation (Romans 5:3-4 NLT).

IV. Read Isaiah 30:18 and Proverbs 3:5-6 and write below what they mean to you.

1. Do you know how profoundly your patient waiting affects God? Explain.

2. What are some specific ways you can "trust in the Lord"?

"Take courage, single friend. You are not alone in your wait; neither are you alone in the feelings and struggles you encounter. Many godly women have waited and won. Many women have lost hope and compromised. Wait patiently and win triumphantly the future your Father has planned for you. It will always be designed with you in mind and is worth being patient to discover."

*Developing patience is hard. Getting married
ahead of God's timing is worse.*

3. Write your response to God's tug at your heart to be a Lady of Patience.

For your husband is your Maker, whose name is the Lord of hosts... (Isaiah 54:5).

Rest in the Lord and wait patiently for Him... (Psalm 37:7).

Now, dear Lady in Waiting, take a moment to consider what your heart has been telling you during the study of this book and take a moment to pen those thoughts as a prayer, as a love letter to the King.

Day: _____ Date: _____ Scripture: _____

What does this Scripture say about me?

_____

_____

What does it say about God?

_____

_____

How will this change my attitude and action?

_____

_____

Prayer:

_____

_____

_____

_____

Day: _____ Date: _____ Scripture: _____

What does this Scripture say about me?

_____

_____

What does it say about God?

_____

_____

How will this change my attitude and action?

_____

_____

Prayer:

_____

_____

_____

_____

_____

Day: _____ Date: _____ Scripture: _____

What does this Scripture say about me?

_____

_____

What does it say about God?

_____

_____

How will this change my attitude and action?

_____

_____

Prayer:

_____

_____

_____

_____

_____

PART III

Devotional

A WORD FROM THE AUTHORS

*H*ave you ever noticed the funny way a pigeon walks? His head moves forward, he stops, then he takes a step. I have read that a pigeon's eyes do not focus unless his head is still...therefore, he focuses—then steps. We could learn a lot from this "pigeon walk."

Sometimes our lives seem to get out of control; our hearts are injured and our steps unsure. We lose focus, and life comes apart at the seams. This journal is designed to help us keep focus—step by step and day by day.

Proverbs 3:5-6 contains key words to live by with regard to our steps: *"Trust in the Lord with all your heart...."* How much misdirection and pain could we avoid if we trusted in and were daily assured of our God's awesome love for us? *"And do not lean on your own understanding...."* What trouble could we avoid if we went to the all-knowing God for daily direction and wisdom instead of fretting, planning, and worrying? *"In all your ways acknowledge Him...."* This is our focus for each step. And the promise? *"He will make your paths straight."*

It really doesn't matter how much we "know"; it matters how much we "live." This type of journaling through the years has helped me to live more of what I know. I pray that, as you use this spiritual journey tool, you will catch yourself refocusing before each step.

May God richly bless your "walk" with Him!

—DEBBY JONES

Thirty-plus years ago, my spiritual mentor shared the secret of her incredible life with Jesus, and I have tried to live the secret since she shared it on that memorable summer day in 1972: "There is no success, no happiness, and no fulfillment in life apart from a consistent, daily growing relationship with Jesus through the Word."

I have watched thousands of women try to find happiness, success, and fulfillment without spending quiet time with Jesus...and I can testify that their efforts have been in vain.

—JACKIE KENDALL

Helpful Tips for the
Lady in Waiting

*I*t is our desire that this journal will help you live in the presence of the Lord every day. It is not intended to simply add new truth to a bag of theological truth that is already full; rather, it is our expectation that it will bring you to a place of new experiences with your God.

It will require that you spend time carefully considering the significance and implications of each individual quotation. Let its spiritual vibrations resonate in your heart. Contemplate their spiritual meaning as you apply them to your life, ultimately letting them lead you to a quiet place of prayer and communion with your Divine Lover, the Lord Jesus.

Begin Your Journey

Few of us have the opportunity for quiet meditation and personal contemplation every day. Therefore, the pages are not dated. It is important that you use this journal when you have the time to give yourself to prayer and meditation. It will not help you if you simply make this experience a part of a daily regimen of religious duty.

To begin the journey, it is imperative that you find a quiet place where you can get alone with your journal, your Bible, and your Lord. Read each quotation several times, making sure that you have captured the essence of the writer's thoughts. Do not be content with a casual glance before quickly moving on to the next quotation. Allow the Spirit of the Lord to enter your thought processes and bring fresh insight. Let the words become a prayer that is formed on your lips.

The practice of contemplative prayer is certainly a lost art in our Western society. We are used to having our spiritual food gathered, prepared, cooked, and delivered to our table by our favorite preachers of the day. This journal will help you break out of this spiritual rut.

You might want to talk to your friends about a quotation and get their thoughts and reactions. How about memorizing a portion of the quotation so that you can reflect on it during the day?

Come back to these words several times. Do not be satisfied with only one look. Often, days down the road, fresh meaning and application will come to you.

Here are a few reflective questions that will help guide you in your meditations:

- What is the main focus and intent of the author's words?

- How does this concept apply to my life?

- What Scripture verses will lead me into further application of the truth?

- What circumstances have I gone through that enrich the meaning of the statements?

- Are there any particular areas of my life that need adjustment so that I can move into a new dimension of experiencing the power of this truth?

- What is preventing me right now from entering into the reality of this compelling insight?

- How can I form the truth of this quotation into a personal prayer to the Lord?

Before you begin, start with this quotation from Madame Guyon's book, *A Short and Very Easy Method of Prayer*:

Meditative reading is choosing some important practical or speculative truth, always preferring the practical, and proceeding thus: whatever truth you have chosen, read only a small portion of it, endeavoring to taste and digest it, to extract the essence and substance of it, and proceed no farther while any savor or relish remains in the passage: then take up your book again, and proceed as before, seldom reading more than half a page at a time.

It is not the quantity that is read, but the manner of reading, that yields us profit. Those who read fast, reap no more advantage, than a bee would by only skimming over the surface of the flower, instead of waiting to penetrate into it, and extract its sweets. Much reading is rather for scholastic subjects, than divine truths; to receive profit from spiritual books, we must read as I have described; and I am certain that if that method were pursued, we should become gradually habituated to prayer by our reading, and more fully disposed for its exercise.[1]

ENDNOTE

1. Madame Jeanne Guyon, *A Short and Very Easy Method of Prayer*, Ch. II, accessed 3 January 2002; http://www.passtheword.org/Dialogs-From-The-Past/methodofprayer.htm.

MY TRUE COMMUNITY

Mother Teresa (1910–1997)

She was born Agnes Gonxha Bojaxhiu in 1910 in Skopje, Yugoslavia (now Macedonia). In 1928 she decided to become a nun and went to Dublin, Ireland, to join the Sisters of Loreto. From there she went to the Loreto convent in Darjeeling, India.

In 1929 she began to teach geography at St. Mary's High School for Girls in Calcutta. In those days the streets of Calcutta were crowded with beggars, lepers, and the homeless. Unwanted infants were regularly abandoned on the streets or in garbage bins. In 1946, Mother Teresa felt the need to abandon her teaching position to care for the needy in the slums of Calcutta.

Initially focusing her efforts on poor children in the streets, Mother Teresa taught them how to read and how to care for themselves. Many former students of St. Mary's eventually joined her order. Each girl who joined was required to devote her life to serving the poor without accepting any material reward in return.[1]

> Keep giving Jesus to your people not by words, but by your example, by your being in love with Jesus, by radiating his holiness and spreading His fragrance of love everywhere you go. Just keep the joy of Jesus as your strength. Be happy and at peace. Accept whatever He gives—and give whatever He takes with a big smile. You belong to Him.
>
> My true community is the poor—their security is my security, their health is my health. My home is among the poor, and not only the poor, but the poorest of them: the people no one will go near because they are filthy and suffering from contagious diseases, full of germs and vermin—infested; the people who

can't go to church because they can't go out naked; the people who can no longer eat because they haven't the strength; the people who lie down in the street, knowing they are going to die, while others look away and pass them by; the people who no longer cry because their tears have run dry!

The Lord wants me exactly where I am—He will provide the answers.[2]

Accept whatever He gives—and give whatever
He takes with a big smile. You belong to Him.

Day: Date: Time: Location:

ENDNOTES

1.   Don Milam, *The Lost Passions of Jesus* (Shippensburg, PA: MercyPlace, 1999), 131.

2.   Eileen Egan and Kathleen Egan, *Suffering Into Joy* (Ann Arbor, MI: Servant Publications, 1994], 22, 89.

A LIFE WORTHY OF ETERNITY

Susanna Wesley (1669–1742)

Susanna (Annesley) Wesley was born on January 20, 1669, in London, England, and is most known for being the mother of the famous Wesley boys, John and Charles. Susanna was the youngest of 25 children. Her father was a minister and often let Susanna take part in theological discussions with his minister friends.

At the age of 19, Susanna married 26-year-old Samuel Wesley. He was a newly ordained Anglican priest who was named rector of the Epworth parish. During the absence of her husband, Susanna began a Bible study within her home. Neighbors, family, and friends quickly heard of the Bible studies, and the crowd soon grew to over 200 hungry souls.

Susanna regularly spent an hour in prayer and Bible reading every day. This practice was built into the lives of her children and bore fruit in their powerful preaching and passionate prayers.

Susanna passed away on July 25, 1742.

> This life is nothing in comparison of eternity; so very inconsiderable, and withal so wretched, that it is not worthwhile to be, if we were to die as the beasts.
>
> What mortal would sustain the pains, the wants, the disappointments, the cares, and thousands of calamities we must often suffer here? But when we consider this as a probationary state…and that if we wisely behave ourselves here, if we purify our souls from all corrupt and inordinate affections, if we can, by the divine assistance, recover the image of God (moral goodness), which we lost in Adam, and attain to a heavenly temper and disposition of mind, full of the love of God, etc., then we

justly think that this life is an effect of the inconceivable good-ness of God towards us....

I have such a vast inexpressible desire of your salvation, and such dreadful apprehensions of your failing in a work of so great importance; and do moreover know by experience how hard a thing it is to be a Christian, that I cannot for fear, I cannot but most earnestly press you and conjure you, over and over again, to give the most earnest heed to what you have already learned, lest at any time you let slip the remembrance of your final hap-piness, or forget what you have to do in order to attain it.[1]

> *...if we can, by the divine assistance, recover the image of God...then we justly think that this life is an effect of the inconceivable goodness of God towards us...*

Day: _____ Date: _____ Time: _____ Location_____

ENDNOTE

1. George J. Stevenson, *Memorials of the Wesley Family* (London, S.W. Partridge and Co., 1876), 185, as cited in Arnold Dallimore, *Susanna Wesley* (Grand Rapids, MI: Baker Book House, 1993), 91-92.

FIRST LOVE, DIVIDED LOVE

Basilea Schlink (1904–2001)

$\mathscr{B}$asilea (Dr. Klara) Schlink was born in 1904. Her education included social welfare training and a doctorate in psychology. She was a leader of the Women's German Student Christian Movement and bravely stood against Nazi policy during the Hitler regime. She risked her life during World War II, publicly speaking out on the unique destiny of Israel as God's people. Mother Basilea appeared two different times before the German Gestapo for boldly proclaiming Jesus Christ as Lord; she was released despite her unwavering stance. As Mother Basilea and another leader, Mother Martyria, led Bible studies for young people (even teaching the Old Testament, which was forbidden by the Nazis), they began to see revival. The young girls encountered God in a fresh way; His holiness, His justice, His Lordship were experienced anew. Those who were lukewarm in their Christianity repented; hidden sins were confessed, and forgiveness flowed.[1]

Jesus, who so often says "Whoever loves Me..." and asks "Do you love Me?" is concerned about our *love!* He is concerned about a special kind of love. It is the love which is shadowed in the relationship between a bride and her bridegroom; that is, it is an exclusive love, a love which places the beloved, the bridegroom, above all other loves, in the first place. As a Bridegroom, Jesus has a claim to "first love." He who has loved us so much wants to possess us completely, with everything we are and have. Jesus gave Himself wholly and completely for us. Now His love is yearning for us to surrender ourselves and everything that we are to Him, so that He can really be our "first love." So long as our love for Him is a divided love, so long as our heart is bound to family, possessions, or the like, He will not count our love to be genuine.

Divided love is of so little value to Him that He will not enter into a bond of love with such a soul, for this bond presupposes a full mutual love. Because our love is so precious to Jesus, because He yearns for our love, He waits for our uncompromising commitment.[2]

As a Bridegroom, Jesus has a claim to "first love."

Day: _____ Date: _____ Time: _____ Location_____

ENDNOTES

1. Adapted from "Who Is M. Basilea Schlink? Who Is M. Martyria Madauss?" Accessed 21 Jan. 2002, http://www.Kanaan.org/Mother. htm.

2. Basilea Schlink, "Bridal Love," 2001, The Watchword; accessed 3 Jan. 2002; http://www.watchword.org/index2.php?option-com _content&do_pdf=1&id=55.

Day 4

DO WE REALLY LOVE GOD?

Hannah More (1745–1833)

Born in 1745 in Bristol, England, Hannah More was to become a champion of the disenfranchised of the world. Instead of quiet domesticity, in obscurity, Hannah blazed a trail for women. As a powerful writer, she earned a fortune which she used to set up a cottage industry that printed millions of moral tracts that were distributed around the world. She became friends with John Newton, the ex-slave trader, who became her mentor. She joined in with William Wilberforce in the battle against the slave trade.

She has the honor of making English ladies the foremost agent in the education of the poor. The intensity of her love for the Lord Jesus was reflected in a life given for His people.

What an example of balance: the hearts of Mary and Martha beating within the same bosom. Hannah More proves that you can be passionate about His presence and at the same time be a servant to fellow man.[1]

> Our love to God arises out of our emptiness; God's love to us out of His fulness. Our impoverishment draws us to that power which can relieve and to that goodness which can bless us. His overflowing love delights to make us partakers of the bounties He graciously imparts. We can only be said to love God when we endeavour to glorify Him, when we desire a participation of His nature, when we study to imitate His perfections.
>
> We are sometimes inclined to suspect the love of God to us, while we too little suspect our own lack of love to Him....When the heart is devoted to God, we do not need to be perpetually reminded of our obligations to obey Him. They present themselves spontaneously and we fulfill them readily. We think not

so much of the service as of the One served. [The motivation which suggests the work inspires the pleasure.] The performance is the gratification, and the omission is both a pain to the conscience and wound to the affections....

Though we cannot be always thinking of God, we may be always employed in His service. There must be intervals of our communion with Him, but there must be not intermission of our attachment to Him.[2]

Our love to God arises out of our emptiness;
God's love to us out of His fulness.

Day: _____ Date: _____ Time: _____ Location_____

ENDNOTES

1. Tommy Tenney, *God's Favorite House Journal* (Shippensburg, PA: Fresh Bread, 2000), 25.

2. Hannah More, *The Religion of the Heart* (Burlington, NJ: D. Allison & Co., 1811), updated by Donald L. Milam Jr., 27, 33, 85-86, as cited in Tommy Tenney, *Mary's Prayers and Martha's Recipes* (Shippensburg, PA: Fresh Bread, 2002), 19-20.

Day 5

WAITING FOR OUR LOVE

Basilea Schlink (1904–2001)

*J*esus is yearning to have fellowship with us and to hear words of love drop from our lips. He is waiting for us. He wants us to be close to Him. He wants to speak to us in our hearts, to cultivate love's intimate relationship with us. Only in times of quiet when no one else distracts us, and nothing else draws us away, can Jesus visit us with His love. Let him who wishes to know the presence of Jesus and who desires to enter into bridal love for Jesus keep his times of quiet holy and faithfully for Him.

> Jesus is waiting for our love. As important as our sacrifices and our obedience to the commandments are for God (the rich young ruler sacrificed, and kept the commandments), they are not enough. Sacrifices and obedience do not necessarily yield the "eternal, divine life." Love does not necessarily pulsate through them. Jesus is pulsating life and love and He wants to impart His nature to us. Therefore, only our love, which stems from the divine, eternal life which He has granted to us, is the proper response to His love for us. This love leads us to keep His commandments, which are His wishes for us. It will lead us to bring Him many gifts, and to offer Him sacrifices—but in a different spirit….
>
> Bridal love for Jesus is filled with delight. There is no greater, happier, higher, richer love.[1]

He is waiting for us. He wants us to be close to Him. He wants to speak to us in our hearts, to cultivate love's intimate relationship with us.

Day: _____ Date: _____ Time: _____ Location_____

ENDNOTE

1. Basilea Schlink, "Bridal Love," 2001, The Watchword; accessed 3 Jan. 2002; http://www.watchword.org/index2.php?option=com _content&do_pdf=1&id=55.

Day 6

REVELATIONS OF DIVINE LOVE

Julian of Norwich (ca. 1342–ca. 1416)

*J*ulian is the most popular of the English mystics. She lived as a Benedictine nun in Norwich, beside the St. Julian Church, from which she most likely took her name. Little is known about Julian's life, although she is mentioned by her contemporary, Margery Kempe.

Julian's book, *Revelations of Divine Love*, entitled her to become the first great female writer in the English language. Despite her disclaimers of being unskilled as an author, she wrote lively prose in a style all her own. She was well trained in the Bible as well as in the teachings of the Church.

Her theology is based upon her mystical experiences. She became ill at the age of 30 and, in the midst of suffering, prayed for a vision of Christ's sufferings. Once in a time of prayer Julian heard the words, "I am the foundation of your praying"—words that greatly influenced her spiritual life. She always pointed to the goodness and love of God, a light in time of darkness for Julian, who lived in an age of social unrest and the fear of the Black Plague.[1]

> ...Oftentimes our trust is not full. We are not sure that God hears us, as we think because of our unworthiness, and because we don't feel right (for we are as barren and dry oftentimes after our prayers as we were before)...For thus have I felt in myself.
>
> And all this brought our Lord suddenly to my mind, and He showed me these words. He said, "I am the Ground of your asking: first it is my will that you have it; and afterwards, I make you to will it; and then, I make you to ask it and you do ask for it. How should it then be that you do not have what you ask for?"

For it is most impossible that we should ask mercy and grace, and not have it. For everything that our good Lord makes us to ask, Himself has ordained it to us from without beginning. Here may we see that our asking is not cause of God's goodness; and He showed that in all these sweet words when He said: I am [the] Ground. —And our good Lord wills that this be known of His lovers in earth; and the more that we know [it] the more should we ask, if it be wisely taken; and so is our Lord's meaning.[2]

I am the Ground of your asking: first it is My will that you have it; and afterwards, I make you to will it; and then, I make you to ask it and you do ask for it.

Day: _____ Date: _____ Time: _____ Location_____

ENDNOTES

1. Tommy Tenney, *The God Chasers Daily Meditation & Personal Journal* (Shippensburg, PA: Destiny Image Publishers, 19980, 80-81.

2. Adapted from Julian of Norwich, *Revelations of Divine Love*, Grace Warrack, ed. (London: Methuen and Co. Ltd., 1901). Ch. XLI, 14th Revelation; accessed 7 Jan. 2002; http://www.ccel.org/ccel/julian/revelations.toc.html.

THE EFFECTUAL TOUCH
IN THE WILL

Madame Jeanne Guyon (1648–1717)

*M*adame Jeanne Guyon was born at Montargis, France. When she was only 16, she married an invalid who was 38 years old. Unhappy in her marriage, she sought happiness in her devotional life. She lived in a convent under royal order for a year and then was imprisoned in Vincennes and the Bastille because of her religious beliefs. More than seven years of her life were spent in confinement. Many of her books were written during that period.

Writing that compels the reader to move into a living experience of Jesus Christ is Madame Guyon's great contribution to devotional literature. *Experiencing the Depths of Jesus Christ* (sometimes entitled *A Short and Very Easy Method of Prayer*) has had a wide influence: Watchman Nee saw that it was translated into Chinese and made available to every new convert in the Little Flock; Francois Fénelon, John Wesley, and Hudson Taylor all highly recommended it to the believers of their day.[1]

> The Soul then receives an effectual Touch in the Will, which invites it to recollection, and instructs it that God is within, and must be sought there; that He is present in the Heart, and must be there enjoyed.
>
> This discovery, in the beginning, is the source of very great joy to the Soul, as it is an intimation or pledge of happiness to come; in its very commencement, the road it is to pursue is opened and is shown to be that of the Inward Life. This knowledge is the more admirable, as it is the spring of all the felicity

of the Soul, and the solid foundation of interior progress; for those Souls who tend toward God merely by the intellect, even though they should enjoy a somewhat spiritual contemplation, yet can never enter into Intimate Union, if they do not quit that path and enter this of the Inward Touch, where the whole working is in the Will.[2]

The Soul then receives an effectual Touch in the Will, which invites it to recollection, and instructs it that God is within, and must be sought there; that He is present in the Heart and must be there enjoyed.

Day: _____ Date: _____ Time: _____ Location_____

ENDNOTES

1. Tommy Tenney, *The God Chasers Daily Meditation and Personal Journal* (Shippensburg, PA: Fresh Bread, 1999), 114-115.

2. Madame Jeanne Guyon, *The Way to God*, paragraphs 2 and 3; accessed 3 Jan. 2002; http://www.passtheword.org/dialogs-from-the-past/waytogod.htm.

You Must Move In

Hannah Whitall Smith (1832–1911)

Hannah Whitall Smith is the author of the popular classic, *The Christian's Secret of a Happy Life*, which was published in 1875. Its spiritual secrets of walking with God have been a great source of spiritual strength to many generations.

The search for God finds its greatest hope as we look within, deep into our spirit, where Christ lives. Smith gives us a series of clues for developing our inner life for receiving the "Divine Seed" and preparing our spirit for ultimate union with Christ.[1]

> A large part of the pain of life comes from the haunting "fear of evil" which so often besets us. Our lives are full of supposes. Suppose this should happen, or suppose that should happen; what could we do; how could we bear it? But, if we are living in the "high tower" of the dwelling place of God, all these supposes will drop out of our lives. We shall be "quiet from the fear of evil," for no threatenings of evil can penetrate into the "high tower" of God. Even when walking through the valley of the shadow of death, the psalmist could say, "I will fear no evil"; and, if we are dwelling in God, we can say so too.
>
> But you may ask here how you are to get into this divine dwelling place. To this I answer that you must simply move in. If a house should be taken for us by a friend, and we were told it was ready, and that the lease and all the necessary papers were duly attested and signed, we should not ask how we could get into it—we should just pack up and move in. And we must do the same here. God says that He is our dwelling place, and the Bible contains all the necessary papers, duly attested and

signed. And our Lord invites us, nay more, commands us to enter in and abide there. In effect He says, "God is your dwelling place, and you must see to it that you take up your abode there. You must move in."[2]

> *God is your dwelling place, and you must see to it that you take up your abode there. You must move in.*

Day: _____ Date: _____ Time: _____ Location_____

ENDNOTES

1. Tommy Tenney, *Mary's Prayers and Martha's Recipes* (Shippensburg, PA: Fresh Bread, 2002), 21.

2. Hannah Whitall Smith, *The God of All Comfort*, Ch. 8; accessed 3 Jan. 2002; http://www.ccel.org/ccel/smith_hw/comfort.html#VIII.

A LESSON IN THE INTERIOR LIFE

Hannah Whitall Smith (1832–1911)

By rejoicing in Him, however, I do not mean rejoicing in ourselves, although I fear most people think this is really what is meant.

It is their feelings or their revelations or their experiences that constitute the groundwork of their joy, and if none of these are satisfactory, they see no possibility of joy at all.

But the lesson the Lord is trying to teach us all the time is the lesson of self-effacement. He commands us to look away from self and all self's experiences, to crucify self and count it dead, to cease to be interested in self, and to know nothing and be interested in nothing but God.

The reason for this is that God has destined us for a higher life than the self-life. That just as He has destined the caterpillar to become the butterfly, and therefore has appointed the caterpillar life to die, in order that the butterfly life may take its place, so He has appointed our self-life to die in order that the divine life may become ours instead. The caterpillar effaces itself in its grub form, that it may evolve or develop into its butterfly form. It dies that it may live. And just so must we.[1]

God has destined us for a higher life than the self-life.

Day: _____ Date: _____ Time: _____ Location_____

ENDNOTE

1. Hannah Whitall Smith, *The Christian's Secret of a Happy Life* (Christian Witness Co.), Ch. 18; accessed 3 Jan. 2002; http://www.ccel.org/s/smith_hw/secret/secret21.htm.

Day 10

THE PRAYER OF THE HEART

Madame Guyon (1648–1717)

Let all pray: you should live by prayer, as you should live by love. "I counsel you to buy of me gold tried in the fire, that ye may be rich." (Rev. 3:18.) This is very easily obtained, much more easily than you can conceive.

Come all ye that are athirst to the living waters, nor lose your precious moments in hewing out cisterns that will hold no water. (John 7:37; Jer. 2:13.) Come ye famishing souls, who find nought to satisfy you; come, and ye shall be filled! Come, ye poor afflicted ones, bending beneath your load of wretchedness and pain, and ye shall be consoled! Come, ye sick, to your physician, and be not fearful of approaching him because ye are filled with diseases; show them, and they shall be healed!

Children, draw near to your Father, and he will embrace you in the arms of love! Come ye poor, stray, wandering sheep, return to your Shepherd! Come, sinners, to your Saviour! Come ye dull, ignorant, and illiterate, ye who think yourselves the most incapable of prayer! ye are more peculiarly called and adapted thereto. Let all without exception come, for Jesus Christ hath called *all*.[1]

> *Children, draw near to your Father, and He will embrace you in the arms of love! Come ye poor, stray, wandering sheep, return to your Shepherd!*

Day: _____ Date: _____ Time: _____ Location_____

ENDNOTE

1. Madame Jeanne Guyon, *A Short and Very Easy Method of Prayer*, Ch. I; accessed 3 Jan. 2002; http://www.iinet.com/~passtheword/ DIALOGS-FROM-THE-PAST/methodofprayer.htm.

Day 11

MEDITATIVE READING

Madame Guyon (1648–1717)

There are two ways of introducing a soul into prayer, which should be pursued for some time; the one is meditation, the other is reading accompanied by meditation.

Meditative reading is the choosing some important practical or speculative truth, always preferring the practical, and proceeding thus: whatever truth you have chosen, read only a small portion of it, endeavoring to taste and digest it, to extract the essence and substance of it, and proceed no farther while any savor or relish remains in the passage: then take up your book again, and proceed as before, seldom reading more than half a page at a time.

It is not the quantity that is read, but the manner of reading, that yields us profit. Those who read fast, reap no more advantage, than a bee would by only skimming over the surface of the flower, instead of waiting to penetrate into it, and extract its sweets.

Much reading is rather for scholastic subjects, than divine truths; to receive profit from spiritual books, we must read as I have described; and I am certain that if that method were pursued, we should become gradually habituated to prayer by our reading, and more fully disposed for its exercise.[1]

*It is not the quantity that is read,
but the manner of reading,
that yields us profit.*

Day: _____ Date: _____ Time: _____ Location_____

ENDNOTE

1. Madame Jeanne Guyon, *A Short and Very Easy Method of Prayer*, Ch. II; accessed 3 Jan. 2002; http://www.iinet.com/~passtheword/ DIALOGS-FROM-THE-PAST/methodofprayer.htm.

Day 12

DISTRACTIONS IN PRAYER

Amy Carmichael (1867–1951)

*A*my Carmichael was born December 16, 1867, in Millisle, Northern Ireland, the oldest of three sisters and four brothers. She was raised in the Presbyterian church.

During her adolescence Amy showed signs of a great poetic gift. In 1885 she had a mystical experience that set the course of her spiritual pursuit.

Amy's passion for missions was ignited in 1887 when she heard China Inland Mission founder Hudson Taylor speak. Five years later, God's words "Go ye" were all the confirmation she needed to set her course for foreign lands. She was rejected by C.I.M. because of her frail health, but in 1893 she served the Japanese mission as a "Keswick missionary," and in 1895 she departed for India. Miss Carmichael soon formed the evangelizing "Woman's Band" and took in her first "refugee."

In 1900 she moved to Dohnavur where she eventually founded the "Dohnavur Fellowship." In 1903, Amy's *Things as They Are* was published, launching her career as a prolific writer. In 1916 she founded "Sisters of Common Life," a spiritual support group.

Miss Carmichael was crippled by a fall in 1931; four years later, she became bedridden. She remained thus until her death on January 18, 1951, and was buried at her beloved Dohnavur.[1]

> Sometimes nothing helps so much as to turn from trying to pray, and instead, to read on the knees of the spirit some familiar passage from the Bible, for those words have a power in them to effect that of which they speak. Another sure way into peace is found in a literal obedience to Colossians 3:16. Turn a psalm or a hymn into prayer, read or repeat it aloud, for to

speak to oneself deep down in one's heart, using words that one knows and loves, is often a wonderfully quickening thing to do, and nothing more quickly and gently leads one into the place of peace, where prayer is born....

Sometimes we cannot find words...do not be afraid of silence in your prayer time. It may be that you are meant to listen, not to speak. So wait before the Lord. Wait in stillness....And in that stillness, assurance will come to you....You will know that you are heard; you will know that your Lord ponders the voice of your humble desires; you will hear quiet words spoken to you yourself, perhaps to your grateful surprise and refreshment.[2]

> *Do not be afraid of silence in your prayer time. It may be that you are meant to listen, not to speak.*

Day: _____ Date: _____ Time: _____ Location_____

ENDNOTES

1. See www.heroesofhistory.com/page49.html, as cited in Tommy Tenney, *Mary's Prayers and Martha's Recipes* (Shippensburg, PA: Fresh Bread, 2002), 13-14.

2. Amy Carmichael, *Thou Givest...They Gather* (Fort Washington, PA: Christian Literature Crusade, 1958), 45-48, as cited in Tommy Tenney, *Mary's Prayers and Martha's Recipes* (Shippensburg, PA: Fresh Bread, 2002), 14-15.

Day 13

PRAYER DIVINELY EXPLAINED

Madame Guyon (1648–1717)

Prayer is the effusion of the heart in the presence of God: "I have poured out my soul before the Lord," said the mother of Samuel. (1 Sam. 1:15.) The prayer of the wise men at the feet of Christ in the stable of Bethlehem, was signified by the incense they offered.

Prayer is a certain warmth of love, melting, dissolving, and sublimating the soul, and causing it to ascend unto God, and, as the soul is melted, odors rise from it; and these sweet exhalations proceed from the consuming fire of love within.

This is illustrated in the Canticles, [Song of Solomon] 1:12, where the spouse says, "While the king sitteth at his table, my spikenard sendeth forth the smell thereof." The table is the centre of the soul; and when God is there, and we know how to dwell near, and abide with Him, the sacred presence gradually dissolves the hardness of the soul, and, as it melts, fragrance issues forth; hence it is, that the Beloved says of his spouse, in seeing her soul melt when he spoke, "Who is this that cometh out of the wilderness, like pillars of smoke perfumed with myrrh and frankincense?" (Cant. [Song of Solomon] 3:6.)[1]

Prayer is the effusion of the heart in the presence of God.

Day: _____ Date: _____ Time: _____ Location_____

ENDNOTE

1. Madame Jeanne Guyon, *A Short and Very Easy Method of Prayer,* Ch. XX; accessed 3 Jan. 2002 http://www.iinet.com/~passtheword/ DIALOGS-FROM-THE-PAST/methodofprayer.htm.

LOVED OF GOD

Julian of Norwich (ca. 1342–ca. 1416)

For as the body is clad in the cloth, and the flesh in the skin, and the bones in the flesh, and the heart in the whole, so are we, soul and body, clad in the Goodness of God, and enclosed. Yea, and more homely: for all these may waste and wear away, but the Goodness of God is ever whole; and more near to us, without any likeness; for truly our Lover desireth that our soul cleave to Him with all its might, and that we be evermore cleaving to His Goodness. For of all things that heart may think, this pleaseth most God, and soonest speedeth the soul.

For our soul is so specially loved of Him that is highest, that it overpasseth the knowing of all creatures: that is to say, there is no creature that is made that may fully know how much and how sweetly and how tenderly our Maker loveth us. And therefore we may with grace and His help stand in spiritual beholding, with everlasting marvel of this high, overpassing, inestimable Love that Almighty God hath to us of His Goodness. And therefore we may ask of our Lover with reverence all that we will.

For our natural Will is to have God, and the Good Will of God is to have us; and we may never cease from willing nor from longing till we have Him in fullness of joy: and then may we no more desire.

For He willeth that we be occupied in knowing and loving till the time that we shall be fulfilled in Heaven; and therefore was this lesson of Love shewed, with all that followeth, as ye shall see. For the strength and the Ground of all was shewed in the First Sight. For of all things the beholding and the loving of the Maker maketh the soul to seem less in his own sight, and most filleth him with reverent dread and true meekness; with plenty of charity to his even-Christians.[1]

---

*For as the body is clad in the cloth, and the flesh in the
skin, and the bones in the flesh, and the heart in the whole,
so are we, soul and body, clad in the Goodness of God.*

Day: _____ Date: _____ Time: _____ Location_____

ENDNOTE

1. Julian of Norwich, *Revelations of Divine Love.* Grace Warrack, ed. (London: Methuen and Co. Ltd., 1901) Ch. VI; accessed 7 Jan. 2002; http://www.ccel.org/j/julian/revelations/revelations.html.

Day 15

THE PRESENCE OF GOD

Jessie Penn-Lewis (1861–1927)

"Oh God when Thou wentest forth before Thy people, when Thou didst march through the wilderness, the earth shook, the heavens also dropped at the Presence of God: even Sinai itself was moved at the Presence of God." (Psalm 68:7-8) What a glorious ringing shout of triumph there is in these words!

They seem to vividly picture the victorious march of an all-conquering King with everything going down before Him. Habakkuk gives us the same conception of the all-victorious Presence of Jehovah. "Thou didst march through the land.... for victory with Thine Anointed." (Hab. 3:13 RV)

The manifested Presence of God will alone move the "Sinais." How foolish we are to attempt to "push" them. The walls of Jericho fell down without one single push, yet we seem to think we must do our little best and then God will do the rest. Nay, it is "stand still and see the salvation of God." It is the manifested Presence of Jehovah we need; He must march forth before us and the biggest "Sinai" will be moved before Him.

Oh the "Sinais"! How we groan over them! That Sinai of self, will it never go? That idol we have surrendered so often and yet there it stands still the same! That Sinai in our Christian work, and many others known best to God and ourselves. How we take our little spades, do our little best, push and push, dig and dig, failing utterly to make the least impression.

"Oh God...when Thou wentest forth...even Sinai itself...!" It is the Presence of God we need. How can we obtain His

Presence, thus moving so gloriously before us? We must first be willing for His manifested Presence in us.[1]

---

*It is the manifested Presence of Jehovah we
need; He must march forth before us and the
biggest "Sinai" will be moved before Him.*

Day: _____ Date: _____ Time: _____ Location_____

ENDNOTE

1. Jessie Penn-Lewis, "The Presence of God," *The Overcomer* (January, 1929), 1.

Day 16

RELIGION OF THE HEART

Hannah More (1745–1833)

God is the fountain from which all streams of goodness flow. He is the center from which all rays of blessedness shine. All our actions are, therefore, only good insofar as they have a reference to Him: the streams must revert to their Fountain, the rays must converge again to their Center.

If love for God is the governing principle, this powerful spring will actuate all the movements of the reasonable creature. The essence of religious faith does not so much consist in actions as in affections. Though right actions may be performed where there are not right affections, they are a mere carcass, utterly devoid of soul, and therefore, of virtue. On the other hand, genuine affections cannot substantially and truly exist without producing right actions.

Let it never be forgotten that a devout inclination which does not have life and vigor enough to ripen into action when the occasion presents itself has no place in the account of real goodness.

What a model for our humble imitation is that divine Person who was clothed with our humanity! He dwelt among us so that the pattern might be rendered more engaging and conformity to it made more practicable. His life was one of unbroken, universal charity. He never forgot that we are compounded both of soul and body, and after teaching the multitude, He fed them. He repulsed none for being ignorant, was impatient with none for being dull, despised none for being loathed by the world, and He rejected none for being sinners. Our Lord encouraged those whose forgiveness others criticized; in healing sicknesses He converted souls; He gave bread and forgave injuries. Christians must seek to express their morning devotions in their actions through the day.[1]

> *God is the fountain from which all streams of goodness flow.*
> *He is the center from which all rays of blessedness shine.*

Day: _____ Date: _____ Time: _____ Location_____

ENDNOTE

1. Hannah More, *The Religion of the Heart*, (Burlington, New Jersey: D. Allinson and Co., 1811), updated by Donald L. Milam, Jr., 27, 33, 85-86, as cited in Tommy Tenney, *Mary's Prayers and Martha's Recipes* (Shippensburg, PA: Fresh Bread, 2002), 18-19.

Day 17

THE LORD OUR DWELLING PLACE

Hannah Whitall Smith (1832–1911)

"Lord, Thou hast been our dwelling place in all generations."

The comfort or discomfort of our outward lives depends more largely upon the dwelling place of our bodies than upon almost any other material thing; and the comfort or discomfort of our inward life depends similarly upon the dwelling place of our souls.

Our dwelling place is the place where we live, and not the place we merely visit. It is our home. All the interests of our earthly lives are bound up in our home; and we do all we can to make them attractive and comfortable. But our souls need a comfortable dwelling place even more than our bodies; inward comfort, as we all know, is of far greater importance than outward; and, where the soul is full of peace and joy, outward surroundings are of comparatively little account.

It is of vital importance, then, that we should find out definitely where our souls are living. The Lord declares that He has been our dwelling place in all generations, but the question is, Are we living in our dwelling place? The psalmist says of the children of Israel that "they wandered in the wilderness, in a solitary way; they found no city to dwell in. Hungry and thirsty, their soul fainted in them." And I am afraid there are many wandering souls in the church of Christ, whom this description of the wandering Israelites would exactly fit. All their Christian lives they have been wandering in a spiritual wilderness, and have found no city to dwell in, and, hungry and thirsty, their souls have fainted in them. And yet all the while the dwelling place of God has been standing wide open, inviting them to come in and take up their abode there forever. Our Lord Himself urges this invitation upon us. "Abide in Me," He says, "and I in you"; and He goes on to tell us what are the blessed results of this abiding, and what are the sad consequences of not abiding.

The truth is, our souls are made for God. He is our natural home, and we can never be at rest anywhere else. "My soul longeth, yea, even fainteth for the courts of the Lord; my heart and my flesh crieth out for the living God." We always shall hunger and faint for the courts of the Lord, as long as we fail to take up our abode there.[1]

> *The truth is, our souls are made for God. He is our natural home, and we can never be at rest anywhere else.*

Day: _____ Date: _____ Time: _____ Location_____

ENDNOTE

1. Hannah Whitall Smith, *The God of All Comfort*, Ch. 8; accessed 3 Jan. 2002; http://www.ccel.org/ccel/smith_hw/comfort.VIII.html.

PART IV

A Lunatic on a Limb With Jesus

ACKNOWLEDGMENTS

*S*pecial thanks to Susan Fonger for her invaluable contribution to these glimpses of my heart in print.

Thanks to my talented editorial team: Colleen Davidson, Susan Fonger, Daniel Dodds, GeorgiAna Larson, Jamie Puckett, Cheryl Stults, and Linda and Virginia Wells and to my encouraging reading team: Christine, DeDe, Kimberly, LeeAnn, Michele, Ruth, Sandy, and Mom.

Special thanks to Tim and Christine Burke, whose financial sacrifice turned a dream into a reality.

Special salute to Linda Wells (Wellsy) for her labor of love. Her enthusiasm never subsided from the first rough draft to the final submission of the manuscript.

Special, special, special thanks to my threesome (Ken, Ben, and Jessica) who were patient while I wrote and rewrote and rewrote this book.

Story 1

CRIME—KEEPING GOOD NEWS TO ONESELF

On April 15, 1967, at a teen Bible study, Larry Munos showed me how I could receive the gift of eternal life. I couldn't resist such a gift! After I left the Bible study, I hurried home to call my best friend. When she answered the phone, I enthusiastically began to tell her how she could receive the gift of eternal life through Jesus Christ. Her response was, "Oh, I already did that when I was in elementary school."

I immediately said, "I probably am not explaining this clearly. I asked Jesus Christ to come into my heart today, and I know I am going to Heaven."

Judy answered in an aggravated voice, "Jackie, I told you I already asked Jesus into my heart when I was at a church camp."

I said, "There is no way you could have such a great gift and not tell me—we've been best friends for two years." We started to argue, and I kept repeating how shocked I was that my best friend could have kept secret something so significant as *knowing how to get to Heaven*. I remember getting off the phone and praying that I would never be the kind of Christian who would keep such good news a secret.

For many years now, I have met Christians who, like my best friend, are comfortable with keeping this good news to themselves. I have always felt it is a crime to keep such good news from those who are needy. I found a story in the Old Testament that verifies my feelings concerning this crime.

In Second Kings 6:24–7:20, famine had overcome the city of Samaria. The desperate condition was reflected in an incident where a mother proposed that parents eat one another's children. Four lepers from this needy city realized they would find no relief for their desperate condition. Men who lived daily with physical and emotional stress, these four lepers left the city of no hope and "happened" upon a campsite that apparently had been abandoned by the enemy. They found horses and donkeys and tents full of food, silver, gold, and clothing. As they were eating and celebrating their great fortune, the four lepers simultaneously said to one another, "Hey, this ain't right!" *(Ain't—appropriate jargon for lepers who have been kept out of the better schools in Israel).* Four desperate men understood that their good fortune was not for their needs alone but for sharing with other needy people. Their leprosy could have convinced them of their justified selfishness, but their non-leprous hearts showed them the crime of keeping good news to oneself.

We are not doing right. This day is a day of good news, but we are keeping silent; if we wait until morning light, punishment will overtake us. Now therefore come, let us go and tell the king's household (2 Kings 7:9).

REFLECTION

_____

_____

_____

_____

_____

_____

THE PRO AND I

The first movie I remember seeing as a child was *The King and I*. I was only in the third grade, but I was captivated by the film as I sat in that theater with my grandmother. Thirty years later, I saw Yul Brynner in a stage production of the movie; I was again captivated, much as I had been as a child.

As a teenager, I was similarly captivated, not by a movie or movie star but by the love of a big retired NFL pro who turned his back on the screaming fans of the NFL to give his energy to a less impressive audience—searching teens. Week after week, that big football player would tackle the challenges of trying to reach teenagers in the public high schools of San Diego. Once Ray "tackled" a teen, he would hold that teen captive week by week in a wonderful Bible study that he led. I had the privilege of attending that home Bible study. That former NFL football player helped lay the original foundation for my walk with Jesus. He taught me as a teen how to not just believe in Jesus, but how to rely totally upon Jesus moment by moment.

Ray never knew about the dysfunctional home that I came from. I was too ashamed to ever share such private pain. He never knew the fear that I often lived with at night regarding my father. But he did know the most invaluable truth—that Jesus is the only One who will ever satisfy my hungry heart. Ray pushed me and several other teens to get into the Word of God daily to search for the answers to our many questions.

Recently I spoke to retired NFL athletes who were conducting high school assemblies as part of an effort to reach teens. I told them about the "Pro and I" and how to this day Ray has no idea what happened to that teenager whom he used to call "Jack the Quack." How shocked he would be if he knew how much Jesus has used me during the last 30 years! I think about the adults who financially supported Ray's ministry, which helped my life and the lives of other teens. Those adults may not know until eternity what their investment produced for the glory of Jesus.

Do you ever feel like you give and give, and your work is just in vain? Do you ever feel like your efforts are fruitless? Do you ever consider quitting? Does the time and money that you have given as a Christian seem to be a good investment? Often I get exhausted and wonder if what I am doing will last beyond the end of the day, much less reach into eternity. Ray *gave* to me without ever seeing any tangible results. I have *given* to many, but I have no idea what they are doing today. A verse that cheers me on when I can't see the eternal results is the following:

> *And so brothers of mine, stand firm! Let nothing move you as you busy yourselves in the Lord's work. Be sure that nothing you do for Him is ever lost or ever wasted* (1 Corinthians 15:58 PNT).

REFLECTION

_____

_____

_____

_____

_____

_____

Story 3

A PEARL IN A PILE OF MANURE

As chaplain for my college dorm, I gave devotions on Monday nights. I used personal stories from my painful background as examples. Time and time again, students accused me of "exaggerating or lying." Years later, I realized that most of my audience (preacher/missionary kids, church-grown kids) on those Monday nights were not ready for the crazy family I had grown up with. Once, when I told a college counselor about my family background, she just cried. We both sat in silence for a long time.

One evening before I left for college, a friend of mine came by my parents' house to pick me up and take me out for a farewell dinner. As she waited for me (I was running late as usual), a fight broke out between my dad and youngest brother. It escalated as other family members joined the battle (there were nine in my family). Finally, I was ready to go, and as we were getting in my friend's car, she said something I never forgot. From the mouth of a conservative southern belle came the following, "Jackie, you are like a pearl in a pile of [bleep]!" At first I was shocked. Then we burst into laughter. Later that night, as I returned to my parents' house, I wondered if God could possibly use someone from such an odorous environment.

In college, I discovered another pearl from an equally unlikely place. This pearl was found in Moab, which is referred to as "God's washbasin." Yet within the dirty rinse water of Moab, God found a pearl named Ruth. He brought that pearl to Bethlehem, and she married a pillar of strength (Boaz). That pearl, found in a washbasin, became part of the lineage of Jesus. She became the mother of Obed, who was the grandfather of King David and the great, great, great-grandfather of Jesus.

I am not in the lineage of Jesus like Ruth, but in 1967 the Pearl of Great Price—Jesus (see Matt. 13:45-46 KJV)—found this pearl (me) in a pile of manure. He not only blessed me with a husband like Boaz, but also with two "godly seeds" (see Mal. 2:15 KJV). I wonder if you have to be a pearl snatched from a washbasin or a pile of manure to appreciate all that the Pearl of Great Price does daily for you. I used to be ashamed of the family I came from, but as the years passed, I realized that my family's dysfunction was preparation for a ministry to other pearls from various piles of dysfunction. As a pearl rescued from the pile, I am often so overwhelmed with gratitude that I feel like the following:

Who am I, O Sovereign Lord, and what is my family, that You have brought me this far? Is this Your usual way of dealing with man? (2 Samuel 7:18-19 NIV).

REFLECTION

CAUTIOUS IN FRIENDSHIP

*I*n 1969, a Campus Life leader was giving me a ride to a teen Bible study. As we rode along in her VW bug, I noticed a sticker on her dashboard: "As one associates, one becomes." I asked her about the quotation, and she said, "Jackie, you will become like those you spend the most time associating with. Your friends are shaping you and your future." I was a new Christian and still trying to hang on to my non-Christian friends, which was causing such inward conflict. That little chat in the VW bug has influenced me throughout my whole Christian life. I have watched my walk with God become lukewarm and my zeal diminish as I spent too many hours with mediocre, apathetic Christians. I have also noticed that my hunger for Jesus increases after spending time with passionate followers of Jesus. *"A righteous man is cautious in friendship"* (Prov. 12:26a NIV).

When I was 20 years old, my closest friend was 30 years older than I was. For two years, I spent every possible free moment with Mamie. She taught me how to study and to teach God's Word. She had a passion for God that I had never seen before, and I wanted to know Jesus as intimately as she did. We were like Elijah and Elisha. I was always praying for a "double portion" of the power I saw manifested in Mamie's life. I was often teased during that time for spending so much time with a woman who could be my mother. I was motivated by the reality of following her as she followed Jesus.

When I went away to a Christian college, the Lord gave me another passionate woman of God (31 years older), and through our friendship I learned that Jesus would take all the hurts that had touched my life and bring good from each painful blow (see 2 Cor. 1:3-5). The Lord took her to Heaven the year I left college.

Friendships often develop because of common goals and ideals: job relating, parenting concerns, school involvement, children's sports programs, church fellowship/ministries, and community affairs. Can two walk together, except they are agreed? (See Amos 3:3.) The friendships in my life that have lasted through all the different stages, dreams, and goals have been the friendships where Jesus was our constant common goal and ideal.

Think about the people with whom you spend the most time, and consider the characteristics that are shaping their lives and yours. Are some of your friends like the one described in Steven Curtis Chapman's song, "Walk With the Wise"? Do you have friends wiser than you? Do you have friends more mature than you?

He who walks with the wise grows wise (Proverbs 13:20a NIV).

REFLECTION

_____

_____

_____

_____

_____

_____

THE SPIRITUALLY ELITE

When I was a senior in high school, Al Kinard came to town. He began teaching at some of the local Bible studies in San Diego, and he became a buzzword connected to "The Spiritually Elite." I was only a year old in Jesus. I must confess that I was one who was *"zealous for God, but* [my] *zeal* [was] *not based on knowledge"* (see Rom. 10:2). When I first heard him speak, Al talked about having power to live victoriously. As a struggling new believer, I found this message very appealing.

I heard him speak several times—he began to talk about leaving San Diego for a farm in Fresno where people could come and live if they "really wanted to live wholeheartedly for Jesus." This was the '60s, so communes were popular in California; I figured this was going to be a Christian commune. Al invited all of us to come if we "really wanted to follow Jesus."

To go with Al, there were *rules* to be followed:

1. We had to leave our families behind, leaving secretly.

2. We could only wear white muslin clothing to all meetings. (We could keep our jeans for the farm work!)

3. We could only bring our Bible, and any money we could donate to the common purse would be shared.

So, five friends and I ran away to "follow Jesus." Of course, our families were frantic, and the search began. In retrospect, here were six teenagers wanting to win their families to Jesus, and their choices were having the complete opposite effect—our parents thought we had lost our minds.

One morning at the commune, I overheard a very harsh conversation between Al (our holy leader) and a young teenage girl. He spoke so abusively that when I went up on the roof (literally) to pray, Jesus spoke so softly and said, "Jackie, would I ever speak to a young person in the manner that Al did?" Wow, with that one question the light went on; I knew we had been deceived, and we needed to escape this commune.

I devised a middle-of-the-night departure. We knew we did not have the courage to try to leave this "elite group" in broad daylight. We knew they would try to "guilt" us into staying by challenging our commitment to Jesus. They had already said that our leaving would only prove we were not of the "true flock," that we were goats and not sheep. The six of us returned to San Diego, and before we went home, we spent a whole day praying and fasting (no money for food—just enough for gas to get home). Jesus gave us a verse to teach us that "spiritual eliteness" is too often deep deception and distraction from focusing on *Jesus*.

But I am afraid that just as Eve was deceived by the serpent's cunning, your minds may somehow be led astray from your sincere and pure devotion to Christ (2 Corinthians 11:3 NIV).

REFLECTION

_____

_____

_____

_____

_____

_____

Story 6

A SCHOLARSHIP ON A SILVER TRAY

Going to college was never up for discussion in our home: surviving day to day and finishing high school were major accomplishments. In fact, I was the only one of seven children who did not drop out of high school. So, graduating from college would be like getting a doctorate in our family. After high school, I got a job as a church secretary and started taking a few courses at the local community college. I loved my job at the church because of the ministry that I was able to have with young people even though I was just a secretary.

Throughout the two years that I worked at the church, whenever I would speak, the pastors and adults always asked me what college I was going to attend. When I would tell them about my job at the church, they would always say, "You need to get your college degree." Their comments often bugged me, and I prayed about my desire to go to a Christian college—knowing full well that such a desire was an impossible dream. I was making 72 dollars a week, and my parents didn't have a dime to spare, especially for a Christian college.

Whenever I would remark about praying for money to go to a Christian college, my father would sarcastically reply, "Do you think God is going to drop a silver tray with money on it out of Heaven?" I would just grin and pray even harder.

A rich elderly couple heard me speak one Sunday afternoon, and the Lord allowed me to find such favor with them! They were so impressed with my zeal for the Lord that they offered to pay for me to go with Campus Crusade to Spain for a special evangelistic campaign. I wrote to ask them to consider a long-term investment in my life. I asked if they would consider giving me the designated funds for college rather than a trip to Spain for two weeks. Mr. Turner was a little put out by my candid request, but Florence, his wife, prayed about it. Mrs. Turner tried to contact me, but I was counseling and teaching at youth camp. After returning from camp, I was invited to dinner at their penthouse condo in Palm Beach.

That evening they told me that God had put on Epa's (Florence's) heart the desire to send me to college. This desire not only included tuition, room, and board, but also a monthly expense account that would cover my airplane flights home, long distance phone calls, clothing, and pizza. I was so stunned that my junker car and I almost did not make it home. I could hardly concentrate on the road in front of me because of the "silver tray" that was holding my full scholarship for college.

Years later, the Lord polished this silver tray when I found out that I am the only young person (outside of immediate family) to whom such a scholarship has ever been given. I am still flabbergasted, though it is more than 25 years later!

How can I repay the Lord for all His goodness to me? (Psalm 116:12 NIV)

REFLECTION

_____

_____

_____

_____

_____

_____

GOD'S NEW CREATURE PROGRAM

An annual event for the college I attended was a sweetheart banquet and the choosing of a sweetheart queen. During my freshman year, my gown went to this banquet, but I was not wearing it. In fact, my clothes had more dates in my freshman year than I ever did. I was not popular with the guys, but my clothes sure were with my dorm mates; my closet was like a costume rental shop.

To my total surprise, I was nominated to run for sweetheart queen my second year at college. The competition was based not only on our external appearance, but also on the degree to which we inwardly reflected the ideals of this Christian college. Each candidate had to go before the whole student body (4,000) and tell how Jesus had made a difference in her life.

Giving my testimony in front of 4,000 people was not intimidating to me. I had been only six months old in the Lord when I was given the privilege of giving my testimony at the San Diego Civic Auditorium in front of 5,000 people. What was intimidating in this situation was the candidates with whom I would be competing; every candidate was either a preacher's kid, a missionary's kid, or a professor's kid. I was just a kid from a very ungodly home. I was convinced that my "bad" upbringing would ultimately disqualify me. In fact, when we were practicing for the night of the banquet, I paid close attention to the part concerning *how to exit the stage when the winner was announced.* I assumed that I would be one of the girls to exit the stage.

Does it sound like I was very insecure in college? Ironically, my insecurity was fueled regularly by someone who works 24 hours a day to challenge the righteousness of any Christian: *"For the accuser* [satan the shamer] *of our brothers, who accuses them before our God day and night, has been hurled down"* (Rev. 12:10b NIV). Whenever I would hear details of the loving Christian homes in which the various students were raised, I would be filled with shame concerning the home I came from—shame, not from God, but from the accuser.

When they announced the winner on the night of the banquet, the first picture taken of the queen captured her eyes looking toward the exit stairway. Yes, I won! And, the accuser showed up on stage for a moment. They put the crown on my head; my escort (my future husband) walked me to the throne and placed roses in my arms. All the while, the accuser whispered in my ear: "If they knew what I know about your past, you never would have won." I was caught off guard for only a moment. Then King Jesus reminded me of my enrollment in His "New Creature Program."

For too many years, I listened to the accuser while he used my past and my ungodly family to shame me. One day the Lord showed me that my painful family origin helped prepare the very platform from which I speak boldly today.

Therefore, if anyone is in Christ, he is a new creation; the old has gone, the new has come! (2 Corinthians 5:17 NIV).

REFLECTION

_____

_____

_____

_____

_____

_____

MAY I BORROW YOUR BODY?

A college roommate borrowed my favorite dress for a very special date. That date turned out to be the night she became engaged. One night during her first year of marriage, she and her husband were dressing for another special date. Her husband asked her to wear his favorite dress. When she asked him what dress he was referring to, he told her it was the dress she had worn on the night they were engaged. She grinned and said that she needed to call Jackie because she had borrowed the dress from me.

Borrowing is not a new concept. Borrowing is limitless. People borrow almost anything: lawn equipment, tools, cars, money, even wedding gowns. (My wedding gown was borrowed by three other women.)

Jesus borrowed a human body so He could leave Heaven, walk among humans, and ultimately offer redemption to all humankind. This borrowing of a human body has a sophisticated theological term—*incarnation*. One day I was thinking about the body in which Jesus was willing to be confined as He walked on this earth. Jesus was able to do the will of the Father in a human body; I realized that I can do the will of the Father in *my* human body. Then, I realized what Paul's reference to the Christian's body being a temple where the Holy Spirit dwells (see 1 Cor. 6:19) really means: it validates that God intends to use my body for His purpose. My free will determines whether I let Him borrow my body today for His will. Doing the will of the Father is allowing *my body to be borrowed by the Holy Spirit to expedite the will of the Father here on earth.* Jesus was incarnated 2,000 years ago; this incarnation process continues in the "borrowed" bodies of His followers.

Knowing that God is borrowing my body gives me confidence whenever I get a chance to do the will of the Father. Whether I am sharing Christ with a stranger on a plane or in the grocery store, whether I am teaching 5 women or 500—all these opportunities are just another chance for the Spirit of God to borrow my body as a heavenly microphone on this planet. The Spirit of God wants to borrow your body to finish the will of your Father.

Consider the irony of a Christian being thrilled to have Jesus purchase her body with His blood so she may go to Heaven, but this same person resists God's desire to borrow her body to accomplish His work here on earth. He purchased us with His blood, but our free will still places our bodies in our control. So, if God is going to borrow my body to speak or minister to someone on this planet, I must be willing to loan my body to Him. Paul felt that loaning my body to God on a continual basis was my "reasonable service." When you let Him borrow your body, you will be thrilled with the things He does with such a frail human frame. "Excuse Me, may I borrow your body?" Body borrowed by Jesus—cool, huh?

I beg you, my brothers, as an act of intelligent worship, to give Him your bodies (Romans 12:1 PNT).

REFLECTION

THE MESSAGE AT THE RED LIGHT

When I graduated from high school, I started to date a wonderful Christian guy (the first Christian I ever dated) who was on staff with Youth for Christ. Our dating relationship seemed to be the talk of the town—and this was no small town—San Diego. We consciously sought the Lord concerning His blueprints for dating, and we enjoyed not only one another but also the Lord together. What could be better? Then my parents moved to Florida, so I made arrangements to continue to live in San Diego—of course, I did not want to move some 3,000 miles away from the man of my dreams.

A year later, returning from a big Youth for Christ rally, David said he needed to talk with me. As he began to talk, I sensed that he was having difficulty with what he was trying to tell me. When he finally blurted out, "The Lord wants me to break up with you," I was so shocked that I just burst out crying. His response to my tears was, "Where is your faith—why are you crying so hard?"

Shocked at his judgmental remark, I was stunned into silence. Then I blurted out, "Faith does not put sand bags in front of a person's tear ducts." He made a few more comments and then got out of the car and went into his parents' home.

As I drove away from his house, I stopped at a red light. I think that I sat there through several lights (it was after midnight, so there was no traffic behind my car). When I finally noticed that the light turned red again, the red light was magnified in the darkness, and it suddenly made me think of the blood of Jesus. A verse I had just memorized came to my mind: *"He that spared not His own Son, but delivered Him up for us all, how shall He not with Him also freely give us all things?"* (Rom. 8:32 KJV). Talk about a moment of truth—if God gave up the best for me, then with the best—Jesus—He will give me what is best for me. When I allowed myself to think that my Mr. Wonderful was not God's best for me, I actually began to smile as I tried to imagine someone who would possibly be better for me than my David. As the light turned green, I drove home to my little rented room with a peace and joy that passed all understanding—knowing that God had only the best in mind not only for me, but also for David. Two years later he married a nurse who can care for him, for he now has multiple sclerosis.

Time and time and time again, I have been able to encourage others with the reality of Romans 8:32. I have watched God prove Himself to those who would dare to believe that life is worth living when life was not on their terms but on God's terms! Oh, the terrible burden to always want life on our terms! What a secure place awaits the woman who has finally surrendered the terrible burden of not trusting that God's blueprints are God's best for her.

He that did not hesitate to spare His own Son but gave Him up for us all—can we not trust such a God to give us, with Him, everything else that we can need? (Romans 8:32 PNT).

REFLECTION

_____

_____

_____

_____

_____

Story 10

OVERCHARGED BY WORRY

*T*his morning while studying I came across the following warning from Jesus:

> *Be careful, or your hearts will be weighed down with dissipation, drunkenness and the anxieties of life, and that day will close on you unexpectedly like a trap* (Luke 21:34 NIV).

> *Watch out! Don't let your hearts be dulled by carousing and drunkenness, and by the worries of this life. Don't let that day catch you unaware, like a trap* (Luke 21:34-35 NLT).

What do I need to watch out for?

1. Carousing (Greek): Refers to a *headache from over-indulgence.* How often do we overindulge on this life and wake up with morning hangovers from being more stuffed by the things of this world than from a feast at the King's table?

2. Drunkenness: As a believer I have never found this to be an issue that would distract me from being ready for my coming bridegroom, or so I thought.

3. Worries of this life (Greek): Lesser things of this life.

As I reflected on drunkenness being a *non-issue*, the Lord pricked my heart with this question: "How often, Jackie, have you been intoxicated by *worry?*" Ouch—that hurt. How often does my day begin like an alcoholic who must have a drink before breakfast, except that my drink of choice is the *wine of worry?* How often have I had a tall glass of Foaming Worry before going to bed? How often have my family members seen me distracted by intoxicating worries about *lesser things, temporal things?* How often have those I loved suffered the consequences of *my heart being weighed down by worry?* How often have I had to take Advil for a hang-over from stress?

The worst aspect of this intoxication is that it is the opposite of trust.

"Because he loves Me," says the Lord, "I will rescue him; I will protect him, for he acknowledges My name. He will call upon Me, and I will answer him" (Psalm 91:14-15 NIV).

As I continued to ponder intoxicating worry, I decided to look up the King James version of Luke 21:34. I gasped when I saw this phrase: *"And take heed to yourselves, lest at any time your hearts be overcharged with sur-feiting, and drunkenness, and cares of this life."*

Wow, *worry overcharges my heart.* Worry demands more than my heart was ever intended to give (or function, or perform).

Let's begin today by resisting that first glass of the wine of worry. Let's switch to a *tall glass of living water.* I may have to start a new chapter of AA—"AA for worriers" who want to be delivered from over-charged, weighed down, burdened, and intoxicated hearts. If we take this exhortation seriously, then our Bridegroom will not have to compete with our worry headaches and hangovers. Our heavenly Bridegroom is the One who spoke this warning. I have not always been a good listener when my husband warns me about particular people or activities, and I have lived with the consequences. Today I want to stop being *over-charged* by worry so that both my earthly bridegroom and my heavenly Bridegroom do not have to handle a woman drunk on worry and stress.

An anxious heart weighs a man down (Proverbs 12:25 NIV).

REFLECTION

_____

_____

_____

_____

_____

_____

A HUMAN SPARKLER

*A*s a group of elected people, Israel had been chosen by God to glorify Him, but they failed miserably. I was deeply moved as I read about this in Dwight Edwards's book, *Revolution Within*.[1] The author's insights pulled at my heartstrings: Israel failed in their purpose because they *profaned* God's name! When I think about what *profane* means, I think of "blasphemy" and "sacrilege." Edwards explained that *profane* also means "common."

Ezekiel 36:20 says, *"And wherever they went among the nations they profaned My holy name"* (NIV).

I looked up *profaned* and, sure enough, in Hebrew it means "to blaspheme," "to curse," and "common." The dictionary definition of the word *common* is "ordinary, mediocre, humdrum, cheap, colorless, dull, drab."

Wow, all of us *profane* God's name when we represent Him as common, ordinary, or dull in our lives. When we do not allow God to sparkle and shine through us, then our extraordinary, awesome God appears common and ordinary to those around us. Yikes! I mourn for our incomparable God who is daily *profaned* in our lives.

When we tremble in the midst of a crisis; when we are anxious, full of doubt; when we show fear; or when we fret, we relegate our God to a position of mediocrity, to ordinariness. When we display these attitudes, we display to others that our God is not big enough to handle our problems, not powerful enough. If He is as incomparable as the Word declares, then we should not be anything but confident in a trustworthy God and His infinite grace.

I have spent hours examining the areas of my life where I don't allow God to shine and sparkle through me. If I want to glorify God, then I need to allow my life to be a display of *His extraordinary capacity*—only then is He glorified and only then do I become a "Human Sparkler."

My prayer today is that I will allow God to sparkle through the display window. I do not want to insult Him by allowing those around me to think I love and serve a common, ordinary, mediocre, dull, or colorless Sovereign.

A popular phrase among youth leaders is, "We are here to make God look good." Kay Arthur captures this thought in her book *To Know Him by Name*. She writes, "You are to live in such a way as to give all of creation a correct opinion or estimate of who God is."[2]

A "Human Sparkler" is the best case in defense of an incomparable, extraordinary God!

So all of us who have had that veil removed can see and reflect the glory of the Lord (2 Corinthians 3:18 NLT)

ENDNOTES

1. Dwight Edwards, *Revolution Within* (Colorado Springs, CO: WaterBrook Press, 2001).

2. Kay Arthur, *To Know Him by Name* (Sisters, OR: Multnomah Books, 1995). 18.

REFLECTION

_____

_____

_____

_____

_____

_____

I BELIEVED A LIE

I was standing on the platform as the matron of honor for a precious young friend whom I had loved and spiritually discipled for several years. As her bridegroom began to say his vows, he began to weep. His best man (his father) began to cry. I did not cry—I sobbed. What people in the audience did not know was the cause of my deep sobbing. Many had assumed that my tears were from the joy of seeing Christina and Michael unite in Christ. I may have begun crying for that reason initially, but the tears of joy turned to painful sobbing after the father of lies whispered: "Your bridegroom did not weep for you because you were damaged goods."

That one lie turned into hundreds of thoughts that spiraled around the lie—thoughts like: God gave Christina a wonderful Christian home to grow up in, with two loving parents and two great brothers. She grew up in a home where laughter and music were a common occurrence. I, in contrast, grew up in a non-Christian, abusive home, where screaming, fighting, and verbal abuse were the music I heard daily. I was not given the blessings that Christina had. And, yes, I was damaged goods on my wedding day.

From one little lie, I spiraled into a deep ditch of self-pity. Jesus saw the self-pity ditch that I had fallen into, and the next day He showed me that my heavenly Bridegroom has wept for me. He wept in the garden and bravely faced the Cross because of the joy that was set before Him—the joy of offering me forgiveness and taking me as His bride. He even gave me the Holy Spirit as my engagement ring (see Eph. 1:13). Jesus is madly in love with me (see Eph. 3:18). I had a choice to make: Believe Jesus or believe the father of lies.

You may be wondering by now: *How can a Christian who has the Spirit of Truth within her believe such a lie?* Let me try to explain. Daily I have the choice to either believe the truth or to exchange the *truth* for a lie. I have the choice to wound myself through lies or to be healed through truths.

Adam and Eve were in a perfect relationship with God Almighty, but that perfect relationship did not keep Eve from believing a lie. We must recognize that as Christians we are following the truth, studying the truth, and living the truth, but that does not immunize us, as believers, from being exposed to lies and even choosing to believe lies. We have a legacy of lies because we were originally followers of the father of lies (see John 8:44). Airwaves are overflowing with lies from the prince of the power of the air (see Eph. 2:2).

Have you been telling yourself the truth? If so, you are en route to emotional health. If you've been telling yourself lies, then you struggle regularly with guilt and feelings of never measuring up.

Then you will know the truth, and the truth will set you free (John 8:32 NIV).

REFLECTION

_____

_____

_____

_____

_____

_____

ARE YOU GUILTY OF ACHAN'S SIN?

*I*n a familiar story, the reader could miss an obvious nugget. Reading through the Book of Joshua, I came upon the story of Achan and his sin of craving the beautiful Babylonian robe, the silver coins, and the bar of gold. Many know the story of how he took these items and hid them in his tent. That was a sin because it directly violated God's instruction concerning the conquering of Jericho (see Josh. 6:18-19). When I reread this familiar story, I was focusing on the lust that drove Achan to disobey and the costly cravings that resulted in the deaths of himself and his family. This deadly craving reminded me of the many addictions that destroy so many American homes. Then the Lord rocked my world by revealing to me another aspect of the tragedy. I had assumed Achan's sin was lust, but it was the deeper sin of presumption.

When God gave the marching orders for Jericho, He said, "No plunder for the warriors." Being a warrior, Achan heard that instruction and proceeded to commit a "presumptuous sin." He *assumed* that the "no plunder for the warriors" would be the marching orders for all the cities they would conquer. So Achan gave in to his lust and cravings. He *assumed* that God would not provide for him as a warrior. Sadly, Achan stole in Jericho what God was going to *freely give him* in the next city of Ai.

When God gave Joshua the marching orders for Ai, the Lord included, "Keep the captured goods and the cattle for yourselves" (see Josh. 8:2). So Achan's ultimate sin was not only lust, but also the presumption that God would not provide for him as a warrior. *Achan stole what God would have given him if Achan had only trusted El Elyon's timing and specific marching orders.*

- How often do we steal *too early* what God *later* wants to give us freely?

- How often do we impatiently pursue what our Father wants to give us when we are sitting still? (see Isa. 64:4).

- How often do we panic and conclude that God is not going to provide? (see Matt. 6:25-33).

- How often do we assume what God is going to do next and we rush ahead, drenched in fear that it is not going to be the best for us? (see Rom. 8:32).

- How many times have you and I suffered because we *assumed* what God would do and then we were knocked down by the surprise turn of events? (see Isa. 55:8-9).

"Lord, forgive me for a propensity to sin like Achan. Forgive me for living even a moment of my life drenched in fear rather than drenched in faith."

This is what the Lord says—the Holy One of Israel and your Creator: "Do you question what I do for My children? Do you give Me orders about the work of My hands?"(Isaiah 45:11 NLT).

REFLECTION

_____

_____

_____

_____

_____

_____

HOLDING HANDS AFTER ALL THESE YEARS

When I was in college, I was very impressed by the love relationship between my English literature teacher (Dr. Evangeline Banta) and her husband. She invited me to spend a weekend at her home where I got a closer look at a love relationship that I had assumed only existed in literature. At the end of our weekend together, I asked Evangeline what was the secret of their love that had flourished and not shriveled after 40-plus years of marriage. I never forgot her remark, and it has been the most important marital advice I ever received. Evangeline said, "We made a commitment on our wedding night that we would not go to sleep angry with one another." This is such a simple remark, but such a foundational truth for love that will last a lifetime.

Jesus chose the marriage relationship to be a reflection of the heavenly Bridegroom and his earthly Bride. *"The marriage relationship is doubtless a great mystery, but I am speaking of something deeper still—the marriage of Christ and His Church"* (Eph. 5:32 PNT). I used to cringe when I heard the symbol of marriage compared with Christ and His Church since so many marriages are in such pitiful conditions today.

Then I realized that the emotional divorce in most marriages— caused by unresolved conflict (too many nights going to bed angry)—is the same emotional divorce I see between Christ and His Church. So many Christians are divorced from true intimacy with God because the Holy Spirit has been grieved (see Eph. 4:30) and quenched (see 1 Thess. 5:19 KJV). Ironically, the Holy Spirit is "grieved" by a separation, a gap, when we do not willingly put away anger and bitterness (see Eph. 4:31).

Our natural marriage relationship experiences the same gaps and grief when we do not deal with our anger and bitterness. Just as

Christians can choose to live with a gap between God and themselves, many couples choose to live day in and day out with gaps as wide as the English Channel.

At my bridal shower, married women were encouraged to give me advice, which was recorded for me by the hostess of the shower. Every married woman gave her version of the advice that Evangeline gave me that weekend. One woman challenged me to be the first one to make the move across the emotional Grand Canyon caused by conflict. Men are so uncomfortable with emotional realities and need marriage to teach them about handling anger before the sun sets daily. This same woman said that the "first move" in resolving conflict is the most difficult moment, but once the first step is taken, one senses the ability to sprint into the rest of the process. Pouting renders one unable to walk, much less sprint, into conflict resolution.

I have often been grateful for the days when the sun shines for a longer period—I feel as though that day is a bonus day in resolving conflict before the sun sets.

If you are angry, be sure that it is not out of wounded pride or bad temper. Never go to bed angry—don't give the devil that sort of foothold (Ephesians 4:26-27 PNT).

REFLECTION

THE ULTIMATE SEDUCTION

hen I fast, my time in God's Word is often quite sensitive and illuminating. One morning, the following verse caught my attention: "*Satan rose up against Israel and incited David to take a census of Israel*" (1 Chron. 21:1 NIV). Satan incited David. What does *incited* mean? I looked up *incited* in my Strong's Concordance and found that *incited* comes from the words: "stimulate, seduce." Satan seduced David to count the military. What was wrong with counting the military? Why would satan seduce David to do something that was not a violation of Mosaic law? Why was Joab so repulsed (see 1 Chron. 21:6) by David's command?

What David did was evil in the sight of God (see 1 Chron. 21:7), but I could not see why. I could understand that David's adultery with Bathsheba was sin. I saw his murdering Uriah as a clearly evil move, but what was I missing in this command to count the military of Israel and Judah? Then the Lord turned on the light in my heart. I saw clearly that the evil done by David was not the *census*, but the *motive* behind David's actions. David wanted to know how many fighting men in Israel and Judah he could depend on. Joab, as well as God, did not see David's actions as being those of a responsible warrior-king. David's actions were manifestations of "self-reliance" rather than "God-reliance." David's *motive*, which is hidden to the naked eye, was obvious to not only an all-knowing God but also to a discerning friend (Joab).

Joab perceived that David was being seduced to trust in his strength, his army, his past military record. Joab tried to counter the seduction with the statement, "*May the Lord multiply His troops a hundred times over*" (1 Chron. 21:3a NIV). Joab was challenging David with the fact that the heavenly Commander-in-Chief is an expert at multiplying what we give to Him—whether it is a military army or a mere sack lunch.

David did not want to hear Joab's challenge to his self-trust. Do you have a Joab who will challenge you when you are being seduced to trust in yourself?

David's momentary self-trust cost the lives of 70,000 men on whom he had wanted to rely. These soldiers died in a battle between the seducer and one of God's children. Satan, the oldest seducer, began this timeless strategy with Eve, and he continues daily to seduce God's children into trusting themselves more than God.

To trust in myself and others more than Jesus,

To rely on myself and others more than Jesus,

To depend on myself and others more than Jesus,...is not a mere character flaw, but *sin*. Too often I have dismissed self-reliance as the flaw of an insecure, controlling person. Forgive me, Lord, for allowing this seduction in my life—I want to trust You with my whole heart, soul, and mind.

> *...you have eaten the fruit of deception. Because you have depended on your own strength and on your many warriors* (Hosea 10:13 NIV).

REFLECTION

HEAVENLY POTPOURRI

*G*ood smells, bad smells, stale smells, fresh smells, sweet smells—each of these scents are picked up by our olfactory nerves. Our family consistently uses and overuses the olfactory nervous system—we are a family of "sniffers." Whenever we kiss, we sniff. Whenever we hug, we snatch a sniff. We struggle with the way allergies affect our freedom to sniff and appreciate our environment. When our daughter was young and I would be speaking out of town, she would go into my closet and "sniff" some of my clothes in order to feel my presence.

Did you know that smells, sniffs, and scents are all a biblical reality? Being a "sniffer," I did some research on the different smells/scents in the Bible. I considered the fact that scents are not only given off by people, but also by animals and objects. I discovered three interesting aromas.

I found the obvious scent of animals in the Levitical offerings. Talk about the smell of barbecue on a consistent basis! Whenever the Jews smelled the offerings, they were smelling the scent of a significant relationship with God. The smell of lamb, bull, or goat cooking on the altar (their grill) was a daily reminder to all the "sniffers" that a relationship with the living God is a viable reality.

Objects that give off scents and smells took me to the New Testament where Paul remarked that the gifts he received from other believers were gifts producing an aroma so pleasing to God. The scents from practical gifts (cloak, parchment, food, money) given to Paul were referred to as a heavenly potpourri. *"Your generosity is like a lovely fragrance, a sacrifice that pleases the very heart of God"* (Phil. 4:18b PNT). Talk about a new perfume! Celebrities are always having new scents named after them. God's children, through giving, produce new scents on a daily basis. Move over, Liz Taylor! You should smell some of this heavenly potpourri!

Lastly, I found the most potent heavenly potpourri. This wonderful aroma was from the intimate aspect of people's lives—that is, the intimate privilege of prayer. How awesome to think that my daily prayers are mingled with incense that burns so sweetly before the throne of God—talk about a heavenly moment for any "sniffer"! I can imagine God taking a deep breath, and into His nostrils flows a sweet aroma that comes from the cry of my heart. My prayers may seem so desperate and painful here, but in Heaven they are transformed into a heavenly aroma that would thrill any "sniffer"!

He was given much incense to offer, with the prayers of all the saints, on the golden altar before the throne. The smoke of the incense, together with the prayers of the saints, went up before God from the angel's hand (Revelation 8:3-4 NIV).

REFLECTION

_____

_____

_____

_____

_____

_____

DIVINE PRAYER ENCOUNTER

I urge, then, first of all, that requests, prayers, intercession and thanksgiving be made for everyone (1 Timothy 2:1 NIV).

While separating this verse into bite-sized pieces, I found something new that I had an absolute praise party about. First, the Lord used the expression "first of all" to remind me of the primary role that prayer is to take in my life daily. Secondly, the Lord used the word "everyone" to remind me of the many people that God anticipates my praying for regularly. Then I found the definition of "intercession," and I gasped big time. *Intercession* has several definitions: "audience with the king," "encounter," "social interaction,"—all intimate terms that I love—and then I found "chance upon." Now, that phrase my not ring your bell, but it triggered a siren inside of me.

Let me explain. Whenever we take the time to pray, we are positioning ourselves to "chance upon" intimacy with our heavenly Bridegroom. Get this—the phrase "chance upon" radically impacted my life in 1972, when I read Ruth 2:3 where Ruth "chanced upon an encounter" with her future bridegroom. Do you see the connection between "chance upon" and "intercession"? Ruth's "chance encounter" was part of sovereign destiny. Such destiny-filled encounters with our heavenly Bridegroom are available 24/7 to each of us.

When Ruth had her "chance encounter" with her future bridegroom, Boaz spoke encouraging words to her needy heart. When you and I pray, our heavenly Boaz/Bridegroom wants to speak very specific blessings and directions when we "chance upon" such a holy, intimate moment with Him.

We need a more conscious holy pause when we pray, aware that this is an opportunity for "chanced upon" intimacy with our heavenly

Bridegroom. Maybe the reason so many of God's people don't hear His voice is this: they know how to beg and implore God with their needs, but they don't expect to hear something specific during their audience with the King! The reality is that most of God's kids know how to pray, but they don't know how to listen. Listening happens in the midst of intimate intercession that is ultimately followed by thanksgiving. Such intimacy with one's heavenly Bridegroom produces a grateful heart that cannot be restrained. This is the sacred romance most people are reading about, yet they are still missing their "chanced upon" intimacy with Jesus.

> *What other nation is so great as to have their gods near them the way the Lord our God is near us whenever we pray to Him?* (Deuteronomy 4:7 NIV).

REFLECTION

_____

_____

_____

_____

_____

_____

MOTOR-MOUTH'S
HEAVENLY DIARY

When I was only two years old, I was already such a motor-mouth. My mother told me that one evening when they were having a dinner party, I was walking about babbling freely when my father decided I needed to be put in my crib. Will putting a two-year-old in her crib close her lips? Wrong! I actually called out to one of the dinner guests and tried to have a conversation from my crib. I can laugh about the story now, but I have several painful memories of being teased throughout my life concerning the motor that propels my mouth.

When I became a Christian, several of the brethren felt called of God to talk to me about my incessant babbling. They used all the typical verses that exhort a person (especially a woman) to be quiet, like: *"study to be quiet"* (1 Thess. 4:11 KJV); *"quiet and peaceable lives"* (1 Tim. 2:2 KJV); or, *"A woman should learn in quietness and full submission"* (1 Tim. 2:11 NIV). Their favorite verse, with which to shame a "motor-mouth," referred to *"the unfading beauty of a gentle and quiet spirit, which is of great worth in God's sight"* (1 Pet. 3:4 NIV). I purchased Strong's Exhaustive Concordance and did a little study on the word *quiet*, especially the use in First Peter 3:4. What a surprise to find that the word *quiet* does not mean sealed lips, but an "undisturbed and peaceful spirit"!

The Book of Proverbs is full of warnings about the misuse and abuse of one's lips and speech. I have always been concerned that I would bless people with my speech and not curse or harm anyone. I also know that where there are many words, the possibility of harmful words exists. I am daily looking to the Holy Spirit to keep a close tab on my speech. I have learned to repent as quickly as He notifies me of my mouth's offense.

In college one evening, I was being teased at the dinner table concerning my "motor-mouth." Just as the shame began to rise in my heart, a young man spoke up and said the neatest phrase this "motor-mouth" had ever heard. He said, "Yeah, she talks a lot, but have you noticed who she talks about incessantly? At least, in all her talking she is saying something worth listening to." A silence fell upon the table. I looked at this young man, smiled, and knew that my "motor-mouth" was being used by the One I loved. That young man eventually became my husband.

Back in my dorm that night, the Lord gave me a verse to remind me how He feels about my incessant chatting with others about Him. Did you know that Jesus listens to the conversations that we have concerning our love for Him, and they are being recorded in a heavenly diary? This "motor-mouth" was liberated that night—for some, that is a blessing, and for others...well, they can buy earplugs at Walgreens.

Then those who feared the Lord talked with each other, and the Lord listened and heard. A scroll of remembrance was written in His presence concerning those who feared the Lord and honored His name (Malachi 3:16 NIV).

REFLECTION

_____

_____

_____

_____

_____

_____

THE GALATIAN DISEASE

*S*ince 1979, I have been a volunteer nurse working the "Galatian Disease" wing within Christianity. To prepare me for this job, the Lord led me to one of the most legalistic Christian colleges in the United States—a college where I spent four years observing the misery of Christians who live with too little grace and too much emphasis on the letter of the law. *"If you try to be justified by the Law you automatically cut yourself off from the power of Christ, you put yourself outside the range of His grace"* (Gal. 5:4 PNT). I spent four years trying to resist becoming infected with the "Galatian Disease."

The "Galatian Disease" has noticeable symptoms: It drains a person of joy and creativity. It fills a person with cynicism. It depletes a person of a loving attitude and replaces it with a judgmental one. This disease-laden individual too often looks like she sucks on lemons on an hourly basis. One of these individuals asked me one day, "Do you sleep with a coat hanger in your mouth so you can smile all day?" Smiling is treated like the ultimate crime. Throughout my four years of training, I almost got my "blesser busted," but I knew how to get immunized against this graceless condition. Whenever I noticed one of the symptoms coming on, I would reread the Book of Galatians, and the symptom would subside.

As I tried to stand firm in the freedom that Jesus had won for me (see Gal. 5:1), I was often attacked concerning my emphasis on grace. I was told that my emphasis on grace would give people license to sin (see Gal. 5:13). That caused me legitimate concern; I would never want to encourage anyone to use grace as a passport into sin. Then I realized that anyone who really experiences God's grace does not have the desire to "sin against God" but, on the contrary, that person wants to please the One who called him or her to live as a beneficiary of such amazing grace.

Do legalistic systems motivate Christians to live more holy lives? I have walked with Jesus only 30 years, but I have not observed legalistic Christians as having more success living holy lives than those of us who are motivated and constrained by the grace of God. I honestly believe that God's grace ultimately produces such gratitude in the recipients that the very spring in the steps of their obedience is the spring of grace. I am sure many people take advantage of God's grace, but that is not cured by more laws and rules. I have read many times about God's children taking advantage of God's grace. This particular group of God's kids were in the Old Testament under the strict Mosaic law.

> *Will you steal and murder, commit adultery and perjury, burn incense to Baal and follow other gods you have not known, and then come and stand before Me in this house, which bears My Name, and say, "We are safe"—safe to do these detestable things?* (Jeremiah 7:9-10 NIV)

REFLECTION

BELOVED DOODLES AND I

I went to the post office to pick up a registered letter from our lawyer. Standing in line, I was a little anxious, wondering what the letter was about. I wondered if the IRS had wrapped some red tape around our lawyer, who had been helping us in applying for a non-profit exemption status for Power to Grow Ministry (a ministry that my husband and I had just formed). As I opened the thick envelope, I assumed that more IRS red tape would be enclosed, but I discovered someone's last will and testament. I immediately assumed that Dick's secretary had mailed me the wrong papers. Being a curious female, I began to read the will, and the first interesting thing I read, as I recall, was:

I direct my Trustee to pay first from income and then from principal, if necessary, the sum of $100 per week to Frieda Houchins, to be used in part for the care of my beloved puppy dog, Doodles, for its lifetime.

As I continued reading, since my attention was captured by Doodles, I came upon the next amazing statement:

I hereby devise the sum of *Three Thousand Dollars ($3,000) to Power to Grow, Inc., Jackie Kendall ministries.*

Well, I started howling like a puppy, I was so shocked. I did not even know the deceased, yet she had placed me in her will just three and one-half months before her death. Etta Munn had decided to encourage me to continue to give myself with abandon to the Lord she and I both love.

As I drove away from the post office, I started thinking about Etta being with Jesus. Her gift was a way that she could still speak out for Jesus: *though dead, she could still speak.* Etta, like righteous Abel, has offered a pleasing sacrifice to God, a sacrifice whose aroma will continue through the years. Etta put other ministries in her will, enabling many to continue working on earth for the One she is now enjoying face to face.

So beloved Doodles and I are presently being blessed by Etta, who now dwells with Jesus beyond Florida's beautiful blue skies.

> *And by faith [she] still speaks, even though [she] is dead* (Hebrews 11:4b NIV).

REFLECTION

_____

_____

_____

_____

_____

_____

EVERYONE NEEDS FRIENDS
LIKE DANIEL'S

I was thinking about Daniel, *"a man greatly beloved"* of God (see Dan. 10:11 KJV). In Hebrew, the word for "beloved" means not only "great delight" and "great desire" but also "delectable." Wow, Daniel's life was actually delectable to God! What amazing favor. Tears filled my eyes because my heart yearned for my own life to be "delectable" to God.

As I looked more closely at Daniel's life, I read about his three friends, and the Lord showed me something truly exciting. We know Daniel's friends as Shadrach, Meshach, and Abednego—the names they were given in captivity in *Babylon*. Their not-so-famous *Hebrew* names were Hananiah, Mishael, and Azariah. As I studied the Hebrew translations and meanings of these names, I discovered what kind of friends Daniel had, the kind we all need: friends who want passionately to follow Jesus.

- *Hananiah* means "the Lord is gracious."
- *Mishael* means "the Lord is my help."
- *Azariah* means "Who is like our God?"

Just imagine! Their very names held the messages those friends needed to give one another when all three were cast into the fiery furnace (see Dan. 3). Their names described the gracious, incomparable, helping God who showed up in the furnace as the fourth man. The Lord, who walked in the fiery furnace with them, was the embodiment of all three of their names!

Do you have friends who remind you that the Lord is gracious (Jehovah-raah), that He is our helper (El Shaddai), and that He is an incomparable God (El Elyon)? As we associate with others, we become a reflection of those with whom we spend time (see Amos 3:3; Prov.

13:20). Can people in your life see that you have been hanging out with friends like those Daniel had?

I want to be like Daniel's friends.

Hananiah's, Mishael's, and Azariah's Babylonian captors changed their names but couldn't change their hearts. The three friends' hearts remained passionately committed to their incomparable God. I used to live in sin's Babylon. When Jesus delivered me from captivity, He changed not only my heart—*"Therefore, if anyone is in Christ, he is a new creation"* (2 Cor. 5:17 NIV), but He also changed my name—*"and will give him a white stone, and in the stone a new name written, which no man knoweth [except] he that receiveth it"* (Rev. 2:17 KJV).

I pray that you and I will be a reminder of God's gracious, incomparable help to those who know us—especially to those who are about to go into a fiery trial.

A despairing man should have the devotion of his friends (Job 6:14 NIV).

REFLECTION

BREAD THAT ALWAYS RISES

*H*ave you ever been given a jar of "starter" for sourdough bread? Well, I have been given a few and have followed the directions when I mixed up the bread dough, but seeing the bread rise to the top of the bowl has never been my experience. My friend Margo always has success with this "starter," and she always makes the most delicious bread. She has even given me some "starter" from her very own refrigerated jar, but the potion always dies in my refrigerator. Other women have declared that the "starter" worked for them, but I tend to be the exception to most circumstances. I did not give up trying to make this tasty sourdough bread until I had tried several times. With every attempt, I ended up with the most depressed looking loaves of bread; in fact, they looked more like cocoons for giant moths.

One day I was reading Deuteronomy 28 ("This woman can't make bread rise, but she can understand the Book of Deuteronomy!"), and I came upon the blessings that God promised to His children who would fully obey the commands of the Lord. As I was reading the following list, I thought of a blessing that was missing from the list:

- blessed womb (verse 4)
- blessed basket and kneading trough (verse 5)
- blessed coming and going (verse 6)
- blessed barns (verse 8)
- blessed bank account (verse 12)
- always the top and never the bottom (verse 13)

As I read about blessed wombs, bubbling bread, bulging barns, and bursting bank accounts, I realized that—even though my sourdough bread remains at the "bottom of my kneading trough," my bank account has never been bursting, and I have sometimes felt as though I was at the bottom rather than the top—I am comforted by a blessing that is not in the above list: the blessing of an ever present Advocate who rises to defend me when I do not fully follow the Lord's commands (see 1 John 2:1 KJV).

As the mystery of the sourdough bread cunningly escapes me, the greater mystery of a relationship with the Bread of Life has captured this baker's heart. This Bread of Life is always nourishing and comforting me, especially on those days when my kids ask, "Why are you baking giant moth cocoons?"

> *Your basket and your kneading trough will be blessed* (Deuteronomy 28:5 NIV).

REFLECTION

JOY FOR A MOTHER'S INNERMOST BEING

While carrying our first child in my womb, I had so much anxiety about my lack of wisdom in the area of parenting. Because I came from such a painful home, I was so afraid that our home would contain the same chaos that I experienced as a child. I began to read everything I could about being a godly parent. I asked many questions of women whose children I knew and admired. I even asked children what they felt their parents did right. I must confess: I was desperate in my search. Parents whom I respected did one consistent thing: They took time to read to their children on a daily basis. This act of love requires some 15 to 20 minutes each day. As soon as our firstborn could sit up, I began reading daily to him. This was not only my privilege, but also that of my husband and any babysitter who would care for our children.

Thirteen years later, one night while Ken was out of town, Ben and I were having devotions together (Ben and his dad usually share this reading time together nightly). After we finished reading in the devotional book, Ben remarked about a verse that he had found in Matthew. I asked him, "When were you reading the Book of Matthew?" I assumed he would say in his Bible class at school.

To my surprise, Ben said, "Oh, I've been setting my alarm to wake me up 15 minutes earlier so I can read my Bible each day."

Of course my response was so intuitive, "Oh, really!"

Then I proceeded to share with Ben what Proverbs says about the joy that a wise son brings his father and mother. I shared with him how several times in the Book of Proverbs we are encouraged to keep the truth as close to us as a necklace around one's neck (see Prov. 3:3,22). When I prayed with Ben, my heart was full of praise for the work God is doing in Ben's private devotional world. I kissed Ben goodnight. Then, Ben walked toward the bathroom and said, "Mom, I love you, and I sure hope you like your new necklace." I confess: I was overwhelmed.

I have often run at a "full-throttle pace," but I can honestly say that I have never allowed busyness to rob our children of this special "soul-quieting time" with their mom or dad. If you've read the best-selling parenting book, *The Key to Your Child's Heart,* you will understand why this reading time was a Kendall family priority. Keeping a child's spirit open to the truth is the most awesome privilege and responsibility for any parent.

All those books, all those hours, all those moments will seem like a blink of an eye when the day comes that your children want to read and discover truth for themselves—when your time to read is over.

My son, if your heart is wise, then my heart will be glad; my inmost being will rejoice when your lips speak what is right (Proverbs 23:15-16 NIV).

REFLECTION

_____

_____

_____

_____

_____

_____

GOD'S LOVE LANGUAGE

On May 7, 1992, I finished reading my Bible and recorded the thought: "I delight God." It was such an awesome concept to consider the delight that I am capable of bringing to God. Psalm 16:3 defines the ones who delight God: *"As for the saints who are in the land, they are the glorious ones in whom is all My delight"* (NIV). Now, that is a verse I could "Selah" (pause and think about) for the rest of my days on planet Earth. When I think about delighting God and loving on Him, it is almost more than I can bear!

One year later, May 10, 1993, I journaled the following: "I have been thinking about Gary Chapman's teaching on the five love languages." As I thought about the different ways of showing love to others, suddenly I felt as though Jesus was sitting down right beside me on the couch. I heard Him say, "Jackie, what do you think My love language is?" At first, I was caught off guard by the question, and then I began to ponder it: *What fills God's love tank?*

You may think this question is ridiculous, but I really allowed myself to consider what God's love language is. I ran through Gary Chapman's list: touch, meaningful communication, acts of service, quality time, and gifts. I could see how all of them—except maybe touch—fill God's love tank.

Then the light went on in my heart, and I said to Jesus, "Your love language is faith/trust, isn't it?" The Lord reminded me of a Scripture in Hebrews that validated my answer. The verse talks about the impossibility of ever totally satisfying the Lord without *faith*. Every challenging situation I face is an opportunity to love on the Lord. Every crisis I face that demands deep faith is a great time for loving on the Lord. As Philip

Yancey says, "God doesn't want to be analyzed; He wants to be trusted." This is another way of saying, "He just wants to be loved by you."

David once wrote, *"He brought me out into a spacious place; He rescued me because He delighted in me"* (Ps. 18:19 NIV). David did not delight the Lord by being perfect; David delighted the Lord because he understood God's love language—trust and faith. Throughout the psalms, you can find David trusting and loving on God during his darkest hours.

Here's a neat project: The next time you read the psalms, whenever you see the word *trust*, circle the word, and let the circles be a reminder of God's love language.

The next time you face a trial, crisis, disappointment, broken dream, or heartbreak, remember that you are facing not only a chance to exercise your faith, but also an opportunity to "love on the Lord."

And without faith it is impossible to please God (Hebrews 11:6 NIV).

REFLECTION

Story 25

THE PERFECT FATHER'S DAY GIFT

*H*ave you ever seen those ladders that have some "give" to them? They are sturdy but can bend a little when someone hurries up them. I told a group of women that I felt the perfect Father's Day gift would be this ladder. Some 80 women looked at me quite puzzled with this particular gift suggestion. I assured them that I had a perfectly good reason for such a gift. I reminded them about the study we had been doing on the topic, "When a Man Doesn't Need a Woman." We had been talking about a woman's tendency to want to control not only her children, but also her husband.

One of the most common techniques employed by women for control is *nagging*. Now, women hate the reference to nagging about as much as they hate the jokes about PMS. One day I mustered enough courage to read some of the common references to a nagging woman (see Prov. 19:13; 21:9,19; 27:15). One of the verses implies that a man is better off being a "roof-top dweller" (see Prov. 21:9) than living in a house with a nagging woman. As soon as I finished reading that verse, I saw a man placing a ladder on the side of his house and hurrying up the ladder to his roof. I started laughing at the thought of a man having to sit on his roof to escape his nagging wife and find a moment of peace with the God who made his wife!

Then I thought about the concept of a place that a man can hurry to when his wife begins to nag—so I brainstormed a trip to Home Depot where a woman could buy a ladder and place it on the side of her house with a ribbon around it for Father's Day. Then the next time Mommy starts nagging Daddy, he can calmly walk out the door, climb the ladder, and wait for her to calm down. I envisioned a whole neighborhood where men were sitting on their roofs just after dinner. Just think of all the fights that this ladder could prevent. What a quiet but potent visual reminder that nagging never changed one individual on planet Earth!

As I thought about the escape ladder, the Lord showed me that most men already have their escape routes down pat—whether it is tinkering in the garage, hunting every weekend (see Prov. 21:19), glaring at the television, or even sitting behind the newspaper. Each man develops his own technique of muting his wife's voice. The saddest aspect of this reality is: When a man must develop a means of muting out his wife's nagging voice, he also carelessly mutes out her voice of love, encouragement, wisdom, and respect.

I was overwhelmed when I asked my husband how he felt when he heard my angry, nagging voice. He said, "I feel powerless." I now own that flexible ladder, and it is for me...I escape to a quiet place where my heavenly Bridegroom calms my heart so I nurture and don't nag.

A quarrelsome wife is like a constant dripping on a rainy day; restraining her is like restraining the wind or grasping oil with the hand (Proverbs 27:15-16 NIV).

REFLECTION

_____

_____

_____

_____

_____

_____

THE LONGEST SHORT TRIP

My mom, brother Michael, sister Mary, and I went to Washington, D.C. for a 25-year Chrest family reunion. We got there a few days early so we could do some sightseeing. Then we decided to drive to Gaithersburg, Maryland, to surprise a group of relatives who had no idea that we had already arrived. We took off early in the morning; my brother was driving, and I was the navigator. Thirty minutes into this one-hour trip, my mom said, "I think we are going the wrong way." We totally ignored her remarks because everyone knows that Mom needs directions to find her way out of her driveway. Mom kept insisting we were going the wrong way; we kept ignoring her remarks. Two hours later, we pulled over to ask directions, only to discover that we had driven for two hours in the direction opposite our destination. We were stunned, Mom was grinning, and Mary was laughing hysterically. Michael and I were completely frustrated by our own stubbornness and unwillingness to listen.

While reading the Book of Deuteronomy, I discovered a group of people who took "the longest short trip." Their prolonged trip made our journey look like a mere U-turn. It took Israel 40 years to reach the Promised Land. The actual traveling distance between Horeb and Kadesh Barnea takes 11 days. Mathematically, I cannot figure the ratio of 11 days to 14,600-plus days, but I do know there is a big difference. What caused such a prolonged trip? What made this the longest short trip in history? No, I was *not* navigating for Moses, and neither was my mom!

The journey for Israel was *prolonged* because of the people's *lack of faith*. Moses and the people roamed the desert for 40 years. Their lack of faith in the One navigating the trip was manifested by their murmuring and complaining in the presence of God's miraculous leadership. *"In spite of this* [all the miracles], *you did not trust in the Lord your God"* (Deut. 1:32 NIV). When Michael and I doubted Mom's word, we had grounds for our doubts. When Israel doubted God's Word through Moses, they had no grounds for their doubts. God mercifully let them roam for 40 years, just as my mom let us drive for two hours the wrong way. He also provided for them the whole time they were roaming in the desert (see Deut. 2:7). His mercy also reminds me of the way my mother did not rub it in when our trip to Gaithersburg took five hours rather than one hour.

Often when the road gets rough, we are tempted to grumble, complain, and assume we are going the wrong way. Rough roads and barren deserts are all part of the journey with Jesus to a place of abundance (see Ps. 66:10-12). We prolong our time in the desert when we don't listen to the One trying to tell us the way we need to go (like good ol' Mom in the backseat that day). Jesus is taking us on a "potentially short trip to a place of abundance." It can take us 11 days or 40 years. Daily I am learning to listen to the Navigator. And next time, I am going to listen to Mom too!

These forty years the Lord your God has been with you, and you have not lacked anything (Deuteronomy 2:7c NIV).

REFLECTION

_____

_____

_____

_____

_____

_____

A HEAVENLY HUG

*D*o you sometimes feel like you need a big hug? I heard a preacher talk about a big man walking up to him after a very moving message. Instead of asking the preacher to pray for him, the man said, "Can I have a hug?" Sometimes we need a hug, and in that moment there is no one we can turn to.

Years ago, as a single youth pastor, my husband was driving home after a long day of ministry to young people, and he realized how very lonely he felt. He loved working for Jesus, but that evening he was feeling particularly lonely. He began talking to the Lord about his loneliness when he suddenly felt a *presence* in his car. He felt a big hug that just warmed him from the top of his head to the tip of his toes. Now, Ken is not an emotional person, so this experience really caught him off guard, and he felt as though he were experiencing a "meltdown." His heart was full of the presence of Jesus, and he was overwhelmed by a "heavenly hug."

Recently a young Christian mentioned going through a very difficult time: she felt as if she were in the "dead of winter" spiritually. Sylvia was driving in her car to visit someone in the hospital (which is very difficult for her) when she suddenly felt as though someone reached from behind the driver's seat and gave her a big hug. At first she was startled, then she was captivated by this comforting gesture from the Father. Both Ken and Sylvia felt this heavenly hug while driving in their cars, but I do not think God's comforting presence is only available in cars. I believe the Heavenly Hugger is available in hospital rooms, funeral homes, lonely hotel rooms, and during the darkest night or the brightest day.

I have met hundreds of people who know volumes about God but who only have pamphlets full of experiences with God. Henry Blackaby, the author of *Experiencing God*, has said, "Merely *knowing about God* will leave you unsatisfied. Truly knowing God only comes through *experience* as He reveals Himself to you...."[1] I know that a person can experience God without ever feeling "hugged by God." But I also believe that we limit our experiences with God because we have Him in such a tight and confining box. Jesus is literally anxious to reveal more of Himself to His children. Are you sometimes skeptical about intimacy with God? I used to be...but the Spirit of "PaPa Sir" (see Gal. 4:6) who dwells within me has confronted my skepticism, and He has transformed my perception from *God* to *Father God*.

I have been hugged by Father God when I did not even know how needy I was. What a heritage for God's kids—our heavenly Father, the great "Heavenly Hugger."

> *Let the beloved of the Lord rest secure in Him, for He shields him all day long, and the one the Lord loves rests between His shoulders* (Deuteronomy 33:12 NIV).

ENDNOTE

1. Henry T. Blackaby and Claude V. King, *Experiencing God* (Nashville, TN: Broadman and Holman Publishers, 2008), 2.

REFLECTION

_____

_____

_____

_____

_____

_____

HOW BOLDLY CAN WE PRAY?

Knocking at Midnight

*I*n Luke chapter 11, Jesus teaches His disciples how to pray. While rereading this familiar passage, I almost missed a most precious nugget: Luke 11:5-8. In these verses Jesus tells a story of a *very inconvenient request from a friend at midnight*. The friend grants the request *not because of friendship*, but because of the *petitioner's persistence*, e.g., *boldness*.

I decided to look up *persistence/boldness*. Hold onto your hats! The Greek word *anaiden*, for persistence/boldness, means "unabashed audacity," "shameless boldness," "brazen persistence displayed," "in the pursuit of something," "an insistence characterized by rudeness."

Wow, when was the last time you or I prayed with "unabashed audacity" and "shameless boldness"? As I pondered this question, the Lord reminded me of the prayer life of my first mentor. As Mamie Hinch prayed with such "shameless boldness," I would wonder if my confidence in God would ever be strong enough for me to pray with such glorious audacity. "I cry out to God without holding back" (see Psalm 77:1 NLT).

As I thought about this boldness in prayer, the Lord reminded me of Heb. 4:16. This speaks about coming before the throne of God with confidence. The Greek word for confidence, *parresia*, means "freedom in speaking all that one thinks," "confident boldness in speaking," "plainness and exactness of speech."

I am fired up that Jesus reminds me today that "shameless boldness" is a critical aspect of prevailing prayer power. May we pray with holy audacity and shameless boldness because prayer can do whatever God can do.

So let us come boldly to the throne of our gracious God. There we will receive His mercy, and we will find grace to help us when we need it most (Hebrews 4:16 NLT).

REFLECTION

_____

_____

_____

_____

_____

_____

A NO-EXCUSE WOMAN

*H*ave you ever been distracted by daily demands? Have you ever felt crippled by your circumstances? Have you ever gone to bed exhausted emotionally? I discovered a woman in the Word of God who did not let her daily demands, crippling circumstances, and emotional exhaustion keep her from doing what was right in a major crisis. No, it is not the superwoman described in Proverbs 31, but she was a relative of the author of the Book of Proverbs.

I found this "no-excuse woman" in First Samuel 25—you guessed it: Abigail. She is described as an intelligent, beautiful woman. It is obvious that this woman of understanding had no choice regarding a mate, because her husband, Nabal, is described as a churlish man, which in our modern language means: "a real jerk." Abigail had no choice concerning her marriage partner, but she did have a choice in how she would live while married to such a mean and unapproachable man (see 1 Sam. 25:3,17).

Abigail did not use the excuse of being married to a wicked man to keep her from making a critical, wise choice in a life-threatening matter. Her servants came to her with the crisis situation because they knew that you "do not present a reasonable request to an unreasonable person (Nabal)." When she was told of the approaching disaster, Abigail quickly did what was right (see 1 Sam. 25:18). Even though she could have been emotionally crippled by the life-threatening circumstances, she wisely moved into an action that kept David and 400 soldiers from killing all the men in her household.

Abigail lived with a cruel man, which is an emotional drain. I believe that the God of Israel must have shown her how to use good judgment rather than excuses when faced with hard decisions and draining demands. She did not use her husband's evil dealings as an excuse to hold weekly "pity parties."

Abigail was not codependent toward Nabal because she saw him for what he was: *"May my lord pay no attention to that wicked man Nabal. He is just like his name—his name is Fool, and folly goes with him"* (1 Sam. 25:25a NIV). She made no excuses for Nabal's harsh response when David and his men needed a blessing.

An anointed earthly king blessed Abigail for her good judgment, and her heavenly King sustained her while she was married to a fool. When the fool died, the earthly king took her as his bride (see 1 Sam. 25:40). Of course, the moral of this story is not: Do the right thing, and God will kill your foolish husband and give you a king in his place. The moral of this story is: if Abigail can bless an earthly king while married to a fool, we can bless our heavenly King, regardless of the biographical sketch of our mate.

May you be blessed for your good judgment and for keeping me from bloodshed (1 Samuel 25:33 NIV).

REFLECTION

A MISSIONARY TO BEVERLY HILLS

*N*ow, the title above may seem to contain a contradiction of terms: *missionary* and *Beverly Hills*. In LeeAnn's case, these terms are completely compatible. A missionary is one who is sent to a foreign place to bring the good news of Jesus to those who have not heard. Trust me, Beverly Hills would be a foreign place for many of us. Almost on a weekly basis, LeeAnn encounters another person who does not know God's way to Heaven. Oh, they have heard mumblings about mystical mountain-climbing efforts to Heaven, but very few know the revealed truth of God.

When LeeAnn first told me that her husband's promotion would transport them from Orlando to Beverly Hills, I immediately thought of the famous people that LeeAnn would rub shoulders with, and I just grinned—because I knew that LeeAnn would never allow celebrity or star status to keep her from looking for every little niche that she could possibly squeeze the truth about Jesus into.

She found a church and told the leadership of her willingness to host a Bible study in her home. When the sign-up sheets were sent out, no one signed up for her group. She called me, and I told her God would show her the women that He had in mind for a "Bible study." It has been so exciting to hear about the women who have found themselves at this Bible study.

After telling a rich young man what he must do to inherit eternal life (see Mark 10:17-22), Jesus turned to His disciples and said, *"How hard it is for the rich to enter the kingdom of God"* (Mark 10:23 NIV). It has been so fabulous to see God use LeeAnn to scale the walls of difficulty in the lives of the rich and famous—and boldly tell them about her Jesus. It is so hard for the rich to ever believe that there isn't enough money, fame, or things in the world to satisfy their hungry hearts. I am so grateful that God placed LeeAnn right in the hub of this mentality and gave her the courage to challenge this vanity.

LeeAnn could waste so many hours by being self-consumed as many of her rich and famous neighbors do. Her passion for God keeps her from squandering the gift of time that she has been given. She is a witness, whether she is shopping at Bloomingdale's or playing on a playground with her daughter and the other children who are there with their nannies. Her Christianity has permeated her role as a wife and mother. She shines in a crowd because her inward beauty magnifies her outward beauty. She is not only a missionary in Beverly Hills, but she also supports missions and goes regularly on mission trips. You should have seen her on a rough job site on a mission trip to Quito, Ecuador. She was a champion girl scout from Beverly Hills.

> *Brothers, think of what you were when you were called. Not many of you were wise...influential...of noble birth* (1 Corinthians 1:26 NIV).

REFLECTION

_____

_____

_____

_____

_____

_____

A PRICELESS BELT IN
A TRASH CAN

or more than 14 years, my mother has strung pearls for stores on prestigious Worth Avenue of Palm Beach, Florida. One day while delivering some work to one of these stores, she was in the back of the store when she noticed a beautiful belt lying in a trash can. When she asked about the belt, the owner remarked that she had "no use" for the belt any longer. My mother, being the humble woman that she is, asked if she could give the throwaway belt to her daughter. The owner agreed, and Mom took the beautiful belt out of the trash can.

My mom looked at the belt to see why it was "useless." Were some of the beads torn off the leather, or was the buckle broken? After examining the belt more closely, my mom realized that the belt was not only in perfect condition, but was also worth at least 300 dollars. The detailed beadwork mounted on leather was awesome! My mom couldn't wait to give the beautiful belt to her oldest child. I never wear the belt without remembering where it was taken from—a trash can in a Palm Beach store.

While reading in Jeremiah 13, I came across another "priceless belt in a trash can." This belt was not created by artists in China; this belt was a people that God had chosen for His glory. What had rendered the belt "useless"? The buckle was not broken, and the beadwork was not torn from the leather. This belt (this people) was useless because of stubborn hearts and a refusal to listen to God's Word.

These people had been chosen and pulled close to God, as close as one wraps a belt around one's waist. The privilege of closeness and intimacy with Almighty God should have resulted in a people who brought God praise and honor, people chosen to be wrapped around God as a priceless belt or a trusted confidant: *"The Lord confides in those who fear Him; He makes His covenant known to them"* (Ps. 25:14 NIV). Being one of God's daughters, I do not want to be found "useless" because of my own stubbornness or be found in a "trash can" because I would not listen to the Father. I find security in being wrapped around the Father and of being of priceless value to Him as He confides in me (see John 14:21; Eph. 1:9).

> *"These wicked people, who refuse to listen to My words, who follow the stubbornness of their hearts…will be like this belt—completely useless! For as a belt is bound around a man's waist, so I bound the whole house of Israel and the whole house of Judah to Me," declares the Lord, "to be My people for My renown and praise and honor. But they have not listened"* (Jeremiah 13:10-11 NIV).

REFLECTION

_____

_____

_____

_____

_____

_____

HOW DO YOU SAY
GOODBYE TO SHAME?

Although we know that Jesus died to pay for our sins, some Christians are constantly assaulted by satan's favorite tool—shame. Although forgiven believers know that there is no *condemnation* in Christ (see Rom. 8:1), we still seem to struggle with shame. Why does shame keep such a tenacious hold on so many Christians? Last night in church, the worship leader read a passage of Scripture, and the Lord so rocked my world that I wanted to jump out of my seat, run to the platform, grab a microphone, and share what God showed me. Wisdom kept me seated, so I share this with you.

The passage was Luke 7:36-50. In my Bible it has a subtitle: "Jesus Anointed by a Sinful Woman." I know this Scripture well and used it in the first chapter of *Lady in Waiting*—describing a woman's reckless abandonment to Jesus. As I looked more closely at the passage, something new came into focus. This sinful, notorious woman walked into a most condemning situation: the home of Simon the Pharisee. It would be like a prostitute showing up for a covered dish dinner at the pastor's house! This sinful woman did not allow condemning shame to keep her from anointing and kissing the feet of the Holy One of Israel. Now, how did a *sinful* woman walk past a judgmental, self-righteous man like Simon? This sinner was so focused on Jesus Christ that she was not tripped up by a "shaming Simon"! This person did something so radical—so passionate. Her single-minded attention on Jesus kept her from being frozen in her steps by *shame's chilly finger of condemnation*.

The judgmental "shaming Simons" of this world are daily used by satan (see Rev.12:10-11) to accuse, confuse and trip up God's less-than-perfect children. When a believer focuses on Jesus, the "shaming

Simons" of this world wield no power over that believer. However, when struggling believers focus on a Simon's comments, they are stopped in their tracks, and they never reach the feet of Jesus. We are to come *boldly* unto the throne of grace (see Heb. 4:15-16). We must resist the "shaming Simons" who continually whisper how "unworthy" we are.

Focus on the forgiving Savior rather than the judgmental Simons.

Do you know how God views our failures?

- He expects them.

- He forgives them.

- He uses them.

The following memory verses will break the finger of any "shaming Simon":

> *Do not be afraid; you will not suffer shame. Do not fear disgrace; you will not be humiliated. You will forget the shame of your youth* (Isaiah 54:4 NIV).

> *Instead of their shame My people will receive a double portion, and instead of disgrace they will rejoice in their inheritance; and so they will inherit a double portion in their land, and everlasting joy will be theirs* (Isaiah 61:7 NIV).

Whenever you get ready to worship Jesus, don't be surprised if "shaming Simon" is in the room—and when this happens, focus on Jesus. Boldly kiss His feet and ignore the groan of a "shaming Simon" in the background!

> *...and the one who trusts in Him will never be put to shame* (Romans 9:33 NIV).

REFLECTION

SURRENDER YOUR JUNIOR GOD BADGE AT THE DOOR, PLEASE

Where did this "Junior God badge" originate? Who was the first person who struggled with the desire to run the universe, or at least his or her part of the planet? I don't mean to pick on our dear mother, Eve, but she was the first woman who decided that control was better than dependence on God. Now, she was not the first "being" who wanted the Junior God title—that belongs to lucifer, whose "love song" of independence (see Isa. 14:12-15) transported him from Heaven to hell. Now he roams planet Earth in an attempt to enlist people in his choir!

This Junior God badge mentality manifests itself in the basic need to control. The woman with this propensity will actually feel the responsibility of living out the very characteristics of God. I know this woman very well, and I have experienced all her propensities.

For example, the omnipresent woman can be found zooming through the day, rushing here and there to be everything to everybody. She is doing her best to be everywhere for everyone so that she can keep everyone in her world happy. This omnipresent woman ends up frustrated and fatigued.

The omnipotent woman has unrealistic, grandiose expectations of herself. Common phrases used by her throughout the day are: "I can do it...I'll get it...I'll fix it...I'll do it...." She is so driven to make everyone happy that she even worries about God's needs.

The omniscient woman is driven by the need to be all-knowing (constantly reading, attending seminars, etc.) so she can use her knowledge to control, pressure, and manipulate those in her world. Controlling them for their good is her reason—but also her blind spot.

The sovereign woman manifests the heart of the need to control. "I am in charge so no one will get hurt." She is afraid to surrender the terrible burden she is carrying—the burden of always wanting life on her terms.

Only God Almighty can be all-knowing, all-powerful, and always present—never fatigued, frustrated, drained, aggravated, and burned out. Wow, I am already tired, and it is only 2:07 p.m.! I think I am going to remove my Junior God badge and put it back in the junk drawer in my kitchen. The Lord has given me the freedom to wear the badge—if I want to burn out myself and others. Once again, I choose to remove my Junior God badge, pour myself a Diet Coke, and let God be in charge; I am just too tired.

...for anyone who enters God's rest also rests from his own work, just as God did from His (Hebrews 4:10 NIV).

REFLECTION

_____

_____

_____

_____

_____

_____

LIBERATING THE CONTROL FREAK

God: the Ultimate Agent of Causation

Recently the Lord gave my daughter something in her devotions that has captured my attention. I can't escape the impact. Jessica was studying John 17 when she came upon verse 17: *"Sanctify them by the truth; Your word is truth"* (NIV). Jessica studied the Greek definition for *sanctify* and found a meaning that thrilled her: "God is the ultimate agent of causation."

That phrase is so incredible when you allow yourself to remove your "Junior God badge" and ponder the depth of what you see in people every day.

Causation is defined in Webster's as "the process of causing." To cause is defined as "to effect by command, authority, or force."

For the woman who longs to be completely delivered from her Eve-like addiction to control, this definition is *most liberating*. The sanctification of a life is the result of Jehovah-mekoddishkem's (the Lord who sanctifies you) glorious "causation" in a person's heart. This reality has changed what I pray for people. Now I pray that God will sanctify them "through and through," and then I can release the outcome of my longings because I know who the agent of causation is—*not me, but God*.

Six years ago, a single gal named Jodi exhorted me with the phrase "It is not about you, but God." That young woman understood that God is the ultimate agent of causation. He alone changes the human heart.

If you love someone whose heart needs changing, just keep asking Jehovah-mekoddishkem to sanctify them through and through.

I can return to the Lord's daily assignments with joy and confidence in the ultimate agent of causation—El Elyon the Most High God.

- Sometimes as spouses we want to be the ultimate agent of causation.

- Sometimes as parents we want to be the ultimate agent of causation.

- Sometimes as friends we want to be the ultimate agent of causation.

- Sometimes as ministry leaders we want to be the ultimate agent of causation.

- Again, I remove my Junior God badge. I have pierced too many holes in my clothes by continually re-attaching it.

I will give you a new heart...And I will put My Spirit in you and move you to follow My decrees and be careful to keep My laws (Ezekiel 36:26-27 NIV).

REFLECTION

_____

_____

_____

_____

_____

_____

Story 35

FRUITFUL IN SUFFERING

After speaking at a youth camp in North Carolina, Ken and I and our children decided to drive home that evening so we could sleep in our own beds. We arrived home at about 2:00 a.m. and put our sleeping children in bed. Since we noticed a large number of messages on our answering machine, we began listening to them as we prepared to go to bed.

The first voice was the shouting of my youngest brother: "Jackie, call us at JFK emergency room!" The next message was the calm voice of my sister-in-law, pleading, "Jackie, please call us right away." The next message was Ken's mother, saying, "Where are you, children? Call home now!" The fourth call was a dear Christian friend, who said, "We are so sorry about your sister; call us if there is anything we can do."

I said to Ken, "Which sister? (I had four.) What is going on?" Ken insisted on calling his mom first, and then I planned to call my mom.

When I heard Ken say, "Oh no," I began to cry. I did not know what had happened, but I knew something horrible had taken place. While Ken and I had been speaking Friday night to young people about saying "no" to drugs, alcohol, and premarital sex, my sister, Bobbie, was dying at the JFK emergency room from a drug overdose.

The news of her suicide was the most painful thing I had ever experienced. I felt as though I had entered an emotional coma. I knew that Jesus wanted to comfort and sustain me, but the grief inside screamed so loud that—for a brief moment—His voice was drowned out. Because He is a man of sorrows who is acquainted with grief, He very patiently waited for me to throw myself into His comforting arms.

One year later (early morn on Mother's Day) in the same emergency room, my dad died of sudden heart failure. He was not ready for eternity, and that reality had me in a state of grief far deeper than words could ever express. I had been trying to reach my father spiritually for 24 years. As my brother drove me home from the emergency room, I kept thinking about facing our children, who had been praying for years for Grandpa's salvation. All I knew to do was weep with them, hold them, and rely on the only One who could comfort us in this unbearable circumstance. When I went to bed that night, I told Jesus that I did not know how He could possibly comfort me in the face of such a horrifying reality.

The next morning, Jesus gave a word to a dear friend (Margo) who called and asked me to look at the name of Joseph's second born. When I read the name *Ephraim*, my heart jumped within me, and peace began to flood my soul. Jesus said, "Jackie, I am going to plant a garden in the center of your pain, a garden that will bless not only your life but also the lives of many others." Out of my sister's suicide and my dad's hopeless death something beautiful has come. I now wear a gold bracelet with the name *Ephraim* as a daily reminder that pain is an opportunity for the planting of another garden. (Note: In 1994, another of my siblings committed suicide. By the grace of God, I continue to learn about being fruitful in suffering.)

The second son he named Ephraim and said, "It is because God has made me fruitful in the land of my suffering" (Genesis 41:52 NIV).

REFLECTION

_____

_____

_____

_____

_____

_____

A BROKEN DREAM IN THE MAKING

I am a planner, a dreamer, and a list maker—I get as much fun from planning and anticipating an event as from the actual event! But the downside of this grand adventure comes when the event never materializes after all my dreaming and planning. When I was a young Christian, I would always preface my dreams and plans with the biblical expression, "If the Lord wills...." Using that phrase in front of my plans always reminded me that I needed to yield my plans, as well as my hopes and dreams, to God. *"Commit to the Lord whatever you do, and your plans will succeed"* (Prov. 16:3 NIV).

A couple of years into my Christian walk, after hearing me use the phrase, "If the Lord wills," an older Christian said, "You do not need to use that phrase to try to sound spiritual." Now, I never thought of the phrase as a way of sounding spiritual. I used that phrase to remind myself who is ultimately in charge of my life's blueprints. Fearing others would think that I was using a "Christianese" expression, I stopped saying, "If the Lord wills" or "Lord willing."

When I grew older and (thank God) wiser, I realized that the phrase, "Lord willing," is not only a wonderful reminder for the one who uses these two words, but also for the one who hears them. This generation is so afraid of spiritualizing and over-using Christian lingo that we have forgotten the awesome reality that God's Word is supernaturally empowered (see Heb. 4:12). Whether it's a verse or an expression used in God's Word, we need to be careful not to discard it like some type of colloquial slang.

Why did the Holy Spirit tell us to preface our blueprints and dreams with the expression, "If the Lord wills"? I think one of the reasons is to remind us to give our blueprints and dreams to the Lord for His authorization on a continual basis. I am only 30 years old in Jesus, but one thing I know for sure:

Every expectation,
every plan,
every dream
not yielded to God,
is a potential broken dream in the making.

I am still a planner, dreamer, and list maker but I am using the phrase "If the Lord wills" more than ever these days.

Now listen, you who say, "Today or tomorrow we will go to this or that city, spend a year there, carry on business and make money."...Instead, you ought to say, "If it is the Lord's will, we will live and do this or that." As it is, you boast and brag. All such boasting is evil (James 4:13,15-16 NIV).

REFLECTION

_____

_____

_____

_____

_____

_____

Story 37

SPEECHLESS IN THE PRESENCE OF PAIN

Sitting in a restaurant across from a beautiful single woman, I listened to her personal story of pain. She had been married for a few years and had been trying to conceive a child. In the meantime, her best friend (who was single) told her that she was pregnant. What irony! Her unmarried friend was with child while she continued childless. The irony turned into trauma when her single friend told her who the father was—her husband. Can you comprehend the devastation caused in this beautiful woman's heart? She had been betrayed not only by her husband, but also by her best friend. Have you experienced a similarly crushing emotional blow?

She told how she had put her life on hold emotionally after her husband divorced her. Such a response is totally understandable. When she had finished her story, I was speechless (which is not my normal state of being). I sat stunned, praying for several minutes. Then the Lord graciously nudged me and said, "Jackie, I am not intimidated by trauma. In fact, I can be closer than ever during such painful times." After this heavenly nudge, I took a chance and I challenged her to give her broken heart, her empty arms, and her loneliness to Jesus. By faith, I assured her that Jesus could touch and heal the ragged tear in her heart.

She accepted the challenge, and Jesus not only performed major surgery on her heart, but He also taught her how to resist feeling sorry for herself and stop living in the arena of bitterness. After she made the choice of recklessly abandoning herself to Jesus as Lord, she was free to serve Him. Jesus transformed her from a crushed, brokenhearted single woman into a fearless witness for Jesus. Years later, a godly man fell in love with this single woman who had been using her free time to serve the Head Surgeon who repaired her broken heart.

When someone tells me about deep personal pain, my initial response is often speechlessness. In those moments of stunned silence, the Holy Spirit reminds me that the "God of *all* comfort" is ready and available. Sometimes a person is not ready to turn to God for comfort. It is very tempting to usurp God's role and try to be *the* comforter. The problem with being this empathetic comforter is the brevity of the effect of our comfort. Only comfort from God lasts into the late hours of the night and throughout the many lonely days ahead. I carefully listen to their pain (even crying when they cry), but I persistently point toward the only One who can truly heal a broken heart. David wrote about the nearness of God when the pain was the deepest. He knew firsthand that only God gives lasting hope and comfort.

The Lord is close to the brokenhearted and saves those who are crushed in spirit (Psalm 34:18 NIV).

REFLECTION

_____

_____

_____

_____

_____

_____

_____

GINGER'S SONG OF VICTORY

After a very loud, upbeat concert with the group New Song, our pastor said that someone very special was going to give a testimony. Onto the platform walked a petite blonde. She began to tell us that the Lord had asked her to stand before the congregation and give Him glory and praise. Now that would not seem like a hard assignment from the Lord, unless you understand the context of Ginger's life.

In only eight years of marriage, Ginger and Kevin had faced many trials—the deaths of their two sons, then a miscarriage, and questions as to whether Ginger could bear more children. Ginger never allowed her childlessness to keep her from being a blessing to someone else's children as an elementary school teacher. Ginger came to accept childlessness as her cross to bear. The cross became heavier when Christmas came, and with this happy time of year she also received word that her precious father had fast-moving, incurable cancer. The questions came as quickly as the cancer came. *How does someone so full of life, strength, and youth get a disease that will take all his strength away so quickly? Haven't I suffered enough with the deaths of two sons and the unfulfilled desire to have children? Why, God, why me?*

While her dad was dying, Ginger was diagnosed with cancer. As Ginger battled for life against this invading virus, a bigger battle was raging within—this battle was the strong challenge to her faith. The challenge came in the form of a painful "why, God?" The battle raged stronger—her dad was dying back home in Alabama while she was waging war on her own cancer in the hospital in West Palm Beach.

Ginger went before our congregation (1,000 people) that night to publicly declare who had won the battle against the painful "why, God?" Only God's grace enables anyone to win against the infamous "why,

God?" Ginger has won against so many challenges to her faith, and I can hear her battle song of victory:

I will declare God's goodness in the face of death,

I will declare God's goodness in the face of loss,

I will declare God's goodness in the face of my own cancer,

I will declare God's goodness in the face of broken dreams.

She concluded her testimony with a powerful statement of faith: "I have learned to trust Him, even when I don't understand" (see Isa. 40:28). Her willingness to live without understanding is the manifestation of her deep faith. I know she is a candidate for God's hall of fame, whose inductees are nominated because of their faith. Living without all the answers is the very heart of the life of faith. (Ginger's cancer went into remission, and she and Kevin adopted a precious baby girl. Six years later, Ginger won the ultimate victory over cancer...Heaven.)

As you do not know the path of the wind, or how the body is formed in a mother's womb, so you cannot understand the work of God, the Maker of all things (Ecclesiastes 11:5 NIV).

REFLECTION

_____

_____

_____

_____

_____

_____

A MIRACLE WORKER

*T*he movie *The Miracle Worker* left such a lasting impression on me through watching a human being with a Herculean task daily attempt the impossible. On January 3, 1992, I watched another "miracle worker." This time the star was not Anne Sullivan but my husband, Ken Kendall. I watched Ken preach his younger brother Mark's funeral. The church was packed to the wall. More than half the audience were not believers (mostly business associates of the Kendall Companies). The Lord showed Ken that he was going to do the impossible: Ken would use Mark's expressions and gestures to preach the Gospel through Mark, titled "A Message From Heaven."

Ten years earlier Ken had performed Mark's wedding, and then the Lord led him to preach at his funeral. As I listened to Ken, I whispered to both our children, "You are watching a miracle. This is not possible to do in one's own strength." As I watched Ken share such a powerful challenge, I knew I was a "miracle watcher." The Lord not only gave Ken the message but also the method of sharing the truth that would challenge and comfort in the midst of grief.

Later that day, I watched another miracle as Ken shared with Tony (a family friend) the good news of knowing the God of all comfort personally. I was again a "miracle watcher" as I witnessed Ken leading Tony in a prayer to receive Jesus Christ.

Eighteen months prior to this funeral, I had spoken at the funeral of my younger sister, who had committed suicide. I knew the task was impossible, but I also knew that "impossible" simply means "possible with God." One year later, I was making arrangements for my father's funeral; six months later Ken was doing his brother's funeral. Three immediate family members died within 18 months, and our friends were "miracle watchers," as they saw God sustain us.

At each funeral, the *God of all comfort* hugged us on the inside while others hugged us on the outside: These were holy moments. Being sustained by God through three seasons of grief (back to back) proved to our family, without a doubt, that God's grace is sufficient. Every trial, every heartbreak, every tragic loss is a chance for another episode of *The Miracle Worker*, God.

> *As a mother comforts her child, so will I comfort you...When you see this, your heart will rejoice and you will flourish like grass; the hand of the Lord will be made known to His servants* (Isaiah 66:13-14 NIV).

REFLECTION

_____

_____

_____

_____

_____

_____

GIFT FOR THE GRIEVING

*B*efore March 23, 1990, I always felt inadequate whenever I was told about death visiting a family I knew. Whether I was going to the funeral, viewing, service, or the following wake, I felt speechless and ill-prepared to comfort those in mourning. Once, after a funeral and wake, Ken asked me, "Why do we have a viewing, a funeral service, and a get-together afterward?"

I said, "I really don't know." The whole grief process was really a mystery to both Ken and me.

Then grief came knocking loudly at our door with the suicide of my younger sister, Bobbie. Grief continued to bang on our door with the sudden death of my father, and grief almost punched a hole in our door with the shocking death of Ken's younger brother. With each death came more understanding about the grief process and the "gift for the grieving."

This gift can be given by anyone who loves the people who have lost a loved one. It involves time, attention, patience, listening—and no rushing of the grief process. Too often, well-meaning (but blind) Christians try to hurry a person through the grief process. They preach at the one in mourning, rather than listen and pray. In their preaching, they encourage the grieving person to shove living feelings underground—only to be resurrected at a later date in an even more grievous way. Being robbed of the freedom to grieve is often as potent as death.

This "gift for the grieving" was given to Jacob's sons by Pharaoh (see Gen. 50:1-14) when their father, Jacob, died. Pharaoh ordered the people to mourn for him 70 days (10 weeks for a stranger). The funeral procession contained not only family but also all the dignitaries of Egypt. When they reached the burial place, they wept *loudly and bitterly*. The healing that takes place during a loud lamenting is only understood by those who have been given the freedom to weep deeply. Too often Christians are constrained to a silent stream of tears…no loud weeping. We have too often been robbed of the "gift for the grieving" by preconceived ideas about proper grieving for the believer. If you postpone grieving, the grief does not go away…you only increase the debt owed to grief and actually *prolong the grieving process.*

A counselor once asked a counselee, "Did you cry when your brother was murdered?"

The counselee responded, "Why cry? It wouldn't bring him back."

The counselor wisely replied, "You're right. But it would have brought you back." Whatever powerful emotions (grief, rejection, shame, anger, hate, etc.) we bury, we also bury a part of ourselves. When faced with those who mourn, encourage them to grieve—to keep them alive and not bury them, too. Grief is so deep, but not deeper than God's comfort.

Mourn with those who mourn (Romans 12:15b NIV).

REFLECTION

_____

_____

_____

_____

_____

_____

A MAN TOUCHED
DEEPLY BY MY PAIN

One night we had some friends over for dinner. As the children ate quickly and went into the garage to play, the conversation at the dinner table moved to an emotionally charged topic. The wife (guest) began to share her heart openly, which resulted in her beginning to weep. Ken and I both looked at her husband—we expected him to move over close to her and put a comforting arm around her. We watched as her husband sat totally still and appeared detached emotionally from her. Finally, I jumped up and put my arm around her. She continued to cry and even remarked about her husband's emotional detachment during her display of painful feelings.

So much is happening in America in relation to the healing of the masculine soul. This focus on the masculine soul has even captured and challenged the attention of the Body of Christ. Organizations are being formed where men are being encouraged to "become emotionally reattached." More and more men are looking for mentors and accountability groups.

So ironic to me is the concept that a man who is capable of "feeling someone else's pain" is considered very exceptional, as though women are the only ones really capable of such compassion and sympathy. I have experienced several "lively" discussions recently where men have complained that "women are trying to make men into women in this area of feelings." I understand their concern, but I believe that men have been shut down by a generational cycle of selfish detachment from feelings— a cycle that also shuts down compassion and sympathy.

Every woman's dream is a man who is not frustrated when she weeps. Every woman's fantasy is a man who can sympathize with the things that hurt her—a man who comforts her, rather than preaches at her when she is weeping. Well, I have found the perfect man of my dreams in Jesus Christ, and as my husband becomes more like Jesus, he, too, is becoming the man of my dreams.

Jesus, all God and all Man, was totally in touch with His feelings. He was capable of not only sympathy but also compassion. Jesus is described in Hebrews as a high priest who can be touched by our pain. The Greek word for "touched" actually means "be touched with a feeling of." So, Jesus, a man's Man, was comfortable with all types of feelings and human frailty. Being detached from emotions and incapable of weeping with those who weep is not Christlikeness. Being uncomfortable in the presence of weakness, lacking compassion for those who struggle is not spiritual maturity. The more a man can sympathize, the more he reflects the compassion that was in Jesus' eyes.

For we do not have a high priest who is unable to sympathize with our weaknesses (Hebrews 4:15a NIV).

REFLECTION

_____

_____

_____

_____

_____

_____

REGINA'S STORY

I was teaching a seminar for single women on "Waiting for God's Best" (now in book form as *Lady in Waiting*). One young lady held my attention throughout the time I taught—her beaming countenance was like a magnet for me. Afterward, she stood in line to speak to me, and when she introduced herself, I remarked about her gorgeous red hair and wonderful smile. She was so excited because she was coming to the town where I live to attend a local Christian college. She would be an education major, as I had been, and her zeal for the Lord reminded me of myself in college.

I saw her only a couple of times in West Palm Beach, and she always had that glow about her. I meet so many people, and I am horrible about remembering names, but Regina's name I never forgot: the redhead on fire for Jesus.

One Easter Sunday afternoon, as my brother-in-law was showing us his school annual, he became especially anxious to show us the dedication pages where the college had given a special tribute to a dear friend of our family. As he opened to the memorial page honoring Dr. Billie, across the page from her picture was a wonderful picture of Regina. I gasped in shock because the students were memorializing the death of such a soul winner—Regina. I asked Tim, "How did Regina die?"

His reply was too horrible to believe. Regina had gone bike riding. When she did not return, the search began. They found her body the next day—she had been raped, and her throat had been slit. I was so shocked that I became quite hysterical for a moment. I wept for such a tragic death of a precious redhead living for Jesus. I had to calm down because the whole family wanted to know why I was weeping so hard. They did not know that I had been blessed in meeting Regina.

As I cried off and on for three days, I kept thinking about her parents aching for their loss. On the third day, my mourning moved into deep anger that godly parents raised a daughter for God's glory but that her destiny had become rape and murder. Of course, I was also selfishly thinking about such a horrible thing ever happening to our daughter, and the angry tears just kept flowing. Then the God of all comfort turned my anger into understanding through the Book of Job. The Lord showed me that He is capable of caring for us when we face our greatest loss. He assured me that His grace can travel as deep as a Grand Canyon of grief. He also showed me that Regina's parents will be given a glimpse of Him, like Job received. A glimpse will not answer all their questions, but it will give strength and hope to keep them from becoming spiritually barren. I have heard through others that God is using her parents, who are truly fruitful and not barren.

One glimpse of Him and hope begins to heal the heart's agony.

My ears had heard of You but now my eyes have seen You (Job 42:5 NIV).

REFLECTION

_____

_____

_____

_____

_____

_____

BLOSSOMS AFTER THE STORM

When we moved into our second home, one of my first concerns was the huge number of tropical plants surrounding it. The house had won the landscaping award in a parade of homes contest. I knew that such beautiful plants do not grow without some attention and care. I was anxious because, instead of having a "green thumb," mine is black. I have single-handedly killed every living plant that I have ever been given. I took my "black thumb" to a nursery to find out the perfect fertilizer for the beautiful bird-of-paradise plants that line our entryway and the even more gorgeous white bird-of-paradise plants that grow outside the master-bath windows. The man told me what fertilizer I needed and when to apply the food to the plants. I went home feeling as though my "black thumb" had hope.

I began spreading the fertilizer and, in my enthusiasm, I put too much fertilizer on all the birds. I ended up "burning the buds" right in their stalks. I was so upset that I actually cried. These tropical plants were so special to me because they represented the first flower my son ever gave me. When Ben was only three years old, he told his dad that he had to get his mom a flower. Ken took Ben to a flower shop, and the first flower that caught Ben's eye was a beautiful bird-of-paradise.

Day after day, I had to walk past the buds burned in their stalks, and my heart just ached for the beauty that was burned by my "black thumb." How ironic to think I wanted to help the plants grow and my heavy-handed touch resulted in stunted growth! The fertilizer actually acted as a soil inhibitor. So often, good seed is kept from sprouting because of soil inhibitors. Similarly, in the lives of many people, the precious Word of God is kept from sprouting because of the soil inhibitors that are in the human heart.

Two months later, we had a tropical storm, and it rained for many hours. A few days after the storm, our daughter began to shout from the front porch. I arrived to see her pointing at a new bud. The rain had washed away the excess fertilizer, and the plant was now free to blossom. I became so excited that I jumped up and down on our porch. I started thinking about the storms of life and how they wash away the things that inhibit our growth. I have begun praying that God will send storms into the lives of people in whom I have planted the precious seed of truth. I have prayed for storms of freedom—freedom to blossom.

If you know someone in whom people have planted the "good seed" of God's Word, start praying for the soil-cleansing storm that will allow the sprouting and blossoming of the incorruptible seed.

> *Being born again, not of corruptible seed, but of incorruptible, by the word of God, which liveth and abideth for ever* (1 Peter 1:23 KJV).

REFLECTION

_____

_____

_____

_____

_____

THE GOVERNOR ON MY GAS PEDAL

One day while Rita was foil-frosting my hair in her kitchen, I was complaining about people who always want to slow me down. I told her how frustrated I get when certain individuals step in front of me just when I am ready to sprint forward. Rita said, "They are God-sent governors for your gas pedal."

I said, "What in the world is a governor for a gas pedal?" Well, I looked it up in a dictionary, which said: "a feedback device on a car or machine used to provide automatic control of speed, pressure, and temperature."

So these people whom I find irritating are sometimes God-sent devices to control the speed of my daily life. Wow! I began to wonder if I could validate such a concept scripturally. Maybe you are already thinking of some "God-placed governors" in your life. I decided to look into the lives of three Bible characters.

First, I looked at King David. Immediately I realized that Saul was not only sandpaper for David's life, but also a God-sent governor. I realized that so many of the psalms that David penned were a result of the consistent input from "governor Saul." To me, Saul appeared to be an obstacle that stood in the way of David as he made the ascent; now I see Saul as the "governor" who controlled the speed with which David ascended the throne. God knew the time it would require for David's character to be shaped into a servant-leader and shepherd of Israel. Saul was used by God to keep David from speeding to the throne prematurely.

My New Testament hero, Paul, also had a governor that he wrote about in Second Corinthians 12:7. Paul called his governor a *"thorn in the flesh."* Paul even asked God to remove the governor (thorn), but God knew that the governor was for Paul's good and His glory. Paul's giftedness, revelation, and wisdom were kept in check by this governor (thorn), lest he become absurdly conceited.

My ultimate hero, Jesus, did not need a governor, but He still submitted to earthly governors as an example for me: governors such as a limited human body, an imperfect family, very inept disciples, religious leaders, and the humiliation of the cross. Jesus took the lead example in teaching us how to submit to "governors" who seem so unreasonable.

When my parents were teens, governors were put on gas pedals so parents did not have to worry about high-speed races through town. I am grateful for a heavenly Father who knows how dangerous I would be if my life did not have some type of monitoring. I am now grateful for the "governors" God has placed in my life—people who love me but aren't as excited as I am about my plans and pursuits.

Although He was a son, He learned obedience from what He suffered (Hebrews 5:8 NIV).

REFLECTION

_____

_____

_____

_____

_____

_____

SHE HAD IT ALL

*H*ave you ever met a woman who is married to the perfect man? Maybe he looks like the perfect husband. Maybe she wants you to think he is perfect.

Have you ever met a woman with the perfect body (sigh, groan, ugh)? She never thinks it is perfect; she can readily point to her flaw(s).

Have you ever met a woman who lives in the perfect house (parade of homes winner)? I have been in several awesome houses, but the head of the manse can always show you something that needs changing or upgrading.

Well, I know a woman who was married to the perfect man (one has lived on this planet); she had the perfect body; she lived in the perfect house. Was she content with all that God gave her? *"But godliness with contentment is great gain"* (1 Tim. 6:6 NIV). Was she a classic example of the lady of contentment? No, she actually believed a lie that God had not provided for all her needs. I know you have already guessed the name of the woman I am referring to—and you are absolutely right—Eve.

Eve believed a lie concerning God's provision for all she needed as a woman. Ironically, the lie that she chose to believe cost her:

- her perfect husband
- her perfect body
- her perfect house

The descendants of Eve have often believed the lies that rob them of things more valuable than a perfect husband, a perfect body, or a perfect house. All of Eve's daughters have believed lies that have robbed them of the security of knowing that they are:

- deeply loved
- fully pleasing
- totally forgiven
- accepted and complete in Christ

(Read Robert McGee's *Search for Significance*, a must for any daughter of Eve who lacks the above security.)

Eve lost what we will never have, but we can have so much more than the liar wants us to believe. We will "lack no good thing" when we understand what it is to fear and seek the Lord.

Fear the Lord, you His saints, for those who fear Him lack nothing. The lions may grow weak and hungry, but those who seek the Lord lack no good thing (Psalm 34:9-10 NIV).

REFLECTION

_____

_____

_____

_____

_____

_____

A MAN'S TRIP THROUGH THE BIRTH CANAL

*A*part from Adam, every man enters the world through a woman's birth canal. Now that is not a brilliant revelation—but today the Lord showed me that a man enters the world of emotional freedom through the woman—like going back into the birth canal. Let me explain.

Time and time again, I have witnessed men dealing with their own stuff spiritually and emotionally (blind spots, generational cycles, hidden struggles) after their wives have already begun this process. Because men are visual, they watch what we do more than hear what we say (see 1 Pet. 3:1). When a woman stops focusing on her husband for her source of love, joy, peace, and wholeness, then her husband takes notice of her behavior toward her heavenly Husband (see Isa. 54:5).

When a woman wants her husband to be her *source* of love, joy, peace, and more, she puts immeasurable pressure on him. God never intended a man to be everything a woman needs—that is an idolatrous mentality and doesn't sit well with our heavenly Bridegroom. The more a woman discovers that Jesus is her *source*, the more she removes such pressure from her husband. Then the man can move into the birth canal for entrance into a world where he will deal with his own issues and his own baggage.

A woman is constantly looking for the best method to change her husband. All the while, her very relationship with Jesus is the most powerful method of impacting her husband. The Bible instructs a man to live with his wife with the ever-present awareness that she is a *science*. She is a "knowledge" to be studied (see 1 Pet. 3:7 KJV). A critical aspect of science is observation—as a man observes a woman dealing with "her inside stuff," he begins to get clues about the existence of "his inside stuff."

My husband is in a men's accountability group. Recently the group members discussed something they had observed as men: a woman's liberty to talk about her "inside stuff" and a man's lack of liberty to speak about his "inside stuff." The men agreed that men, in general, are only comfortable with talking about the superficial "outside stuff" (sports, hunting, business).

I have observed God both breaking and healing the wives who are married to the men in my husband's group. As each wife deals with her own stuff, there seems to be a parallel movement on the part of her husband. One by one, I have witnessed the husbands moving (though nervously) into the "birth canal," where they are being made ready for entrance into a new world, a world where they will have to deal with their "inside stuff" and learn to be more comfortable talking with other men about the "inside stuff" (see Ps. 51:6). Is the man you love in the "birth canal" yet? What is he observing in your life concerning your dealing with your "inside stuff"? Your freedom through being complete in Christ (see Col. 2:10) is a pitocin drip to bring on labor and move him into the birth canal.

If any of them do not believe the word, they may be won over without words by the behavior of their wives (1 Peter 3:1b NIV).

REFLECTION

_____

_____

_____

_____

_____

_____

FROM THE SCHOOL BUS INTO THE ARMS OF JESUS

The lump in my throat is so large that I can't swallow. The ache in my heart is so deep, I feel as though my breathing is labored. I can't get to sleep because I am so burdened for Rachel's mommy, a single parent holding three jobs in order to care for her four daughters.

Not even the president of the United States has a job as difficult as the role of a single parent. The single parent does not have a mate, a cabinet, a full office staff, or thousands of civil servants to help with the demands of life. Rachel's mom must face three jobs and the countless needs of four daughters—with very little help.

This struggling single mom was dealt a tragic blow that was felt not only by the Christian school her children attend, but also by our whole community. While parking her school bus, Rachel's mom accidentally ran over her youngest daughter. Rachel was killed instantly. When the story of this tragedy hit the local news, a gasp spread throughout the Christian community. It is incomprehensible how any parent can face the accidental death of a child. Yet, as I sit here writing after midnight, I know that as deep as the pain is, God's grace is equally as deep. I know from the testimony of other parents who have faced the tragic death of a child that the grace of God sustains where the mind and emotions cannot comprehend.

Rachel's mom used to be our children's bus driver; our daughter, Jessica, knew who Rachel was; Rachel's sister was in sixth grade with Jessica. Rachel, who was four years old, was the youngest of the four sisters. Our Jessica was so upset about this tragic death and asked so many questions that I could not answer...like the questions that run through each of our minds whenever we face a crisis or tragedy.

Jesus whispered something to me about little Rachel that comforted Jessica. I told Jessica that in a split second, Rachel went from the school bus into the arms of Jesus where she will be kept safe until her mom and sisters arrive in Heaven, *"away from the body and at home with the Lord"* (2 Cor. 5:8b NIV).

When Rachel's daddy walked out on his wife and four girls, his abandonment sent a crushing blow to their hearts. God has taken care of this family: He has been a compensatory Father to these fatherless girls. I am praying that in this most distressing circumstance, Rachel's mom will allow her faithful and dependable heavenly Husband (see Isa. 54:5) to comfort and carry her through this numbing, breathless time in her life. The community of believers is rallying around Rachel's mom and three sisters. God's comfort and love is being delivered with "flesh on it."

> *For He stands at the right hand of the needy one...* (Psalm 109:31 NIV).

REFLECTION

_____

_____

_____

_____

_____

_____

A SNARE IN MY SOUL

*R*ecently I watched a segment of a television program, 20/20, which focused on the physical hazards directly related to anger. For several years I have been aware of the damaging physical effect of anger: higher susceptibility to sickness and serious illnesses such as heart disease, cancer, ulcers, etc. Ironically, whenever you go to a doctor, he asks for information on your family's medical history: heart disease, cancer, and diabetes—but I have never seen "anger" on the medical form. My father died from congestive heart failure. I believe that the specific root of all his physical complications could be traced to the raging anger that pulsed throughout his life.

"Do not make friends with a hot-tempered man, do not associate with one easily angered, or you may learn his ways and get yourself ensnared" (Prov. 22:24-25 NIV). I never had a choice about living with a hot-tempered father. I never had a choice about associating with a huge clan of easily angered people. Attending family get-togethers was always another occasion for a big fight. One Thanksgiving, arguing broke out during dinner. One by one, my brothers and sisters (I'm the oldest of seven children) and their families began to leave. When the noise subsided, my husband was the only one remaining at the table. I grew up with the mindset that anger was an unavoidable daily reality.

When I became a Christian, I realized that I had a "snare" in my soul. I often cried and asked Jesus to remove my propensity toward anger (see Heb. 12:1). I realized that I had a choice to be angry or not—a choice to decide what I associated with anger. After years of studying and soul-searching, I am learning how to manage my propensity for anger. The Holy Spirit has taught me that I can be angry and not sin (see Eph. 4:26). Just repent and forgive before sunset! The Holy

Spirit also gives me the power to not harm myself or others with the anger I sometimes experience. *"Better a patient man than a warrior, a man who controls his temper than one who takes a city"* (Prov. 16:32 NIV). Controlling anger is not merely "pushing it underground," a process that looks like control but will allow anger to erupt later in bitterness and/or depression.

Anger has many sources; many substances fuel its fire. I was not only raised in an angry family, but I am also living in an angry nation. My heart aches for the wounded hearts hovering behind so much of the anger that I see daily. I am committed to controlling my anger by looking honestly at my own wounded heart and at the fuel such woundedness provides. As Jesus heals my wounded heart, my anger is decreasing. My soul is not so ensnared.

Too long have I lived among those who hate peace. I am a man of peace; but when I speak, they are for war (Psalm 120:6-7 NIV).

REFLECTION

_____

_____

_____

_____

_____

_____

HE CAN GIVE A SONG IN HELL

*H*ave you ever felt proud of God? Have you ever cheered for something awesome He did: "Way to go, God!" Recently, I learned about something that God did to make me so proud of the incomparable God whom I serve. A friend of ours, who went on a mission trip to the Dominican Republic with Prison Fellowship International, told us the following story.

He went to minister in a prison called "La Victoria," originally designed for 700 prisoners but now housing 4,000 men for crimes ranging from petty theft to murder. Conditions were so crowded that he literally waded through a mass of humanity. The smell was beyond the point of being overwhelming. It brought tears to his eyes, not just from the inhumanity, but also from the mixture of aromas, none of which was pleasant. The men were housed in huge, dimly lit cells that were about 20 feet by 100 feet (2,000 square feet). In each of these cells lived more than 170 men. The restroom facilities for this mass of men consisted of a small room at one end, a room with a couple of holes in the floor, and a couple of faucets. There the prisoners bathed, washed clothes, and carried out other basic necessities. Everywhere, men were cooking over primitive hot plates to supplement their daily allowance of a dime's worth of food given by the prison at the two feedings per day.

As our friend moved through this inhumane, decrepit prison, he began to hear loud a cappella singing of Christian songs. He came upon the dining hall/chapel where 300 or more men were singing songs of praise. In this horrible circumstance, God was able to develop unbridled spiritual enthusiasm in the hearts of men. When our friend preached, the men cheered for God. When he had finished preaching, the men all cried out in Spanish—a deafening unison: "Jesus Christ has set me free! Jesus Christ has set me free!"

This story just knocked my socks off. I was overwhelmed to think about singing praise in such a despicable place. I was stunned that men, while in such a dreadful prison, could declare freedom in Jesus. God was able to give hope, passion, and praise in a place as hopeless as "hell." I am so proud of my heavenly Father who can supernaturally put a song in the heart of people who live in the most putrid sewer. *"He leads forth the prisoners with singing"* (Ps. 68:6 NIV). I am so proud of my heavenly Father who can give strength and hope in the unspeakable situations of life. Our God is incomparable, and throughout the world He is proving this reality. It is my privilege to be one of His witnesses to His "numero uno" status in the universe.

Did I not proclaim this and foretell it long ago? You are My witnesses. Is there any God besides Me? No, there is no other Rock; I know not one (Isaiah 44:8 NIV).

REFLECTION

_____

_____

_____

_____

_____

_____

I Do Not Want to Be Buried With Moses

*D*o you become angry when things do not go the way you planned? Do you become frustrated when other people are upset because you cannot fix what is wrong? I used to assume that my anger was just a manifestation of the sin that so easily trips me up. Then God used a chapter in the Book of Numbers to shed some new light on my aggravation and frustration with life, circumstances, and people.

Moses and Aaron were faced with an angry crowd (more than two million strong) who were upset by a life-threatening situation: no water for so many in the middle of the desert. The people wanted Moses and Aaron to tell them what they planned to do about the need for an ocean of water in the middle of the desert. Moses and Aaron took this enormous need to God, who told them exactly what to do: *"Speak to that rock before their eyes and it will pour out its water"* (Num. 20:8 NIV).

As Moses and Aaron gathered the grumbling people in front of the rock, I believe that Moses moved from faith in God to anger with the complaining crowd. Instead of speaking to the rock, Moses struck the rock in anger (see Num. 20:11). Moses' anger with the rebellious, grumbling people robbed him of the trust that he had demonstrated in the presence of Pharaoh and at the edge of the Red Sea. God saw Moses' anger with the people as a missed opportunity to honor God in front of the people:

> *Because you did not trust in Me enough to honor Me as holy in the sight of the Israelites, you will not bring this community into the land I give them* (Numbers 20:12 NIV).

That passage just broke my heart because I am sure that Moses knew what it was to trust, but he was blinded by his anger with the people. Instead of focusing on God and the rock, Moses took his eyes off the glory of God and focused on the murmuring community he was leading. The people's problem with trusting the God of Israel became Moses' problem.

For several years, whenever I would read about Moses' anger and the consequence—not entering the Promised Land—I would grieve that my anger, like that of Moses, would cost me the "promised land." (I don't mean Heaven, but my inheritance in Jesus.) This year, when I read through this passage, I saw that Moses' anger was a symptom of his lack of trust. I would never have correlated my anger with circumstances or people as a deeper root issue: a lack of trust in a sovereign God. For years I have felt sorry for Moses because I felt that his frustration and anger with a rebellious group of people were justified. I felt that Moses was frustrated with a people who could doubt after witnessing the parting of the Red Sea.

Then God showed me that even Moses, a man of great faith (see Heb. 11:23-29), struggled with trusting God, which was manifested through his anger. Whenever I am angry, I consider not only the person or circumstance, but also the extent to which I am failing to trust God. I do not want my tombstone in Moab (see Deut. 34:1,5-6).

This is because both of you broke faith with Me in the presence of the Israelites (Deuteronomy 32:51 NIV).

REFLECTION

GET BEHIND ME, GOD

*W*ho would ever say to God, "Get behind me, please"? If any-thing, we want to be following closely behind God. Can we thrust God behind our backs? What could possibly place God behind us rather than in front of us? The key to such bizarre behavior is in the area of idolatry.

> *You have done more evil than all who lived before you. You have made for yourself other gods, idols...you have provoked Me to anger and thrust Me behind your back* (1 Kings 14:9 NIV).

Now you are breathing easier because you know you are not into the worship of idols.

Let's look a little closer at the word *idol*. The last verse in First John is a warning about Christians "keeping themselves from idols" (see 1 John 5:21). That verse has always intrigued me because I know it is not just a cultural warning for the first-century believer. I have learned that an idol is any substitute for Jesus at the center of my life. I know that an idol is anyone (or anything) from whom (or which) I try to draw love, joy, and peace.

Here's a little "check for idols" in your life. Can you think of any person or thing that has robbed you of your peace and/or joy this week? We constantly hear the remark, "_____ just ruined my whole day!" You can fill that blank in with a person's name or the name of a mate-rial possession. You may fill the blank in with your car breaking down, or a phone call from your mother-in-law. A person is an idol in your life when that person can ruin your day. A possession is an idol in your life when its damage or loss can rob you of your peace and joy.

Keeping myself from idols simply means considering the place and power that I give to certain people and things in my life. For example, if my husband can ruin my day and rob me of peace and joy—then he has moved from a mate's proper place in my life to God's place. My husband is now in front, and God is thrust behind me. When a child can ruin my day, then that child has moved from a special place in my world to the "center" of my world. That is a place for only Jesus (see 2 Kings 17:41).

My husband, my children, my mother, my mother-in-law, my ministry—and the list goes on—each of these can remain in their proper place in my life, or they can shift to God's place. Jeff VanVonderen calls this shift an "impulse toward idolatry." People and things can cause us pain, but if the pain controls us and keeps us from God's peace, then we have given this person or thing God's place in our lives.

The saddest aspect of this "impulse toward idolatry" is what we forfeit when we cling to people and things more than we cling to God. Ironically, when we are in pain, we turn to people and things to comfort us; consequently, we forfeit God's grace—our greatest comfort—which becomes sacrificed by our idolatrous choice.

Those who cling to worthless idols forfeit the grace that could be theirs (Jonah 2:8 NIV).

REFLECTION

_____
_____
_____
_____
_____
_____

EVERYTHING SAID WAS WISE AND HELPFUL

One verse made me slam on my brakes this morning. It described Samuel's verbal ministry:

> *As Samuel grew up, the Lord was with him, and everything Samuel said was wise and helpful* (1 Samuel 3:19 NLT).

What powerful six words: "Everything said was wise and helpful." This became the cry of my heart for today. What did Samuel do that made his words so effective in helping people? Jesus led me to a previous passage: *"Speak, Lord, for your servant is listening"* (1 Sam. 3:9 NIV).

In Hebrew, listening is *sama*—this refers to "undivided attention." I ponder the impact of a person giving God this kind of attention. The Holy Spirit brought to my remembrance another prophet who gave God "undivided attention."

> *The Sovereign Lord has given me an instructed tongue, to know the word that sustains the weary. He wakens me morning by morning, wakens my ear to listen [sama] like one being taught* (Isaiah 50:4 NIV).

Hooray, Isaiah knew the key to "wise and helpful words"—listening morning by morning to the Sovereign Lord's instruction. The Hebrew word for "sustain" is used only once in the Old Testament. *Sustain* means "to hasten to help support." Now it's getting intense—why? Because I know that so often Christians rush to provide answers to suffering and trials, and in their rush they offer utter nonsense to those in pain. In this light, our words are not helpful, and our words hit the ground where they rot.

First Samuel 3:19 says, *"The Lord was with Samuel as he grew up, and He let none of his words fall to the ground"* (NIV). Yikes—words that fall to the ground. What is usually on the ground? Rotting vegetation, road-kill, and trash. This question echoed in my mind: what are rotten words? What words belong in the trash rather than in a gift package sent to a suffering person?

You won't believe what the Holy Spirit showed me next:

> *Do not let any unwholesome talk come out of your mouths, but only what is helpful for building others up according to their needs, that it may benefit those who listen* (Ephesians 4:29 NIV).

Well, knock me off my chair already.

Unwholesome talk—the word for *unwholesome* in Greek means "rot/decay." Remember the words of Samuel that the Lord kept from falling to the ground. If we are to avoid *unwholesome* words pouring out of our mouths in the presence of the needy, we need to give the Lord our "undivided attention." I used to say of my son: "If I don't have his eyes (looking at mine), I don't have his ears." If our eyes are not focused on the truth of God's Word, we will be vulnerable to "rushing to say things that are not beneficial to those who are listening."

The word for "building others up" in Greek implies "spiritual profit." Is it spiritually profitable for people to hear what you are getting ready to say? What does an undivided listener have to offer a needy listener? Benefit! The word for "benefit" in Greek is *charis*, which means "grace, a gift causing delight in the recipient." Do our words cause delight in the recipient? Are they a gift to the listener? Do our words build up or tear down? The Hebrew word for "fall" (words fall to the ground) refers to "being brought down, a violent fall."

How ironic that for years I have heard youth leaders use Ephesians 4:29 to keep teens from saying "cuss words." Instead, these leaders could have challenged teens to consider that their conversations have the power to be "a gift" or to be "roadkill rot."

One last thought—Isaiah remarked about the sovereign Lord being his instructor. What is so impressive about Isaiah referring to God's sovereignty is that only a sovereign God knows what benefits the wounded heart! Without "undivided attention" on God's sovereign understanding, we are incapable of being helpful encouragers.

Timely advice is lovely, like golden apples in a silver basket (Proverbs 25:11 NLT).

REFLECTION

_____

_____

_____

_____

_____

_____

AILING HEART, ANGRY MOUTH

*H*ave you ever seen a simple discussion turn into a heated argument and said to yourself, "What was that really about?" Have you ever said something hateful, and your immediate response was, "Where did that come from?" What is fueling such harsh remarks and argumentative statements? *"For out of the overflow of the heart the mouth speaks"* (Matt. 12:34b NIV). How disappointing to realize that harsh remarks and argumentative attitudes are the "overflow" of my heart, mind, will, and emotion!

In Luke 2:50-51, Jesus made some remarks that His parents did not understand, and His mother pondered them in her heart for years. The remarks that she pondered were words of such deep wisdom that she would only comprehend them when Jesus was a man. As a child, I heard remarks that I did not understand. I, too, pondered them in my heart for years. The remarks were not full of wisdom but were very harsh and deeply painful. Now, as an adult, I understand the impact of the harsh words that I heard so regularly. My heart's overflow is too often a painful reminder of what I stored those years ago. The sarcastic and critical things I heard as a child, I kept hidden in my heart; I was often angered by what I did understand. Such anger in my young heart took root to produce a debating, argumentative teenager and young adult.

I have struggled for many years with anger and harsh remarks. Only in the last ten years have I understood the correlation of the angry remarks and an "ailing" (sick) heart. I found a verse in the Book of Job that refers to the anger that flows from an ailing heart. I looked up the Hebrew word for "ailing," and it means "pressed to pungent, to irritate."

Talk about a searchlight being turned on in my soul! Suddenly I understood the source of the angry overflow: past hurt feelings of abuse, injustice, criticism, and rejection—all of these have been pressing on my heart, and the overflow has been pungent. Years of stored feelings of pain have fermented in a very angry, sick heart. By God's grace, I have been given the strength to look at the issues that I have pondered over the years. Through forgiving so many who contributed to the "pungent overflow," my ailing heart is getting better. My angry mouth and argumentative attitude are becoming more of a distant memory than a daily occurrence.

The next time you are with an argumentative person, pray for insight into the things that have been pressing on that person's heart to cause such an angry overflow. The past is not an excuse for our present anger, but it can give us clues to deal with the pungent storage that is a constant fuel line to an angry, argumentative attitude. Knowing what is in the storage areas of one's heart allows one to confront those things that supply the crushing remarks spilling out of an ailing heart through angry lips.

What ails you that you keep on arguing? (Job 16:3b NIV)

REFLECTION

IF GOD IS FOR ME, WHO CAN BE AGAINST ME?

Have you ever been criticized so harshly that the pain knocked the breath right out of you? I lived in a household where this was a part of the daily schedule! One day a godly woman said to me, "Whenever you are criticized, consider the source and that will help you monitor your reaction." I thought a long time about the expression, "consider the source," and I became so excited about this *fact*: God, who knows me through and through, still chose me for Himself.

God's foreknowledge did not keep Him from choosing a sinner like me. Without foreknowledge, people make some serious mistakes—but God, who is all-knowing, never makes mistakes and is never caught off guard. This all-knowing God did not choose against me, but for me.

Whenever I am criticized, I first ask the Lord to show me any aspect of the criticism that may be truth, so I can repent and let Jesus transform that blind spot in my life. When the criticism contradicts something that Jesus says about me, I choose to value Jesus' opinion rather than people's opinions. Whatever people say about me, I accept but lay the comments alongside Jesus' biographical sketch of me—that is where I live, rest, and have confidence. Jesus' biographical sketch for one of His girls would read something like this:

- She is chosen and dearly loved by *Me* (see 1 Thess. 1:4; Col. 3:12).

- She is a child of *Mine*, part of My family (see Rom. 8:15-16).

- She is free to call *Me* "Daddy" (see Gal. 4:6).

- She was on *My* mind before I spoke the world into existence (see 2 Tim. 1:9).

- She is a one of a kind, custom designed by *Me* (see Eph. 2:10).

- She is getting better with every passing moment (see 2 Cor. 5:17).

- She is part of a royal calling and responsibility (see 1 Pet. 2:9-10).

- She is an heir of an unshakable kingdom (see Gal. 4:6-7; Heb. 12:28).

- She is aware of her enemy, but is dauntless (see 1 Pet. 5:8).

The next time someone speaks to you in a harsh and critical manner, just pause and think: *Excuse me, do you know with whom you are speaking?* That thought always puts a smile on my face, which puzzles the one who would slay me verbally.

Why do we continue to allow people's rejection to control us more than the acceptance that we have received from God Almighty through Jesus?

In face of all this, what is there left to say? If God is for us, who can be against us? (Romans 8:31 PNT).

REFLECTION

ARE YOU FIGHTING SOMEONE ELSE'S BATTLE?

*H*ow often I have fallen into bed totally exhausted by a day full of so many demands, so many voices, and so many needy people! Too often I have been drained because I fought battles that were not mine. I had listened to a voice full of pain and assumed that I needed to do something. I had heard about a crisis situation and immediately considered how I would squeeze this need into my full schedule. Because of my tendency to fall prey to the "messiah complex," I have too often charged into a battle that was not even in my territory.

This tendency is not necessarily a lack of spirituality; one of the greatest kings of Judah died because he rushed out to fight a battle that was not his. It is said of King Josiah: "As long as he lived, [he] did not fail to follow the Lord" (see 2 Chron. 34:2,33). So when he charged into battle against the king of Egypt, Josiah was a righteous king. Yet, his spirituality did not keep him from the deception of a stubborn "messiah complex." King Neco sent a messenger to tell Josiah that this was not a battle between King Neco and King Josiah—who totally disregarded the warning, disguised himself, and charged into battle where he was mortally wounded.

Josiah used a disguise to get into someone else's battle. I, too, have used several disguises to "justify" my involvement in conflicts that are not mine. Maybe you have some of the same disguises in your closet:

- "Selfless Caring Christian"
- "Sensitive Servant"
- "Sacrificing Saint"
- "Sincere Counselor"

* "Strong Rescuer"

These names are sometimes disguises for an exhausted approval addict who is trapped into performing by spiritual peer pressure. Often I have felt that because the need was presented to me, it was an automatic "go" for me to jump into my chariot and charge forth to do battle for God. When I am fighting a battle that is not mine, I, like Josiah, will be wounded by arrows not intended for me. Fighting battles that are not mine is like being a masochist—wounding myself through stubborn over-involvement.

Lord, I do not want to die prematurely (ministry-wise through burnout) from engaging in battles that are not mine! Help me to judge each demand, each cry for help, and each desperate need on the basis of whether or not it is part of Your "yoke" that is easy and Your "burden" that is light.

After all this, when Josiah had set the temple in order, Neco king of Egypt went up to fight at Carchemish on the Euphrates, and Josiah marched out to meet him in battle. But Neco sent messengers to him, saying, "What quarrel is there between you and me, O king of Judah?" (2 Chronicles 35:20-21a NIV).

REFLECTION

_____

_____

_____

_____

_____

_____

A WORSHIPER SEDUCED

*A*groundbreaking book has raised my antennae about a believer's capacity for seduction. The book is Beth Moore's *When Godly People Do Ungodly Things: Arming Yourself in the Age of Seduction.*

This morning while studying, I came across a passage that just shouted "seduction alert!" The passage is Numbers 3:4a (NLT):

> *But Nadab and Abihu died in the Lord's presence in the wilderness of Sinai when they burned before the Lord the wrong different kind of fire, different than He had commanded.*

This is a familiar story to many, but its significance might escape the reader. I was inspired to look up the names *Nadab* and *Abihu* in Hebrew. It is breathtaking how the meanings of names illuminate and unveil the rich message within a passage of Scripture. *Nadab* means "spontaneous volunteer." *Abihu* means "worshiper of God."

Here you have Nadab, a "hand-waving, pick-me, enthusiastic volunteer" and his brother Abihu, the "God worshiper." However, they died because they disobeyed God. How do such prime candidates for the priesthood make such a foolish choice? Just like Eve (see 2 Cor. 11:3), they were seduced by the dragon of all lies. This fire-breathing evil one is prowling our earth with the intent to exact revenge on God by wreaking havoc on His children.

My burden today is that I will never think for one moment that I have immunization against making a foolish, costly choice (see 1 Cor. 10:12). I have been an "enthusiastic, spontaneous volunteer" since I met Jesus, and I am reminded of the price tag of disobedience. I am even more sensitive to the subtle seduction that can enter the life of a spontaneous volunteer and worshiper of God. My heart's cry for myself and for you is that we would finish well the race set before us and that not one of us would become a statistical casualty.

> *Therefore I do not run like a man running aimlessly; I do not fight like a man beating the air. No, I beat my body and make it my slave so that after I have preached to others, I myself will not be disqualified for the prize* (1 Corinthians 9:26-27 NIV).

REFLECTION

_____

_____

_____

_____

_____

_____

RELYING ON A PIERCING SPLINTER

When you are hit with a tragedy/disappointment, who do you call first? Do you call your husband, or maybe your mom, or even your prayer partner? I call all three—they are like a human trinity to me. It is wonderful to have people who love you and will stand by you in a crisis. The limitation of this earthly trinity is captured in a phrase my first pastor used to say to us, "Rely upon people, and you can only get what people have to give. Rely upon God, and you get all He has to give." My earthly trinity becomes a *piercing splinter* when I rely totally upon it and neglect my heavenly Trinity.

Israel had the support of the heavenly Commander-in-Chief, but would often turn to earthly generals for necessary support.

> *Look now, you are depending on Egypt, that splintered reed of a staff, which pierces a man's hand and wounds him if he leans on it! Such is Pharaoh king of Egypt to all who depend on him* (Isaiah 36:6 NIV).

The armies of Egypt were awesome and intimidating and would appear strong and reliable to the naked eye. God refers to this army as a "reed and piercing splinter."

God knows that the earthly people and things that we rely upon ultimately wound us. God has known for years how much I want to totally rely upon Him, so He has permitted several difficult circumstances to invade my life and test whom I would rely upon—the strong arm of my earthly trinity or the omnipotent arm of my heavenly Trinity.

I can look back over the years and see the people upon whom I would rely totally rather than Jesus. Very often these people are a reminder to me of my disobedience of trusting people more than God. Israel had this reminder in the very nation of Egypt: *"Egypt will no longer be a source of confidence for the people of Israel but will be a reminder of their sin in turning to her for help"* (Ezek. 29:16a NIV). Just think: Egypt, a nation once giving Israel confidence when they were allies, eventually became a memorial to Israel's disobedience. At one time Egypt put a cocky grin of confidence on Israel's face; then she put on a face of shame.

The next time you face a crisis, consider carefully upon whom you are going to rely—the piercing splinter of people or the *One who was pierced* so that you and I can rely on Him. Relying on Jesus turns me toward Him; relying on people turns me away from Him.

> *Cursed is the one who trusts in man, who depends on flesh for his strength and whose heart turns away from the Lord. He will be like a bush in the wastelands; he will not see prosperity when it comes. He will dwell in the parched places of the desert, in a salt land where no one lives* (Jeremiah 17:5-6 NIV).

REFLECTION

_____

_____

_____

_____

_____

_____

THE ABUNDANTLY
BLESSED WRESTLER

Who is the abundantly blessed wrestler?

Many of you would immediately think of Jacob wrestling with God in Gen. 32:28: *"Your name will no longer be Jacob, but Israel, because you have struggled with God and with men and have overcome"* (NIV). Jacob was blessed after struggling and wrestling with God and man.

Have you been struggling with God or men recently? I have. This morning in Deuteronomy 33:23 (NLT) I found a nugget that I couldn't wait to research and then share with those I love. *"Moses said this about the tribe of Naphtali: 'Oh Naphtali, you are rich in favor and full of the Lord's blessings; may you possess the west and the south.'"* Immediately I wondered: "Why was Naphtali so rich in favor and full of blessings?"

Here are the Hebrew interpretations:

- "Rich in favor" means that a superior is gracious and kind in reacting to an inferior; the superior is taking delight and pleasure in this servant!

- "Full of the Lord's blessings" means the completion of something that was unfinished and the filling of something that was empty.

Do you need the completion of something that is unfinished?

Do you need the filling of something that is empty?

Now prepare for takeoff!

Naphtali means "wrestling and struggling." If you've been struggling and wrestling, you are a likely candidate for God's favor and full blessing of completion of what is yet unfinished in your life. The struggle is part of the path to completion. The wrestling match does not mean you have missed the blessing; the wrestling match is an aspect *of* the blessing—like a frame around a masterpiece.

Like Jacob and Naphtali—to wrestle with God or men or circumstances is a blessed wrestling event. It's a time when you and I remember that our superior, incomparable God is pleased with us in Christ and He is going to complete the good work He has begun in each of us. God is going to use our wrestling and struggling to continue to sanctify us through and through.

For our struggle is not against flesh and blood, but against the rulers, against the authorities, against the powers of this dark world and against the spiritual forces of evil in the heavenly realms. (Ephesians 6:12 NIV).

REFLECTION

NO ACCELERATED
GROWTH COURSES

When I was young, I wanted results without having to sweat. Can't I just take a pill to change? I wanted to learn in a week what others had learned in a lifetime. I was sure that I could take some accelerated course for spiritual growth. I understood that salvation cost me nothing and discipleship would cost me everything. But I was convinced (proof of my immaturity) that I could appropriate the wisdom of the ancients without having some wrinkles and gray hair. I even found a verse to support my naïve thinking: *"I understand more than the ancients, because I keep Thy precepts"* (Ps. 119:100 KJV). Too often for me, "Ps." did not stand for the Psalms but for a "pretty silly" child of God.

Then I discovered that my desire for:

- "a quick fix"
- "an instant spiritual depth"
- "an accelerated growth process"

…was a typical sign not only of being immature, but also of being *human*.

In Jeremiah chapters 28 and 29, the Jews were in exile among the Babylonians, and they wanted to know how long their lesson was going to take. A false prophet, Hananiah, told the people that God was going to break this yoke in two years (see Jer. 28:11). The people were pleased with his false prophecy because they were in a hurry to return to their homeland. The people couldn't bear the thought of prolonged captivity, so they were open to any quick fix for their struggle.

When Jeremiah prophesied that their learning process or discipline was going to take 70 years (see Jer. 29:10), can you guess whom they wanted to believe? Ironically, one of the most popular verses in Jeremiah follows the verse declaring that the people would be part of a 70-year growth process. God's promises are for us whether we are in captivity or the "promised land." Growing spiritually is a lifelong process. God's hope and peace are not only available when we are grown, but also for the entire growth process.

Are you tempted to want to believe a "Hananiah" concerning an accelerated escape from frustrating spiritual immaturity? Or do you know that spiritual growth is a lifetime process that climaxes in Heaven? That is why it is called the "Christian life" rather than the "Christian day" or the "Christian moment."

In high school I ran away to a commune in Fresno, California, in search of this "accelerated spiritual depth," and all I received were hysterical parents and a visit from the police. The next time someone tells you about a program/formula for "accelerated spiritual growth," just say, "No thank you, Hananiah."

The reply to you will be: "Who?"

And you can respond, "Oh, it's an inside joke!"

> *"For I know the plans I have for you," declares the Lord, "plans to prosper you and not to harm you, plans to give you hope and a future"* (Jeremiah 29:11 NIV).

REFLECTION

_____

_____

_____

_____

_____

_____

SINNING IN THE FACE
OF GOD'S GOODNESS

*B*ecause of the spiritual abuse that takes place in Christian circles, I sometimes hesitate to share what I have learned from God's Word because I do not want to wound the brokenhearted with strong teachings that may feel abrasive. Now that I have expressed my reservation, I want to share what Jesus showed me on June 20, 1993.

As I was reading Second Samuel, I came upon the passage that records Nathan's confrontation of David's sins of adultery and murder (see 2 Sam. 12). Through the prophet, God asked David how he could sin in the face of His goodness:

> *I gave your master's house to you, and your master's wives into your arms. I gave you the house of Israel and Judah. And if all this had been too little, I would have given you even more* (2 Samuel 12:8 NIV).

How much more could God have given David to keep him from sinning against Him? How much more could God have given Adam and Eve to keep them from sinning in the face of His goodness?

As I grieved about the freedom that God's kids feel while they sin in the face of His goodness, God reminded me of one of His children who actually resisted sexual temptation by using the goodness of God as an effective chastity belt. Joseph resisted Potiphar's wife's charming seduction by referring to the incomprehensible choice of sinning against a God who had been so good to him (see Gen. 39). Ironically, Joseph resisted the sin of adultery and found himself in prison. David surrendered to the sin of adultery and continued to live in the palace. Of course, both men ultimately reaped what they sowed—Joseph went from prison to the palace, and David was driven from the palace by his own son, Absalom.

Ultimately, God saw David's sin as despising Him and His Word (see 2 Sam. 12:8-9). *Despising* seems so strong a term, but I decided that, within the context of God's abundant blessings on David, to sin in the face of such abundance is to choose to despise the Giver. God's goodness should be an impetus for obedience, not a permissive gesture to indulge oneself. How amazing to think that God's goodness is further manifested as He forgives the one who repents of despising God's Word and Person (see Ps. 51)!

Joseph resisted adultery in the context of God's goodness; David committed adultery in the context of God's goodness. The choice is ours daily. May we follow Joseph's example of resisting sin because of the context of God's goodness to us.

> *No one is greater in this house than I am. My master has withheld nothing from me except you, because you are his wife. How then could I do such a wicked thing and sin against God?* (Genesis 39:9 NIV).

REFLECTION

_____

_____

_____

_____

_____

_____

MINING FOR CONCEALED JEWELS

I was talking on the telephone with the wife of a retired ball-player. She remarked about my knowledge of the Old Testament and said the Old Testament has always been a place where one could get too easily bogged down. So she avoided it and remained in the New Testament. My first mentor taught me that I would only understand the New Testament when I had learned the Old Testament, especially the first five books (The Pentateuch). As a teenager, I studied the Old Testament with adults who were sometimes twice my age. I loved the New Testament and couldn't bear the thought that I was merely skimming the truth because I didn't know the Old Testament.

An even more powerful impetus for learning the Old Testament came when I read what the apostle Paul considered a bonus for the believer—words hidden in the Old Testament: *"For all those words which were written long ago are meant to teach us today...that we may be encouraged to go on hoping in our own time"* (Rom. 15:4 PNT). God is able to inspire men and women to endure the most horrible circumstances. He can give encouragement during the darkest hour—He pumps this inspiration into our souls through the many lines written so long ago. To neglect the Old Testament is to neglect the bonus of encouragement, endurance, and loyalty that our Christian life requires in such a cynical, painful world.

One of the biggest bonuses I have gained by reading the Old Testament is finding out that the troubling things I see human beings doing are not new for this generation. The self-consumptive American way is not new, any more than the homosexual movement is; *"there is nothing new under the sun"* (Eccles. 1:9). Since the beginning of time, men have done what was right in their own eyes (see Judg. 21:25 KJV), regardless of the consequences.

I have a friend who stopped at one of those "tourist mining areas." For 15 dollars she was able to go mining for a stone. She left with an eight-carat pink stone that she figured must be worth at least the 15 dollar admission fee. She discovered through a jeweler that her stone was worth 800 dollars. She was thrilled to mine for a precious stone whose value was concealed to both the owner of the mine and the one mining. Her experience in that California mining site parallels the success one can have when one goes digging around in the Old Testament. The Old Testament is not only a gold mine, but also a deep shaft full of many precious stones. Are you searching for comfort, hope, wisdom, truth, direction, and encouragement? These, and more, are waiting for you to search and discover what the glory of God has concealed—concealed only to those who have not ever tried mining for these jewels. Just as man has mined for wealth, we as believers can mine for eternal riches that are ours.

It is the glory of God to conceal a matter; to search out a matter is the glory of kings (Proverbs 25:2 NIV).

REFLECTION

"GOOD" BAD EXAMPLES

We are told that if we do not learn from history, we may repeat it. I have always been receptive to learning from history, especially from the many "good" bad examples. I have witnessed several parents' mistakes that have resulted in much pain for their children. These "good" bad examples have been a good guide for me as a mother. I have also seen the mistakes made by many married couples, and their bad examples have been good for me as a willing learner who wants a marriage that will go the distance.

Since there is nothing new under the sun (see Eccles. 1:9), and we always reap what we sow even under grace—then why are we not learning from so many of the "good" bad examples in the Word? I believe that God allowed the mistakes of men to be recorded to give us a warning—to help us learn from these "good" bad examples that are grace to us.

> *Now in these events our ancestors stand as examples to us, warning us not to crave after evil things as they did. Nor are you to worship false gods as they did.... Now these things which happened to our ancestors are illustrations of the way in which God works, and they were written down to be a warning to us who are heirs of the ages which have gone before us* (1 Corinthians 10:6-11 PNT).

One of my biblical ancestors has been a very "good" bad example. The consequences he faced after his devastating choice have been a most potent warning to me as a wife, mother, and woman after God's own heart. David made a choice to commit adultery and murder; his children paid for the consequences of his sin. There were times in the early years of my marriage when it might have seemed easier to quit and leave my husband, but David's "good" bad example was a warning that was ever present in my mind. I knew that committing adultery carries too high a price tag—whether you are a king or a mere maid.

I know a parent who made the choice that David did with Bathsheba. When I was counseling his daughter at youth camp and discovered that she had just been raped, I wept hard. She made me think of the rape of David's daughter, Tamar—who had been a virgin until she was raped, just like this teenager I was counseling. Even though people would deny any correlation between a father's choice and a child's suffering, I have never forgotten that moment with that teenage girl. Whenever I read about the rape of Tamar, I always think of the father she had and the choices he made that cost her virginity.

That story is so painful, yet I think the consequences of sinning against the light that many of us have been given is a grave reality that we often want to cover up and psychoanalyze away. I believe that disregarding the many warnings we have been given through "good" bad examples is like the illusion that we can sow but not reap because God's grace will abort any consequences (see Gal. 6:7).

I applied my heart to what I observed and learned a lesson from what I saw (Proverbs 24:32 NIV).

REFLECTION

THE PROSPERITY OF THE WICKED—A MIRAGE

One of the most awesome music directors who ever lived became captivated by an illusion, and this mirage resulted in a cynical attitude. I am referring to Asaph, who was appointed chief of the choir (see 1 Chron. 15:16-17). As a leader in worship and praise, he was not immune to being distracted by those who had a great deal of this life in their hands. (Of course, he did not notice that they had nothing of the other life in their hearts.) Asaph became captivated by the illusion that the wicked seem to prosper more than the righteous. Remember, a mirage is a distortion of light, and Asaph's eyes were focused on a serious distortion. Notice some of the aspects of this mirage, which he wrote about in Psalm 73. He resented these apparent blessings on the wicked:

- Beautiful bodies (verse 4)—they always have the best bodies and the most elaborate wardrobe.

- Immune to sickness (verse 5)—they always seem healthy and in peak physical condition.

- Opulent necklaces of pride (verses 6-7)—they seem to have no limit to their pride and conceit.

- Claim real estate even in Heaven (verses 8-9)—they can sound as religious as the guy next door.

- Irresistible charm and charisma (verse 10)—they can wow any audience.

- No fear of God (verse 11)—they are not anxious about their spiritual condition.

- Carefree and wealthy (verse 12)—they do not seemingly have a care in the world.

This list could breed jealousy in any warm-blooded human being. All these qualities of the mirage became oppressive to Asaph as he focused his attention on them. God allowed Asaph to "drool" for a while. Then God mercifully opened Asaph's eyes during an awesome quiet time with Him. Quiet times are great opportunities for God to draw attention to the drool that is escaping through the right side of our gaping mouths.

Job gave a powerful drool warning (see Job 24:22-24). King David also understood the tendency to drool in the presence of prosperity, and he said, *"Do not be overawed when a man grows rich, when the splendor of his house increases; for he will take nothing with him"* (Ps. 49:16-17 NIV). David also knew that prosperity was not proof of God's blessing. For example, Joseph resisted sexual temptation and ended up in prison; David yielded to sexual temptation and continued living in his palace. Too often, Christians mistake material blessings as approval from God. May we stop drooling, adjust our vision, acknowledge the mirage, and proceed toward lasting riches—life in Christ.

When I tried to understand all this, it was oppressive to me till I entered the sanctuary of God; then I understood their final destiny (Psalm 73:16-17 NIV).

REFLECTION

_____

_____

_____

_____

_____

_____

SECURITY FOR OUR CHILDREN

Today at lunch, the vice president of a huge corporation in Atlanta mentioned that he has a neighbor who is a doctor, and two of his sons have committed suicide. They lived in the lap of luxury, and death was more appealing than life. Later in the day, I was driving our daughter to gymnastics, and out of the blue, she said, "Sara's (a fellow student at her school) cousin committed suicide yesterday. She was only fifteen years old." A young teenage girl, from a freshly broken home, decided that death was better than life. I started to cry. Jessica said, "Mom, why are you crying? You didn't even know Sara's cousin."

I said to Jessica, "I am crying because my heart is hurt by the things that hurt the heart of God, and I know that God's heart grieves for those who choose death rather than life." I know teen suicides are a constant reality, but my heart grieves for these teens who are too often victims of homes where there was no security for them.

Where was the fortress these teens needed? Where was their place of refuge to give them the ultimate refuge? Whatever these teens turned to for security and significance must have collapsed, and they decided that death was better than life. The security and significance that the world offers teens is like a "spider web," and it cannot support life.

The Word of God clearly states that we can offer our children a secure fortress and refuge. *"He who fears the Lord has a secure fortress, and for his children it will be a refuge"* (Prov. 14:26 NIV). Consider the blueprints of this security system:

- My fear of the Lord…good for my children

- My zeal for the Lord…good for my children

- My trust in the Lord…good for my children

- My tears before the Lord...good for my children
- My struggles before the Lord...good for my children
- My love for the Lord...good for my children

When my children see where I turn when I am in need of security and significance, this fortress for me will become a refuge for them. My fear and love for the Lord is the greatest security that I could ever offer our children.

They will be My people, and I will be their God. I will give them singleness of heart and action, so that they will always fear Me for their own good and the good of their children after them (Jeremiah 32:38-39 NIV).

REFLECTION

_____

_____

_____

_____

_____

_____

TOOTHPICKS IN EYEBALLS

W hat a gory topic! What could I possibly be referring to? This topic refers to the pain people inflict upon themselves when they disobey an ancient principle:

> *But if you turn away and ally yourselves with the survivors of these nations that remain among you and if you intermarry with them and associate with them, then you may be sure...they will become snares and traps for you, whips on your backs and thorns in your eyes* (Joshua 23:12-13 NIV).

As a new Christian, I was taught this ancient principle by one of my spiritual mentors. The principle was simple: Do not date nonbelievers. I have given this same counsel to many teenage girls and single women throughout the last two decades. This counsel is not from a backwoods, legalistic mentality; it is one of the oldest principles for a *"holy race"* (see Ezra 9:2).

Even though this principle is clearly stated in both the Old and New Testaments, I continue to meet women (young and not so young) who think it is a rule created by religion and not a principle instituted by a loving heavenly Father. I know so many unhappy women who are married to nonbelievers. Time and time again, they admit that they had disregarded this biblical principle when they were dating. In disregarding the principle, these women inflicted whips, snares, and thorns on themselves—masochistic behavior. When a person knowingly disregards any biblical injunction, it will result in self-injury. God's principles are for our protection, but it takes faith to believe that God is not a killjoy.

I always ask women who are married to nonbelievers if anyone warned them about their choice to date and eventually marry a nonbeliever.

Often they say, "No one challenged or even warned me about dating a man who didn't know Jesus personally." I am concerned that those of us who know the Lord intimately would have the courage of a Micaiah (see 2 Chron. 18). Micaiah would tell the truth even if the person ended up hating him for what he said. We need courage to speak the truth to any teenage girl or single woman who is considering dating a nonbeliever—warn her about the inevitable pain of "toothpicks in her eyes." I would rather make a gal miserable for a little while by telling her the truth than have her spend years in a miserable marriage because I didn't have a "Micaiah spirit" when it came to telling the truth.

When the great leader, Ezra, was informed about God's children intermarrying with an unholy race, his response was brutal. He tore his clothing, tore hair out of his head and beard (ouch!)—he cried and wept before the Lord. Ezra was appalled that a child of God would carelessly choose to "mingle the holy with the unholy." I, too, have grieved with women who have made this choice, but I also grieve for the casual attitude that too many women take toward a friend or an acquaintance who is dating an unbeliever (see Ezra 9:2). We cannot keep a woman/gal from disobeying God, but we can at least warn her about such masochistic behavior on her part.

Do not be yoked together with unbelievers (2 Corinthians 6:14a NIV).

REFLECTION

Story 66

GET YOUR OWN
MARCHING ORDERS

Once, while speaking at a singles' conference in central Florida, I heard a dramatic story of reconciliation between a daughter and her alcoholic father. When I asked details about this wonderful reconciliation, the woman (also a speaker at the conference) encouraged me to go home and "do thou likewise." I did not have an alcoholic father, but I did have a father who abused seven children. Challenged by this woman's story, I returned home with her "marching orders for 'daughter-father reconciliation.'" Well, to make a long story short, my attempt was not only futile but also nearly fatal emotionally. My attempt backfired violently, and it took me a long time to recover.

The Lord took the pain I experienced from using someone else's marching orders to teach me a very deep spiritual truth. God's ways are not a standard recipe to be duplicated by everyone. God's ways are unique and specific. What He does in one circumstance does not necessarily predict what He will do in a similar situation. God will not be boxed in by presumptuous thinking—that we can second-guess His tactics. The prophet Isaiah warned us about such presumptuous thinking (see Isa. 55:8).

King David demonstrated in Second Samuel 5:17-25 that each battle requires a separate and specific set of marching orders. In this chapter, the Philistines attacked at two different times. Even though it was the same enemy, David inquired of the Lord about the strategy he should use on each occasion. Ironically, David could have relied on his great past experience or on former marching orders, but he wisely sought God's specific marching orders for each separate time the enemy attacked. If you read this chapter, you will see that the strategy was different, even though it was the same group attacking in the same valley.

Why such a variety of marching orders? I believe it is all part of our Father's desire that we come individually to Him in our time of need. I believe that He knows that we will never learn to depend upon Him if we can find a "pre-packed, pre-digested, pre-mixed" version of intimacy with God. Of course, the Father knows how complex and subject to deception the human heart is; each emotional battlefield requires very specific "marching orders."

Please do not send people into battle with your marching orders. The next time you go into battle, check your marching orders and make sure the name stamped on them is yours and that the stamp on them is "present tense."

> *For My thoughts are not your thoughts, neither are your ways My ways* (Isaiah 55:8 NIV).

REFLECTION

_____

_____

_____

_____

_____

_____

THE BEST MEAL YOU'VE EVER MISSED

A couple who is close to us decided to fast and pray to decide whether the wife should go back to school. They chose Monday as the designated day to seek the Lord concerning the need of 8,000 dollars for the wife to finish her college degree. They had not told anyone about their financial needs for Stephanie's schooling. The next day, the husband's mom called and proceeded to tell her son that she and his step-father had decided on *Monday* to help with the college tuition expense. They offered to pay the full amount. Now, I do not see fasting as a "magic formula" or a "fluffy rabbit's foot," but I do believe that it is a wonderful discipline neglected by the saints of God. Let me try to explain.

One day Jesus was challenged by the "religious elite" concerning the fact that His disciples did not fast. Jesus' defense was that His disciples are not to mourn (fast) when the Bridegroom is present, *but* they will fast when the Bridegroom is taken (see Luke 5:33-34). When I read this passage, the words of Jesus grabbed my heart and I began to search the Old and New Testaments concerning the practice of fasting. Jesus, my heavenly Bridegroom, is gone, and He said that *I would fast.*

I discovered occasions for fasting, what to do while fasting, the conditions of fasting, and those who fast. This was an extensive study, and I invite you to also get a concordance and discover the best meal you have ever missed.

I could literally write a book on the results of fasting. I have a fasting journal to record my prayer requests and the truths that God shows me from His Word on the day of fasting. I have fasted with my prayer partner on a weekly basis, and now my husband and I are fasting together regularly.

Are you a potential member of "who's who in fasting"? Here are some of our members:

- Disciples (see Matt. 9:14-15)
- Widows (see Luke 2:36-38)
- Truth seekers (see Acts 10:30-31 KJV)
- Kings, queens, warriors, prophets, ambassadors, even children (see 2 Chron. 20:3)

Pass me my fruit juice, my Bible, and my fasting journal...why don't you join me?

> *Then John's disciples came and asked him, "How is it that we and the Pharisees fast, but your disciples do not fast?" Jesus answered, "How can the guests of the bridegroom mourn while he is with them? The time will come when the bridegroom will be taken from them; then they will fast"* (Matthew 9:14-15 NIV).

REFLECTION

_____

_____

_____

_____

_____

_____

_____

OUTWITTED THROUGH UNFORGIVENESS

Are you ever aggravated when someone cleverly outwits you? Don't you just hate when you discover that you fell for a scam? I was outwitted by an easy-going, smooth-talking police officer in Kentucky as he took 90 minutes to write up a report on a very minor accident. The outwitting continued as I talked to the insurance agent who tried to place blame where it did not belong. Well, the outwitting ended when my husband entered the picture. He challenged the one trying to outwit (intimidate) me. When Ken was finished, we received a written apology from the insurance company with the assurance that our premiums would not be affected. Ken boldly challenged the insurance company concerning their efficiency in securing the truth about the accident. (They were drawing conclusions without having consulted the witnesses.)

My heavenly Husband is ready to help whenever I am being outwitted by the father of lies (see John 8:44). The outwitting ends when the lie is exposed and confronted with the Truth. For longer than I would like to admit, satan has outwitted me in the area of "unforgiveness." I had assumed that I had really forgiven a particular person because I was not trying to get revenge for the hateful things she had done. One day a young pastor's wife asked me why I did not like this particular person, and I said, "What do you mean?"

And she said, "You are always full of compliments, but you are dead silent whenever her name is mentioned." Well, I had assumed that silence was better than slander, and it was. But I still was harboring hurt feelings mingled with anger. Satan outwits me when I use "excuses" for my unforgiveness:

- Why forgive her? She'll only do it again!

- Why forgive him? He doesn't care how much I've been hurt!
- Why forgive her? I know she'll hurt me again!
- Why forgive him? He'll never say he's sorry!
- Why forgive her? She knows better than to do such a thing!

Then my wonderful heavenly Mate reminds me that unforgiveness hurts me more than it does the one I am not forgiving. When I am unforgiving, I don't even want to pray for the capacity to love this person; I'd rather ignore her. Wow, talk about being outwitted with such unloving reasoning! I have defended my unforgiveness, but I have never won in the "courts of truth." In fact, I was found guilty one day when I read Paul's strong warning to the immature saints at Corinth. Paul understood satan's greatest device—to keep the forgiven ones from forgiving. Satan wants us to live in the condition he lives in daily—"unforgiven and unforgiving." For me to believe it is acceptable to be unforgiving when I have been so forgiven, this is the ultimate outwitting. I am most like Jesus, not when I am perfect, but when I am forgiving.

And what I have forgiven—if there was anything to forgive—I have forgiven in the sight of Christ for your sake, in order that Satan might not outwit us. For we are not unaware of his schemes (2 Corinthians 2:10b-11 NIV).

REFLECTION

_____

_____

_____

_____

_____

_____

_____

THE BRIDE BELONGS TO THE BRIDEGROOM

or almost 30 years, I have been involved in serving the Lord. My ministry has been in the local church and also in para-church ministries. The more involved I have been, the more acquainted I have become with the grief of seeing men and women in places of leadership abuse their privileged positions and neglect the legitimate needs of God's people. After years of witnessing firsthand many incidences of spiritual abuse in churches and ministries, a root of bitterness had taken hold of my heart. As this root continued to grow, I never noticed the extent of the root system in my heart because I was always consoling myself with the parallel grief that Jeremiah, the prophet, wrote about in relation to shepherds (leaders) who do not feed their sheep (people).

One passage that painfully paralleled the biographical sketch of some pastors and ministry leaders I knew was the following:

> *The shepherds are senseless and do not inquire of the Lord; so they do not prosper and all their flock is scattered* (Jeremiah 10:21 NIV).

As I watched the scattering of sheep being driven away by senseless shepherds, I became more and more bitter. Then the God of all mercy and compassion sent a humble preacher to my home one day in August. I was sharing with him my grief and anger with certain spiritual leaders. He listened patiently, and then he asked, "Do you have any oil?"

My remark was, "Sure, I have some Puritan oil."

I asked him what he needed it for, and he said, "I want to pray for the sick."

My spiritual mentor had come with him, and I looked at her and said, "Is Mamie sick? Are we going to pray for her?"

And he said, "No, Jackie, you are sick!" I was embarrassed, yet I knew he was right. As he and my mentor anointed me with oil and began to pray for the uprooting of my bitterness, my heart broke, and I began to confess my anger and rage for the abuse I had seen in the church and ministry. When our time of prayer was over, I felt as though I had vomited much of the toxin I had ingested. Pastor Lamb (that is really his name) told me that God would affirm the healing of my bitter heart.

The Lord knows that I always want my experiences to submit to the Word of God, and so He graciously showed me that the Bride belongs to the Bridegroom. He showed me that the Church—His Bride—is ultimately in the capable hands of her heavenly Bridegroom. He kindly, not harshly, reminded me that He is the Head of the Body of Christ. No matter how sick the body seems, the Head is not spinning out of control. Jesus also showed me that as Head of the Body of Christ, He will accomplish the work He intends even within a Body that daily struggles with chronic pain and dysfunction.

The bride belongs to the bridegroom (John 3:29a NIV).

REFLECTION

BE CAREFUL WHAT YOU PRAY FOR

I have always been impressed with Hezekiah's prayer life. When he received a life-threatening letter from Sennacherib, instead of panicking, he went into the temple and spread the letter before the Lord. Then he spread himself out before the Lord in prayer. The Lord's answer to Hezekiah's prayer is recorded in Second Kings 19 and Second Chronicles 32. Talk about a heavenly terminator! The angel God sent annihilated all the fighting men, leaders, and officers under Sennacherib. Great answer to prayer! Quite impressive!

Sometime later, King Hezekiah became ill, and the prophet Isaiah told him to get his house in order because he was going to die. Hezekiah knew firsthand about answered prayer, so he turned his face to the wall, wept bitterly, and begged the Lord to heal him. Another impressive answer to prayer: Isaiah had not even left the palace when the Lord spoke to him and told him to go back and tell Hezekiah that he would be healed—and God was going to give him 15 additional years (see 2 Kings 20:5-6).

Now, I have always been impressed with the 15 additional years aspect of this answered prayer *until* a few summers ago when I was doing thorough research on the kings of Israel and Judah. Why I never noticed this before I do not know, but I just about flipped when I read Second Kings 21. I realized that during the 15 additional years of Hezekiah's life, a child arrived who did great evil. This evil person was Manasseh, born to Hezekiah during the 15 additional years he was given in answer to his bitter crying. Hezekiah's tears and prayers granted a life extension that gave birth to an evil offspring and heir. That child inherited his father's throne and rebuilt all the altars that his father had torn down, resurrecting all the offensive high places that his father had removed: *"Moreover,*

Manasseh also shed so much innocent blood that he filled Jerusalem from end to end" (2 Kings 21:16 NIV).

Let Hezekiah's example challenge each of us to be careful what we cry and weep for. Rather than crying for our will, maybe we should copy the tears of another One who wept in prayer and follow His example rather than Hezekiah's:

Father, if You are willing, take this cup from Me; yet not My will, but Yours be done (Luke 22:42 NIV).

REFLECTION

_____

_____

_____

_____

_____

_____

THE SECRET OF THE ALABASTER BOX

*I*n the days of Jesus, when a young woman reached the age of availability for marriage, her family would purchase an alabaster box for her and fill it with precious ointment. The size of the box and the value of the ointment would parallel her family's wealth. This alabaster box would be part of her dowry. When the young man came to ask for her in marriage, she would respond by taking the alabaster box and breaking it at his feet. This gesture of anointing his feet showed him honor.

One day when Jesus was eating in the house of Simon the leper, a woman came in and broke her alabaster box and poured the valuable ointment on Jesus' head (see Mark 14:3-9). The passage in Luke 7:36-50, which refers to this event, harshly describes the woman as a woman in the city who was a sinner. Were there actually people from the city who were not sinners? Anyway, this woman found Jesus worthy of such sacrifice and honor. In fact, Jesus memorialized her gesture in Matthew 26:13: *"I tell you the truth, wherever this gospel is preached throughout the world, what she has done will also be told, in memory of her"* (NIV). Can you imagine how angry people were that Jesus memorialized a "sinner"? Way to go, King Jesus! Your gesture of such grace is the theme of a song that is sung throughout the world by sinners—"Amazing Grace."

This broken alabaster box is full of great meaning. The woman not only anointed Jesus for His approaching burial, but she also gave her all to a heavenly Bridegroom. Yes, she was a sinner. Who isn't? (See Romans 3:23.) But this sinner had her dreams, and she wisely broke her alabaster box in the presence of the only One who can make a woman's dream come true.

What is in your alabaster box? Is it full of dreams begun as a little girl while you heard, and even "watched," fairy tales about enchanted couples who lived happily ever after? Have you already broken your box at the feet of a young man who has not fulfilled your dreams and has even broken some of your dreams? Or have you been holding on tightly to your alabaster box of dreams, forever searching for a man worthy of the contents of your box? Whether your alabaster box is broken or sealed tightly shut, I encourage you to bring your box and place it at the feet of Jesus.

When you've placed your alabaster box at His feet, then you will be able to respond like Mary to a Heaven-sent assignment. When Mary was asked to become pregnant while engaged to Joseph, she did not argue with the angel. Her response was that of a woman who had already broken her alabaster box at the feet of Joseph and was now ready to take her broken box and lay it at the feet of a heavenly Bridegroom:

I belong to the Lord, body and soul (Luke 1:38 PNT).

REFLECTION

_____

_____

_____

_____

_____

_____

A Busybody and a Murderer

Have you ever considered what a busybody and a murderer have in common? Well, God allowed Peter (are you not surprised it was Peter?) to write about not being ashamed of suffering for doing good. Then Peter wrote the comparison of the understandable suffering for doing evil, such as, *"a murderer or thief or any other kind of criminal, or even as a meddler"* (1 Pet. 4:15b NIV). I remember thinking that the word *meddler* did not fit my concept of a criminal behavior. Have you ever known anyone who has been put in jail as a convicted "meddler—a busybody"? Maybe you know a certain busybody who *should* be constrained behind bars!

I decided to do a little research on the origin of the word *meddler*. I learned that meddler is taken from the word *supervise/supervisor*. So, when a woman is a busybody, that is just another word for a woman who is supervising someone else's family, business, etc. Why would that be such a crime? I realized I was onto something far deeper than a busybody mentality.

One aspect of a woman's role that is nullified by the busybody is the privileged role as "keeper of the home." That is not a role that means to "keep a woman at home." The word *keeper* in Greek refers to "guarding what enters the home." A woman is free to choose what she wants to do outside her home, as long as she does not neglect the guarding of what is entering her home. Too often, when I am supervising someone else's life, family, home, business, etc., it is easy for me to neglect the guarding of my home. For me to not stand guard over my home makes our home vulnerable to all types of enemies who would enter our home and destroy my marriage and our family life. Such neglect is criminal, and it happens on a daily basis in America, even in Christian homes.

The debate concerning a Christian woman working outside her home can be settled with a simple question. How much time can you give to things outside your home and still stand guard over the things that could enter your home and harm those whom you love? With such an awesome responsibility as the keeper of our home, I am sensitive to the self-inflicted suffering that is mine when I am being a busybody. Some busybodies are bored, silly women, but many are competent, gifted women who sometimes neglect evaluating where they give their attention. Does this person, household, ministry, or task qualify under my God-given responsibilities, or is this part of a "busybody crime"? Am I supervising a marriage, a family, or even a job that is not mine? Do I let my "busybody attitude" escort me into someone else's area of responsibility?

> *They should be examples of the good life, so that the younger women may learn to love their husbands and their children, to be sensible and chaste, home-lovers, kind-hearted and willing to adapt themselves to their husbands—a good advertisement for the Christian faith* (Titus 2:4-5 PNT).

REFLECTION

_____

_____

_____

_____

_____

_____

ARE YOU A PAIR OF CLEATS OR A PARACLETE?

When a person in your life is hurting, are you a crushing pair of cleats or a comforting paraclete (a helper, comforter, or advocate)? When a woman shares her pain with you, do you further rupture her wound (like a pair of cleats) or do you help refine her faith through your comfort (paraclete)?

To be a paraclete rather than a pair of cleats, we need to be able to show genuine acceptance of the hurting person's strong feelings of disappointment and anger. Too often we react to a person's pain by giving advice rather than listening and quietly asking questions.

A paraclete will not rupture the wounded by trying to give advice prematurely. She understands that her willingness to listen encourages the healing process (see Prov. 20:5). Job's friends hurt him and angered God by giving too much inappropriate advice. Job's friends were paracletes during the first three days when they sat silently with their hurting friend. They turned into a pair of cleats when they began rambling about the *why* of Job's painful circumstances. Job's friends spoke more than 400 verses as they tried to tell him: "You shouldn't feel that way…you're just reaping what you sowed." Note God's perspective on their *advice*:

> *After the Lord had said these things to Job, he said to Eliphaz the Temanite, "I am angry with you and your two friends, because you have not spoken of Me what is right, as My servant Job has"* (Job 42:7 NIV).

Why do we tend to move into "panic preaching" in the presence of someone's pain? Why do we preach rather than weep with the hurting? I think I know the answer. When we, like Job's friends, come face to face with such suffering in the life of such a godly man, we panic—because we are overwhelmed that such a horrible thing can happen to someone so close to God. We start rambling and preaching in order to drown out the painful reality we are witnessing. Such panic in the presence of pain is the making of another pair of cleats. Nothing slams the door on the hurting soul faster than judgmental, panicked preaching.

The paraclete is so comforting because she has embraced her own pain. For years, people have said to me, "You seem to attract hurting people." Now I understand why. The most effective path in understanding the pain of another is through facing and embracing my own pain! J.B. Phillips captured this in his paraphrase of Second Corinthians 1:5: *"Indeed, experience shows that the more we share in Christ's immeasurable suffering the more we are able to give of His encouragement."* Being a paraclete to another is not only for their comfort but also for their spiritual protection.

We are indwelt by the Paraclete (Holy Spirit), so our capacity to comfort is an automatic potential. May we allow the Paraclete to use us in such a hurting world.

...He will give you another Counselor to be with you forever (John 14:16 NIV).

REFLECTION

_____

_____

_____

_____

_____

_____

_____

ONE OF THE DIVINE SECRETS OF YADAH YADAH

*I*n one sermon my pastor spoke of people being crippled by their emotions and therefore being escorted away from their destiny. As a woman, I do understand that emotions can cripple us and that we might miss a heavenly assignment because we don't feel like obeying the Lord. Everyone started laughing as my pastor went into a physical, bodily depiction of people needing "their feelings" understood. He said that if a person needs someone to listen to her feelings, he will send her to his wife or the counseling staff. He mentioned that as a "former foot-ball coach," he doesn't have the heart for such a "feeling" ministry! The audience roared, and so did I. Then I pondered a question: Is a "feeling" ministry for women only?

Later as I studied for a message God has loaned me ("The Divine Secrets of the Yadah Yadah Sisterhood"), I came across some nuggets that address this "feeling ministry."

Note: The Hebrew word *yadah* means "a sense of understanding and perceiving that comes from a face-to-face/heart-to-heart knowing" (Moses with God, Deut. 34:10: *"Moses, whom the Lord knew face to face"*).

"God gave Solomon wisdom and exceedingly great understanding, and largeness of heart like the sand on the seashore" (1 Kings 4:29 NKJV). To lead and impact people, a person needs not only wisdom and understanding, but also largeness of heart.

This largeness of heart is reflected in the ministry of encouragement. Dr. Larry Crabb has said, "Encouragement is the kind expression that helps someone want to be a better Christian even when life is rough."

"Carry each other's burdens, and in this way you will fulfill the law of Christ" (Gal. 6:2 NIV). The Greek word for "burdens" means "burdened

under pressure, difficulty, grief, savage-fierce weight" (all mental and emotional realities).

Are women the sole humans meant to deal with the "emotional aspects" of people's burdens? Our Lord reminded me of some verses. My soul jumped out of my chair! Consider the ultimate representative of the "feeling ministry"—and this leader was not a female! *"Even though Jesus was God's son, He learned obedience from the things He suffered. In this way, God qualified Him as a perfect High Priest"* (Heb. 5:8-9a NLT). Suffering sets the stage for the perfect leader. If you doubt for a second that Jesus escaped any emotional trials, revisit the garden and the anguish that He experienced.

"For we have not an high priest which cannot be touched with the feeling of our infirmities..." (Heb. 4:15 KJV). This is one of the first verses I learned as a young believer living in an abusive home. If I didn't believe that Jesus was touched by the feelings of my anguish, I would never have been confident enough in Him to keep following Him.

Now here is the kicker: I looked up the word *touched*—oh my goodness! The Greek word for "touched" means

* compassion

* experience pain jointly

* touched with sympathy

* having fellow-feelings

To someone who's suffering, we can offer the exceptional good news that Jesus is *touched*...by their painful feelings. Jesus is a *conjoined experience of sympathy and compassion!*

God called David a man after his own heart. This man was a king, a warrior, a leader, a man's man...but also *a man capable* of experiencing "pain jointly, having fellow-feeling." This man did not miss his destiny because he felt things so deeply. This man was used by God to write poetry/psalms that have comforted millions.

And look: *"Praise be to the God and Father of our Lord Jesus Christ, the Father of compassion and the God of all comfort, who comforts us in all our troubles..."* (2 Cor. 1:3-4 NIV). The Greek word for "compassion" means "pity, mercy, a distinguishing mark of a child of God." Our compassion for people when they are in trouble is a distinguishing mark of our relationship with the High Priest who is touched by our struggles. The Greek word for "comfort" means "encouragement and strengthen; establish a believer in his faith." I love this because God does not comfort us just to erase our sadness and make us happy. God sends specific consolation to purposely strengthen our faith in Him. The Greek word for "who comforts" means "comes to the side to aid with encouragement."

Note: When Jesus said He was going to send another like Himself, He called this "another" the Comforter/Counselor (see John 14:26). He didn't refer to the Holy Spirit as a great leader but as a Comforter!

John Maxwell has said, "80 percent of ministry taking place in churches is done by women." Why? I know there are many factors that explain that statement, but I know without a doubt that a woman's propensity for largeness of heart is one reason God can use her so freely with so many people. I know that a woman's capacity for compassion and sympathy enables her to be "touched" by the needs of others, allowing her to cooperate more freely with the agenda of our Father.

In my 35 years of walking with Jesus, I have met a few men with largeness of heart—may their tribe increase. Personally, I praise God for all the suffering that has broken my heart, time and time again. This breaking made more room for God to accomplish my "largeness of heart." Suffering leads us to the cross, and the cross connects us to God

He comforts us in all our troubles so that we can comfort others (2 Corinthians 1:4 NLT).

REFLECTION

_____

_____

_____

_____

_____

_____

A HOLY WINK FOR MOM

*H*ow would you like to see God wink at you in the middle of your busy day? That's one of the delicious goodies our Lord gave me as I was reading Numbers 6:24-26. The deeper I dug into the Hebrew words, the more good stuff I found! These verses have become my new "blessings" prayer—an alternative to the prayer of Jabez!

This passage reveals the coolest blessings that you can pray for others. In fact, verse 27 states that these blessings were exclusive to those who are God's people, and God is the one who will fulfill the promises. Here are the goodies I found (my translations from the Hebrew are in parentheses):

- "The Lord bless you and keep you (tend you like a garden); (see Num. 6:24)

- the Lord make His face shine (a splendid glow—like a face that lights up when gazing upon one who is loved) upon you and be gracious (kindness and favor for the weak [needy]) to you; (see Num. 6:25)

- the Lord turn His face toward you (this is the ultimate "nod of affection"—like a "holy wink" in a crowd from the One who loves you) (see Num 6:26a)

- and give you peace (establish, set down a satisfied condition and well-being)" (see Num. 6:26b).

The next time you pray for someone, consider praying that she (or he) will allow God to tend her like a garden (this may involve pruning). Pray that she will see God's look of love and "holy wink" in the midst of a crowded day, and that she will not fear weakness or neediness because God *"gives grace to the humble"* (James 4:6). Finally, pray that she will let

Jehovah-shalom be her supernatural peace and well-being in a less-than-perfect world.

These verses were like an early Mother's Day gift to me. I wrote them on an index card and attached it to my car visor. I hope they are a blessing to you and those you pray for. As you pray, you'll receive His "holy wink" too.

Know that the Lord has set apart the godly for Himself; the Lord will hear when I call to Him (Psalm 4:3 NIV).

REFLECTION

_____

_____

_____

_____

_____

_____

AUDACIOUS PRAYER REQUESTS

I am taking a great risk by recording the following thoughts; the topic is one that has disturbed my heart for such a long time. For more than two decades I have been teaching men and women, some who claim to be believers and others who are slightly interested in spiritual things. Time and time again, I have been knocked down (not knocked out) by some of the prayer requests that I have been given by certain people. I have no hesitation whatsoever about praying constantly for the men and women I am trying to minister to—but I really struggle with the audacity of some of their prayer requests.

I struggle with prayer requests from a woman who claims to love Jesus but is living with her boyfriend. I struggle with praying for women who are bearing children out of wedlock, but they ask for God's blessing on their little ones. I struggle with a young woman asking me to pray that she doesn't test positive for AIDS, when I know she is still doing drugs and living with her boyfriend. I struggle with believers who can stubbornly resist God's leadership but wholeheartedly place their many prayer requests before Him. Maybe this audacity is a result of the many religions in America that serve up "a god on our terms," "a god that we don't have to obey." However, many expect their "god" to obey their requests—a "god" who does not expect anything from its followers but whose followers expect everything from their god.

While struggling with the unrestrained presumption with which people ask things from God, I came upon a people in the Old Testament who approached God with the same audacity (see Jer. 21). Here are people who are supposed to be followers of the true God, yet they attack His prophet (Jeremiah) with their tongues and pay no attention to anything he says. These same people continue to backslide further and further away from God, yet when the time of need arrives—King Nebuchadnezzar getting ready to attack their city—they call upon the very prophet they have rejected and expect him to ask God to rescue them from the enemy.

How did God respond to this stubborn, backslidden people and their cry for help? *"I myself will fight against you with an outstretched hand and a mighty arm in anger and fury and great wrath"* (Jer. 21:5 NIV). Lord, I do not want to encourage people to pray with such unrestrained presumption without first challenging them to turn from the sin that so easily besets them.

What does an "audacious prayer request" sound like? (Read Jeremiah 21:2.) Here is a strong warning for prayer requests from people living in stubborn disobedience.

> *If anyone turns a deaf ear to the law, even his prayers are detestable* (Proverbs 28:9 NIV).

REFLECTION

_____

_____

_____

_____

_____

_____

GOD STOOPS DOWN

*W*henever a child asks for help, the adult often needs to stoop down to reach that child. You know how it is when you are carrying several packages: you drop one, and someone stoops down to pick up the package for you—such a helpful gesture.

One of the definitions of this gesture of "stooping" is "condescend/ abasement." The only true God parted the heavens and stooped down to earth in the form of a man in order that humankind could know what it is like for "God to stoop down" on behalf of needy people. This abasement is willingly done on a daily basis for children of the King. Look with me at just a few of the ways that *He stoops down for His own*:

- God stoops down to sustain me (see Ps. 119:116).

- God stoops down to keep me from hurting myself (see Ps. 18:36).

- God stoops down to give me strength (see Neh. 8:10).

- God stoops down to make the way clear for me (see Ps. 18:32).

- God stoops down to train me for life's battles (see Ps. 144:1).

- God stoops down to give me light so I can walk through the darkest night (see Job 29:3).

- God stoops down to give me the capacity to scale the walls people build (see Ps. 18:29).

- God stoops in delight to rescue me (see Ps. 18:19).

- God stoops down to confide in me (see Ps. 25:14).

- God stoops down to bless me in the sight of men (Ps. 31:19).

- God stoops down to place a song in the heart of a former "slime pit dweller" (see Ps. 40:2).

- God stoops down to quiet my anxious heart with His love (see Zeph. 3:17).

How awesome to think that God condescends in order not only to meet the needs of His children but also to make them great! *"You stoop down to make me great"* (Ps. 18:35b NIV). As God stoops down to meet our needs, He is singing a love song over us. Have you heard the love song?

> *The Lord your God is with you, He is mighty to save. He will take great delight in you, He will quiet you with His love, He will rejoice over you with singing* (Zephaniah 3:17 NIV).

REFLECTION

_____

_____

_____

_____

_____

_____

Suggested Reading

Eros Defiled by John White

Too Close, Too Soon by Jim Talley and BobbieReed

Passion and Purity by Elisabeth Elliot

The Pursuit of God by A.W. Tozer

Finding God by Dr. Larry Crabb

Search for Significance by Robert McGee

Trusting God by Jerry Bridges

About Debby Jones and Jackie Kendall

For More Information

Both authors are available for speaking engagements. For more information, call or write:

Debby Jones
Crossover Communications International
P.O. Box 211755
Columbia, SC 29221
1.803.691.0688

Jackie Kendall
P.O. Box 220836
West Palm Beach, FL 33422-0836
1.561.689.6082
www.jackiekendall.com

Help for Finding God's Best in a Mate

How to Avoid a Bozo
Jackie Kendall

Why are so many Christians making such poor choices in life-mates? Do you want to find God's best—Mr. Right? Learn from this video the differences between a man worth waiting for and a Bozo. Discover how to avoid the counterfeit and find the real thing!

IN THE RIGHT HANDS, THIS BOOK WILL CHANGE LIVES!

Most of the people who need this message will not be looking for this book. To change their lives, you need to put a copy of this book in their hands.

> *But others (seeds) fell into good ground, and brought forth fruit, some a hundred-fold, some sixty-fold, some thirty-fold* (Matthew 13:8).

Our ministry is constantly seeking methods to find the good ground, the people who need this anointed message to change their lives. Will you help us reach these people?

> *Remember this—a farmer who plants only a few seeds will get a small crop. But the one who plants generously will get a generous crop* (2 Corinthians 9:6).

EXTEND THIS MINISTRY BY SOWING
3 BOOKS, 5 BOOKS, 10 BOOKS, OR MORE TODAY,
AND BECOME A LIFE CHANGER!

Thank you,

Don Nori Sr., Founder
Destiny Image
Since 1982